WHO *Really* GOES TO HELL?
THE GOSPEL YOU'VE NEVER HEARD

What a Protestant Bible written by Jews says about
God's work through Christ

(A book for those in the church and those offended by it)

by David I. Rudel

BIBLICAL
HERESY
PRESS

The Bible is best read with
your own eyes... preferably open

www.biblicalheresy.com

Scripture quotations are represented in **bold sans serif font**. Other than short quotations (quotations that do not contain an entire verse) all un-attributed quotations are quoted (with sometimes different capitalization) by permission from the *New English Translation* Bible or its notes.
NET Bible®

An online index of the Bible verses cited (allowing for instant viewing of the biblical text) is available at `Scripture.John173.net`

Version 1.3

Due to the author's zeal overrunning his good judgment, an uncorrected version of this work made it into retail channels previously. If you or someone you know purchased one of these defective versions, please apprise the publisher, who will gladly swap the uncorrected copy with a corrected one.

The NET Bible (along with a raft of useful textual and cultural notes) is available in its entirety as a free download or for online web use at `www.nextbible.org`

ISBN-13: 978-0-9818266-0-8
ISBN-10: 0-9818266-0-1

⊗ The paper used in this book meets the requirements of the American National Standards Institute/National Information Standards organization Permanence of Paper for Publications and Documents in Libraries and Archives, ANSI/NISO Z39 : 48 – 1992

CONTENTS

FOREWORD

Well, their it is. You cannot see it because you are reading the text on a printed page. The annoying green wiggly line is only on my computer screen, flagging "their it is." Sometimes I see wiggly lines that are green, sometimes red, but no matter what color they are, they irritate me and I know that the only way to make them disappear is to stop what I am doing, stop what I am thinking, and deal with them.

I am required to hover the cursor over the wiggly line, right click the mouse, and read and respond to the dialogue box that appears. If the line is red, the computer tells me that my word choice deviates from the standard dictionary, and if the line is green, the problem is my grammar. Then, my computer asks me (ever so gently) if I really meant to spell the word that way or if I really meant to use the word in that peculiar fashion. I can respond with several options. I can insert a correctly spelled word from a list, I can insert a grammatically corrected sentence, I can scrap what I have written and begin again, or I can ignore the problem and settle for being incorrect.

I am sure that somewhere in my computer software there is a way for me to disable my annoying wiggly lines. I choose not to. As annoying as it is to have my thought processes interrupted, I realize that when misspelled words and poor grammar appear in a text that bears my name, I inevitably lose credibility in the eyes of discerning readers. How convincing can my argument be if I cannot choose the right word for a sentence?

I call the wiggly lines essential annoyances.

You are holding in your hands a book that may well become for you an essential annoyance. David Rudel's *Who Really Goes to Hell? — The Gospel You've Never Heard* is an important book. He will posit ideas and ask questions about the Bible's teachings and about the Church's use of those teachings that may trouble you. The questions are honest, thoroughly researched, meticulously argued, and will wash over you like incessant waves. Most annoyingly, his questions are always referenced to scripture as the standard.

I don't agree with all of Rudel's conclusions and I question some of his

iii

Biblical-critical methods, but it isn't his conclusions that annoy me. Somehow, the questions that he asks have become embedded in my mind—in my operating system. They open in a dialogue box in my head, and they require a response. Rudel's questions have become a kind of annoying filter through which I must pass my sermons and my sermon preparation, my Bible teaching and the reading that informs it, my public prayers and the very personal contemplation that gives birth to them, and even my intimate thoughts about salvation, damnation, eternal life, death, heaven, and hell.

Well, there it is. If you love God's Word and treasure God's Church, this book will be an essential, albeit annoying, challenge.

2-15-2009
Edward Hopkins
Pastor
Hinton Avenue United Methodist Church
Charlottesville, VA

Introduction: What is This?

WARNING: Cigarette Smoke Contains Carbon Monoxide.

You probably do not read the warning labels on cigarettes. You know the gist and purpose of the warning; reading the text is unlikely to provide any new insight. The warning could say almost anything, and you would read it as, "Hey, perhaps willfully inhaling fumes isn't a good idea."

In fact the label itself does not say smoking is hazardous, even if you assume everyone knows carbon monoxide is dangerous. Perfectly safe substances can contain chemicals that would be deadly in isolation — Chlorine makes up over half of common table salt. But we know the warning really means that the carbon monoxide in smoke, unlike the chlorine in salt, can cause us harm when we put it in our bodies.

Furthermore, we know this warning is different from, say, caution labels on curling irons suggesting you not put them in your ear. The cigarette's warning is not meant to stop you from using the product in a dangerous manner; it discourages you from using the product at all.

We would know these things even had we never read such a label, for the media, our doctors, our parents, etc. tell us smoking is unhealthy. We don't need to read the text; we've already been told what it says... and if we do read it and find something unfamiliar (e.g., *carbon monoxide*), it doesn't stop us from determining the intent. Like watching a foreign version of a film you've already seen in your native tongue, you know the plot without reading the subtitles.

Had the warning read "Exposure to gelid hydroxylic acid can result in horripilation," we might assume cigarettes contain gelid hydroxylic acid and that horripilation is some terrible medical disorder. In reality the label would simply be saying that cold water can cause goose bumps.

My point? *Our assumptions color not only how we read things but also the conclusions we draw as we make the text meet our expectations.*

Our presuppositions are unlikely to lead us astray when we read warning labels on cigarettes, but what about when we read the Bible?

Almost everyone is told what Christianity is about and what to expect from the Bible long before reading it carefully. In addition to these assumptions, we

1

have our own opinions on what we'd like the Bible to say. In the end, it's very hard to simply read the Bible for what it says. Instead, we read into it what we think it should say or what we have been told it says... or we don't read it at all, having decided its teachings (as described by others) make no sense.

What people think Christianity "is all about" is largely based on the views presented by active spreaders of the gospel. From these messages, a consensus has formed among non-Christians of the basic principles of biblical Christianity. For understandable reasons, non-believers tend to define Christianity in terms of its claims regarding how the Judgment works — Who goes to heaven? Who to Hell?

This book emerged as the product of a spiritual, scriptural journey that began when I realized the claims we assume to be *what the Bible says* do not appear to be motivated by scripture at all. Rather, the Bible seems to have been bent to match our assumptions. I eventually found the Bible describes a perfectly reasonable, logical, God-centered story of salvation far afield from what people in America perceive based on evangelists and evangelicals.

I was once a conservative Calvinist, so I'm hopeful this book will turn upside down the worlds of a few who are now as I once was. But I also hope it shows liberal Christians that a literal reading of the Bible makes a good deal more sense than they realize, and (perhaps most of all) I hope it speaks to non-believers who may have judged Christianity too soon based on modern dogma.

The first four chapters demonstrate the motivation for constructing a different salvation paradigm fitting naturally with scripture as a whole.

Chapters five through seven investigate the Judgment, engaging the question in the title of this book. I do not suggest skipping forward to it.

Chapters eight through eleven build up a biblical understanding of salvation. They also serve to defend the paradigm described in the first four chapters and fill a void left by the castles torn down in the middle three.

In short, this book is for anyone who thinks Jesus knew what He was talking about and wants a second opinion on what that entails. I've tried to make the book meaningful to evangelicals, liberal Christians, and non-believers. To do so has required that it not be the perfect match for any one group. This is an *interactive* book in that you can go to www.john173.net to connect with others, see discussion of reader questions, and/or submit your own.

Questing —
Seeking and Finding

– I –

A Journey Begun by *Don't Walk*ING

DON'T WALK

The sign screamed mutely in 216-point font, eerily shining through the October night air, which still bore the texture of a recent rain. The street was empty, but I obeyed the sign anyway. You'll just have to believe me (or not) when I say the attractive student (let's call her Danielle[1]) also standing at the corner wasn't the reason why.

I had come from dining alone, likely at *Everything But Anchovies* (a misnomer — but I forgive them on account of their Pasta Osborne). It's pretty much the only place in Hanover open late, and thus a favorite for Dartmouth students.

Eventually, the sign changed, and we crossed the slick street. I altered my gait to match hers down the sidewalk a few hundred yards. I figured anything more direct would frighten her. (As though having a tall, stocky, scruffy guy in a black fleece keep pace with you down a block at night is no big deal.... Let's just say *Social Intuition 101* was not required for my degree.)

We neared a fork, and she braved a "Good night" in my direction, which I took as license to ask, "Why did you wait at the light?" — the question I had considered posing all along.

She managed to ask me my own question without answering it herself; I cannot for the life of me remember how she did it.

I stuttered, "I'm a believer in Kantian ethics and feel citizenship is tacit agreement to live by the laws of the land... and there are some other reasons as well." Yes, I really said "tacit agreement" in a midnight conversation with a woman I had never met. Did I mention I was in theoretic mathematics?

She answered after my suave response, saying she was starting to believe obeying laws should be part of her Christian faith.

Her response at once humiliated and encouraged me. Though I considered myself a devout believer, I had avoided mentioning it — the "other reasons" in

---

[1]because that was her name

my answer — for fear it might color her opinion of me. Of course this humiliation did not stop me from declaring my own faith after I heard of hers.

She invited me to join The Navigators, a campus Christian fellowship, for their weekly Wednesday meeting. I figured it would be a replay of the dry InterVarsity Bible studies I had sampled at Grinnell, but the opportunity to be in the same room with her outweighed such minor sufferings. I would have even gone to a strictly vegan restaurant to spend more time with her.

I could not have been more wrong regarding The Navigators. Nearly 100 students worshipped with a full praise band, and a student gave a message. I was floored by the enthusiasm and vibrancy of the worship. On the downside, I assessed my chances of capturing Danielle's heart as rather slim.

A calculus student I tutored named Karen invited me to a Campus Crusade for Christ meeting the following week. I took her up on the offer and joined a score of students in a cozy room outside the mess hall. Chris West, the leader, gave a talk on *Romans 12:1–2*:

> **. . . present your bodies as a sacrifice — alive, holy, and pleasing to God — which is your reasonable service. Do not be conformed to this present world, but be transformed by the renewing of your mind, so that you may test and approve what is the will of God — what is good, pleasing, and perfect.**

His talk left me feeling like Dorothy upon landing in Oz, exposing me to God's expectations. I had utterly compartmentalized my faith. I realized I could not wear my belief in Christ as a stamp, a label adorning the hellfire-retardant shrink-wrapping of my soul.

I had always considered myself a serious Christian. My dad was a devout conservative Lutheran. He died when I was seven, and soon thereafter we stopped going to church, but I eventually returned in seventh grade, just in time to begin catechism class. By high school I knew basic doctrine and often got into arguments with my atheist and agnostic classmates. (Most of them, of course, attended church, this being Texas and all. In my home town, there was no law strictly requiring you to go to church, but there was also no law strictly requiring you to breathe or worship football.) On the other hand, I never studied my Bible much. I packed it every time I moved to a new place, but somehow I never found time to read it, much like people "never find time" to floss.

Energized by Chris' talk, I began reading the Bible voraciously. As a graduate student with a knack for his subject, I had the type of free time typically reserved for the unemployed. I read and read, awash in newfound passion.

The ensuing months of study presented an odd puzzle — ***Jesus and Paul appear to fundamentally disagree about the Judgment!***[2]

Let me explain. Paul writes things like **. . . for all have sinned and fall short of the glory of God, . . . a man is not justified by the works of the Law but through faith in Christ Jesus**, and **For by grace you have been saved through faith.** It sounds like Paul is saying everyone deserves to go to hell[3] *by default* while those who have faith in Christ are saved from this fate.

This message is at the core of the gospel you have likely heard from any number of evangelists (and quite possibly have preached yourself). It can be packaged in several ways but generally boils down to the following:

- All humans sin, making them unrighteous in God's eyes and hence disqualified from heaven.
- Jesus died so that believers could receive forgiveness through His sacrifice, allowing them to enter heaven without upsetting God's justice.

Most assume the above is *what the Bible says*, whether or not they agree with it. I'll call this general idea the *modern gospel* or the message of *modern Christianity*. The first half of this book is mostly devoted to engaging that message, and I'll call people who believe some variation of it *evangelicals*, though given how broad of a term that is, perhaps "Conservative Evangelicals" would be a better label. I apologize beforehand for any overgeneralizations that come from addressing this large school of thought while not being too concerned with the differences within it.

Now, evangelicals have much more to say than this, but when it comes to the Judgment, the above crudely captures the essentials for all practical purposes. The only escape from hell is belief in Christ, which means we need to spread the message so everyone has a chance to "make it." There **appears** to be no other conclusion if we believe, as written in *2nd Timothy 3:15*, we are saved by **faith in Christ**. Clearly, people cannot have faith in Christ if they never hear of Him. (Lest you get the wrong idea, I too believe we are saved through faith.)

I found while I read Jesus anew that His teachings on the Judgment just don't jibe with the modern gospel. It's as though He and Paul speak of two different things, and most of what Jesus says just makes no sense if you accept the message presented by evangelicals (or Catholics, for that matter).

---

[2] I use "Judgment" (with a capital J) to refer to the "final judgment" throughout this book.

[3] By "hell" I mean "whatever happens to those who do not pass the Judgment." I'll use "heaven" as the opposite, though we'll find later that this is mildly imprecise.

As a Lutheran, I had grown up on Paul. The gospels almost seemed foreign to me. Sure, I had read all the "important parts" that get stressed in church. I think that's how most Christians read the Bible;[4] we know the parts we like and doze off during the parts we might not understand or do not want to hear. Now, as I read Jesus again for the first time, a surprise lurked on every page. Frankly, He seemed to be saying everything a good Protestant is *not* supposed to believe.

You are likely skeptical of this last point, especially if you are an evangelical. I give several examples in chapter two, but page *173* has a summary of the points covered throughout the book. I bet you've read several passages yourself that looked strange while studying the gospels, and each time you convinced yourself it wasn't perplexing enough to fret over. I further suspect the reason is that you thought *you had no choice.* You were told the only option, if you wanted to believe the Bible, was to agree with the message of modern Christianity.

Keep in mind that those verses that pricked your conscience are the tip of the iceberg. We generally do not find what we are not looking for: If we do not want to see *apparent* contradictions between Jesus and Paul, or contradictions between what the church teaches and what the Bible actually says, our psychology will happily oblige us. Add to this the pressure Christians feel to fit into their local fellowship and support each other's faith, and it's easy to see why problem verses are easily glossed over.

That's much of this book's aim, reading the Bible without sprinkling arcane theological pixie dust over everything that conflicts with what we are told (or want to believe). If you can do this, the Bible as whole (and the Living God it reveals) makes far more sense. But you'll have to leave your dogma at the door.

Note: This book is about God's Word and has over 1000 scripture citations. I suggest first reading through without looking everything up. After getting the general idea, go back and dig into your Bible on anything you want to check or explore. For an easy way to see the passages I cite, go to `Scripture.John173.net`

---

[4]By "most Christians" I mean "the majority of the small number who read the Bible at all."

A Classic Question: A Simple Answer

Luke 10:25 raised my eyebrows as I was reading the Bible anew. A scribe asks Jesus, point-blank, **Teacher, what must I do to inherit eternal life?**

Isn't that the question most see at the heart of the gospel?

No evangelical would give the answer[5] Jesus gives — *Love God and your neighbor.* They might answer, "There is nothing *you* can *do* to inherit eternal life," and should be surprised that neither "faith" nor "Christ" enters into Jesus' answer. A minister who gave Jesus' response would be accused of teaching "works righteousness" or saying we can "earn our way into heaven."

I've heard some rather strained attempts to explain what Christ *really* meant here, but the simple truth is that Christ's Jewish audience took His answer exactly as it sounds[6] — that those who loved God and their neighbor would inherit eternal life — so efforts at explaining away His answer paints Jesus as a rather odd Savior who willfully misleads those He was sent to help.

Today we see the whole Bible as a single package of truth given to us by God. While we should consider all scripture before arriving at a conclusion, we must also keep in mind that the gospels are not merely opportunities for God to speak to us 21st-century types. When Luke wrote his gospel, he may have known of Christian literature, but he could not assume all his readers had access to any particular epistle or gospel. Furthermore, the Jews were not mere foils used for dramatic effect to allow 21st-century Gentiles a better understanding of God. Jesus *loved* the Jews, a people He wept bitterly for in *Luke 19:41–44.*

The anguished *Matthew 23:37* is not the anger of a resentful ruler, but rather the wailing of a mother whose children have refused all efforts at aid. Whenever Jesus speaks plainly to the Jews, we have to assume it is for their benefit. We cannot go around claiming *He says* **you have answered correctly; do this and you will live**, *but He really* means … There's nothing in the narrative, and in particular the conclusion (*Luke 10:37*), suggesting Jesus is misleading or rebuking the scribe. His answer and the narrative is instructive, like Jesus' sermon in *Matthew 5:13 – 7:29*, which begins on a note similar to *Luke 10:28*.

Furthermore, the gospels written by Matthew, Mark, Luke, and John did not originally go out bundled with each other and all of Paul's letters. They were read (or, more likely, heard) by people who may well have had no other accounts

---

[5] He said to him "What is written in the Law? How do you understand it?" The expert answered "Love the Lord your God with all your heart, with all your soul, with all your strength, and with all your mind, and love your neighbor as yourself" (quoting *Deuteronomy 6:5* and *Leviticus 19:18*). Jesus said to him, "You have answered correctly; do this and you will live."

[6] Though they might well understand the *question* differently than we do. More on that later.

of Christ. To interpret them in the light of Paul's letters or 1900 years of religious philosophy is to read them with a lens their writers never intended and their original readers did not have. If Luke thought Jesus' answer was ambiguous and needed clarification, he would have provided it himself.

The only context given by Luke is that this discussion introduces the parable of the good Samaritan, a story not told to answer the question "who goes to hell?" but rather the question **who is my neighbor?**

Matthew Henry's Commentary claims the questioner takes Jesus' commendation in *Luke 10:28* as a conviction because he knows it is impossible for him to keep the requirement perfectly. That commentary then says his second question is an effort at looking for a way out.

This explanation might make sense if the scribe has a 21st-century evangelical understanding of God's justice, but it hardly fits the actual context. First, he answers his own question with a standard Jewish response, so it's hard to imagine it throws him into a fit of terror. Second, the Jews have lived for centuries knowing their obligation to the Law without any emotional trauma. (Indeed, Luke begins his gospel [*Luke 1:6*] referring to two people **blameless** and **righteous before God** by keeping the Law!) Jesus' answer affirms rather than attacks that concept. Third, the scribe's second question would hardly get him out of the hot seat even if we assumed a modern understanding of the situation — even if Jesus tells him only other Jews count as his neighbors, would that really change whether he can keep the command to our 21st-century standards?

Another explanation I've heard is that Christ is "meeting this man where he is" — that this one Jew has a problem with treating his neighbor as himself. Thus, Christ is not teaching fundamental truths but rather showing this particular man the one thing he has to change to follow Jesus.

In truth, the question "who is my neighbor?" is[7] highly debated during Jesus' day. It makes perfect sense for a scribe (whose profession depends on interpreting the Law) to test Jesus' understanding because Jesus is considered a rabbi or prophet at the time. Note the address: **Teacher, what must I do...**

Jesus' answer goes far beyond anyone's expectations. Not only does He claim that anyone can be our neighbor, but He further indicates we should actively try to *be a neighbor* to those God puts in our lives. Note how He changes the question from **who is my neighbor?** to **which of these became a neighbor to the man who fell into the hands of the robbers?**

One Jewish sect holds that only upstanding, righteous people count as their neighbors. Another sect believes *almost* everyone can be a neighbor. But *no*

---

[7] I prefer the present tense for describing the historical context of scenes depicted in the Bible.

one thinks Samaritans (hated by the Jews) are included. The scribe cannot even bring himself to say "the Samaritan" in answer to Jesus' question. Instead he simply says **The one who showed him mercy.**

Jesus' response is revolutionary in its answer to **Who is my neighbor?** It is definitely *not* revolutionary in its answer to **How do I inherit eternal life?** The scribe answers his own question and Jesus commends him: **You have answered correctly; do this and you will live.**

The fact that Christ's response is a prelude to the parable of the good Samaritan does not make it any more compatible with modern Christianity, though I suggest you keep it in mind next time you see a hitchhiker.[8]

A Wild Gospel Chase

You can generally find a Bible verse or two to support almost any viewpoint you want. If you want to show God is a vegetarian who roots for the New York Yankees, you could probably find verses to support that. It's called proof-texting, and it is not very constructive.

On the other hand, I submit you'll have trouble finding even *one* verse in Matthew, Mark, or Luke that closely matches conservative Christianity's understanding of the Judgment, where all are judged as guilty and God grants forgiveness to believers based on Christ's sacrifice.

It is hard (impossible?) to read Matthew, Mark, or Luke in its entirety and come away with anything similar to the gospel you've likely heard. That's a pretty serious problem — that a gospel's message has nothing to do with what we today consider the crux of Christianity. Remember, these early writers had to assume their readers might have no other New Testament writings. Anything critical should be found stenciled in purple Technicolor, jumping off the page. Yet the modern gospel is hard to find clearly portrayed anywhere, let alone spelled out in each work. Evangelists today can sketch out their message in five minutes; you'd think if it were an accurate depiction of Christ's work, each writer would clearly write it *somewhere* in his *gospel.*

So, either now or soon, read all of Mark and ask yourself how much of "the gospel" is in his gospel. The only place Mark mentions hell is *Mark 9:38–50,*[9] a

---

[8]Have you ever heard a sermon on how Jesus says we should pick up hitchhikers? Unfortunately, neither have I. It is incompatible with Christians' interest in "prudence." Course, most of what Jesus says is rather anti-"prudence."

[9]This presumes we ignore Mark 16:9–20, which practically all scholars claim was added later.

passage failing to do traditional Christianity any favors. *Mark 10:21–31* is closer to what we expect, speaking of **the kingdom of God** and linking it to following Jesus, but then *Mark 12:28–34* makes clear that this phrase (**the kingdom of God**) does not mean "heaven" *in the sense we generally use the word.*

Pretend you've never read any of the New Testament. Consider all of Mark and ask yourself *Why was this written? What would I believe about Jesus if this is all I had to go on?* You won't come up with anything resembling the modern gospel. We expect Mark to clearly weave it throughout his work if it were true, yet there's nary a trace. I'm not "throwing away" everything but Mark here, just asking you to ponder his message based on what he wrote.

Even using liberal dating of these gospels, where we assume the writers thought their readers had other information, it is hard to understand why they would not affirm the modern gospel (if it were true); instead they chose (or the Spirit chose for them) to relate teaching after teaching that chafes against it.

Similarly, after you read any of these gospels, you are not drawn to go out and save people from eternal torment in hell by teaching them to believe in Christ. You might come away with many ideas, but "I need to go proclaim Jesus to others *or else they will go to hell*" is certainly not one of them.

Even "The Great Commission" does not suggest this. Read *Matthew 28:18–20* carefully, and you'll find Jesus directs His disciples to spread the *commandments* He taught while on earth. Jesus tells them to make *disciples*, not *believers*, and the reason given is not *otherwise they will go to hell*. What's the reason? — **All authority in heaven and earth has been given to me.**

When pondering what the disciples think they are doing, keep in mind *they initially only go to the Jews!* Note the shock and surprise in *Acts 11:18* when Peter defends his baptizing of Gentiles over a decade after Christ's resurrection. Unless we believe these holy men of God are so callous that they want all Gentiles to be eternally damned, we simply cannot think that Jesus' disciples spread the good news in an effort to save souls *from hell*.

It appears the Greek version of Matthew we have today might come from an earlier Hebrew version written before the Gentiles were welcomed into the church. The original version may not have included the part about **all nations**. This would explain the apostles' action but does not let the modern gospel off the hook. *The fact that **all** the original apostles thought Jesus' work was only for the Jews certainly says something about what Jesus taught them.*

Evangelicals make certain claims about our status in God's eyes. These axioms are the basis of their gospel. Let's look at what Christ had to say on the matter.

Introduction to the Sermon on the Mount

Commencing a sermon spanning three chapters, Jesus says, **anyone who breaks the least of these commandments and teaches others to do so will be called least in the kingdom of heaven, but whoever obeys them and teaches others to do so will be called great in the kingdom of heaven. For I tell you, unless your righteousness goes beyond that of the experts in the law and the Pharisees, you will never enter the kingdom of heaven.** (*Matthew 5:19–20*)

This seemed strange to me as I read through the Bible because Christ not only links righteousness to obeying the commandments, but also links obedience to entering the kingdom of heaven. Evangelicals firmly deny both connections.

Some people read this verse with an eye patch, seeing only part of it at a time. They first disregard all the stuff about commandments and claim Jesus is saying the works the Pharisees had done did not make them righteous. Then they disregard the part about righteousness and focus on the first sentence to say breaking one commandment one time is as bad as breaking all of them all the time. These conclusions ignore the middle part — **but whoever obeys them and teaches others to do so will be called great in the kingdom of heaven**.

The cut-and-paste theology also ignores the context of the passage. He says **these commandments**. What commandments? He means the commands *He is going to articulate next*. Surely the focus cannot be about the futility of trying to follow laws ("works") when He is about to give some of His own! Immediately after this introduction, Christ clarifies God's commands and stresses the danger of ignoring them. If you read it as saying "you have all already broken one of these, so all of you are already cursed," it provides no motivation to do God's will in the future. Thus, the common treatment of the passage destroys the very thing Christ was trying to accomplish in His address!

He's not saying the works of the Pharisees are insufficient because people have no hope of doing God's will. He is saying the Pharisees kept the letter of the Mosaic law without respecting the deeper desires of God shown within it. He makes the same observation in the "Seven Woes" proclaimed in *Matthew 23:1–36*. He shows this clearly in *23:23–24*.

> **Woe to you, experts in the law and you Pharisees, hypocrites! You give a tenth of mint, dill, and cumin, yet you neglect what is more important in the law — justice, mercy, and faithfulness! You should have done these things without neglecting the others. Blind guides! You strain out a gnat yet swallow a camel.**

Jesus is saying it is not enough to follow the letter of the Law. They must respect the weightier aspects God displays in the Law: compassion, mercy, and love. This is what the Pharisees missed, just like their forebears. To correct this, Jesus gives them a taste of the new covenant's law in the "Sermon on the Mount," just as Moses brought the commandments of the old covenant down from Mount Sinai. (To the Jews of Jesus' day, it would seem that Jesus was a rabbi with authority to reinterpret the Mosaic law, but to Matthew's audience the comparison to Moses would be obvious.)

Jesus is definitely not saying it is impossible to please God through obedience (that would make the second half of *Matthew 5:19* look stupid). He's indicting the Pharisees for doing a lousy job because they are manipulating God's law, twisting it to their political needs. Worse, their hypocrisy and mis-teachings are causing well-meaning Jews not to know how to please God either, thus the frustration Jesus shows in *Matthew 23:13–15* and why He speaks in *Matthew 5:19* of both obeying and teaching others to obey. He's addressing the two errors the Pharisees made, and He is going to do the opposite. He keeps the commands, and later sends His disciples out to teach others to do so as well.

Incidentally, this passage makes it hard to believe that those who came before Christ have their fate determined by whether or not they believed a savior would come. The Pharisees of Jesus' day definitely believed *that*, as did the Pharisees who came before them and the Jews who stoned the prophets.

Questions: All Who Wonder Are Not Lost

I've given just one example of how Jesus casts the Judgment. We'll investigate that topic more in chapter two. Jesus' words made me wonder about other things as well. It was terribly hard to accept that what I had been taught and had told others might be wrong. Conservative Christianity has such a tight structure that people are generally given the choice of accepting the entire ensemble or none of it. Each point of doctrine is protected with so much zeal that you would think Christ's existence was being attacked.

Many have questions along the lines of *Why would a loving God only let some people into heaven?* or *Why does God treat those who never heard of Jesus the same as those who rejected Him?* The questions that perplexed me back then had more to do with the internal consistency of the gospel I had been taught.

Forgiveness

For example, Christ says **For if you forgive others their sins, your heavenly Father will also forgive you. But if you do not forgive others, then your Father will not forgive your sins.**[10] What happens to believers who do not forgive others? Are their sins forgiven or not? What about someone who forgives others but does not believe in Christ? Jesus gives no impression that He is only speaking of present-day forgiveness. This verse is part of a sermon where He discusses hell multiple times.

Why does Jesus even say this if the only thing that ends up determining if our sins are forgiven is faith in Him? It would be like a professor (Jesus) telling you that passing (forgiveness by God at the Judgment) his course is based entirely on the quizzes (forgiving others) and then being told by the course's teaching assistant (evangelicals) that passing is based only on class participation (faith in Christ).

Judging Others

In the same vein, Jesus often discussed judging others. Given the stereotypes the church has earned, one has to wonder what **Do not judge, and you will not be judged** (*Luke 6:37*) and **For in the way you judge, you will be judged** (*Matthew 7:2*) mean for judgmental believers. What do they imply for those who are non-judgmental but never hear or perhaps even reject Jesus?

Some claim, "Jesus is just talking about present judgment here — we are judged as we judge others now. But at the final Judgment, we must be judged against God's perfect standard."

I don't know about you, but I do not find that explanation very fulfilling. How could God forgive my sins today (when I forgive others), but then unforgive them later at the Final Judgment (if I was not a believer)? Why would Jesus say we are judged as we judge others, but omit that this fundamental truth does not extend to the most important judgment of all?

The context of these passages does not suggest Jesus' message is limited in scope. *Matthew 18:21–35* in particular appears to have an eternal time frame in mind. Similarly, one of the anti-judgment passages, *Matthew 7:1–2*, comes in the same sermon as verses with the end-times in sight (e.g., *Matthew 7:13*). If different rules apply between present and eternal judgment, you'd think Jesus (or Matthew) would have said so — His Jewish audience would be even less likely than we are to think such a thing.

---

[10]*Matthew 6:14–15*, see also *18:34–35*; *Mark 11:25–26*; and *Luke 17:3–4*. Jesus stressed our forgiveness of others far more than modern Christians do.

Evangelicals hold that all of us are essentially judged as unwelcome in heaven on our own. Those who don't believe in Christ are condemned because, as Paul says in *Romans 3:23*, **all have fallen short of the glory of God.** Believers pass the Judgment not due to their righteousness but because God has forgiven their sin. If that's true, then what does it matter how I judge my neighbor, either lightly or harshly? Why is Jesus wasting His listeners' time (and misleading them as well) by saying **For in the same way you judge others, you will be judged** if the reality is that a single sin is enough to disqualify you from heaven?

Evangelicals believe it is our sin against God that makes us unworthy of heaven. Our judgment of others or lack thereof cannot change that… can it?

Fate of Earlier People

In *Luke 13:28*, Jesus says a whole slew of personages will enter the kingdom of heaven who could never have known Jesus while **evildoers** are not allowed in. How is a 1st-century Jew to take that warning, especially since the only thing Jesus asks of these people is to **repent**?

Jesus refers to Abraham, Isaac, Jacob, and all the prophets "making it in," but these people could not have "had faith in Christ" the way we are told people need to. In fact, the Hebrews before King David did not even look forward to a singular Messiah. Abraham had received a promise that all nations would be blessed through him, but it was not made clear how that promise would come to fruition until after Israel fell. After all, Israel was looking for a political savior, and until they had been defeated they didn't have anyone to be *saved* from.

Or consider Rahab, the prostitute in Jericho who helps the Israelites (*Joshua 2:1–4*). She has no understanding of Judaism and certainly no understanding of a coming savior (or the need for one), yet the writer of Hebrews praises her in *Hebrews 11:31*. She has no gospel to believe in, yet it is hard to see Christ telling her "no" on Judgment day. It is equally hard to see what makes her any different from those after Christ who had no inkling of the Living God's gospel.

These people of the Old Testament who Jesus said will survive the Judgment had *faith in God* and were *faithful to God*, but the same could be said of many people in the past, present, and future.

Finally, how could Enoch (*Genesis 5:24*) or Elijah (*2nd Kings 2:11*) be taken to heaven if their sins were not forgiven, for Christ had not yet died? Suggesting God forgives their sins "early" by looking forward to Christ's sacrifice throws the entire Old Testament into chaos. In any event, the Old Testament writers certainly saw no need to make excuses for God or explain how these ascensions did not break the Almighty's supposedly rigid code of justice.

If believing in a coming savior were important for eternal safety, you'd never know it from reading the Old Testament. In all the teachings of the ancient Hebrews, there is not one vignette of a savior coming to deliver individuals from hell, nor is the importance of *belief* in such a savior to be found in all the pages of the Jewish Torah. You'd think that if the patriarchs who spoke to God and the prophets who spoke for God thought such faith were critical to avoid eternal hellfire, they would have mentioned it somewhere.

Early Gospel

The early apostles thought that Jesus was returning very soon, signalling the end of the age, and this itself poses a problem for the modern gospel. If the apostles were going around telling people that Jesus was the only way to survive the Judgment that was coming very soon, what would that say about God? Why would God put Jesus through so much suffering to allow a single way out of hell *and then send Him at the very end, so as few people as possible can be saved?*

Of course, that isn't what the apostles taught or believed, but what gospel did they spread? Keep in mind that most of the Christian church kept the Mosaic Law for its first 15 years. What does it say about the gospel if the early Jewish Christians required Gentile Christians to keep the Mosaic law?

And, going further back, we reach an intriguing point concerning Jesus' own gospel: *No one knows Christ is going to die!* Jesus *begins* to hint at His coming death in *Mark 8:31*, but only to His disciples and only after two years of preaching. Furthermore, His disciples have no clue what He means — either at that time (*Mark 9:10*) or after several more months (*Luke 18:34*). As Jesus points out in *Luke 24:26–27*, they *should* have figured it out, but they don't. John confirms this in *John 20:9*.

Let me be very clear. Jesus *does* allude to His coming death, and Jesus *does* rise again. I'm simply saying those items are not in the gospel He and His apostles teach the Jewish crowds because not even His disciples understand what will happen to Jesus later. When the gospel authors write that people **believed in Christ** it evidently has nothing to do with His death or resurrection.

I realize this observation may have thrown you into confusion, so I have included in the appendix (beginning on page *177*) a more detailed description.

It turns out that these questions, and many more, can be answered by simply letting Jesus and others mean what they say. However, I am getting ahead of myself. Just like any other jigsaw puzzle, it helps first to put the frame together; then you can place the pieces in later.

The framework I describe in this book allows all the following:

- Jesus' words are truthful and make sense to the Jews He spoke to without needing retroactive reinterpretation based on letters Paul would write to Gentiles 20 years later.

- The individual gospel accounts, as well as the specific teachings within them, transmit the core truths of Christianity to their original readers.

- Paul's writings make sense to his audience without conflicting with the teachings Jesus gives.

- Jesus fulfills the work described by the Old Testament prophets, work the modern gospel leaves mostly untouched. (Evangelicals are happy to show how Jesus fulfills the prophecies *identifying* the Messiah, but their understanding of the gospel ignores the hundreds of pages in God's Word describing why He was needed and what He was to accomplish.)

- Jesus works to heal the problems we see all around, and in, us. He brings *more* than hope — He brings good news.

Summary and Final Notes

In this chapter I simply wanted to share part of my journey and give a flavor for what put me on the path I hope to show you in this book. Nothing in this chapter is meant to *prove* anything, just indicate why the modern gospel does not seem the natural conclusion from Jesus' teachings for a number of reasons. I promise the later chapters will feel less like a whirlwind.

Initially, I found differences between Jesus' teachings (which we will investigate more deeply in the next chapter) and the interpretation we draw from Paul's letters. This got me exploring what, exactly, Jesus teaches as *the gospel* before His death. Through most of His ministry, people think of Him as a rabbi or a prophet, and no one, not even His disciples, knows He is going to die. So what message is Jesus spreading? If you take away Jesus as Messiah, Jesus as Sacrifice, and Jesus as Lord, what do you have left to tell people as the **gospel**? When Jesus says **repent and believe the gospel** what **gospel** does He mean?

And what gospel do His disciples spread afterward? Mark begins his gospel by saying **The beginning of the gospel of Jesus Christ, the Son of God** and then proceeds to give an entire narrative containing practically nothing we would consider the **gospel**.

I am not claiming the Bible is wrong. I'm not claiming Jesus wasn't crucified or that He wasn't resurrected. I'm not saying anything against these basic truths the Bible states clearly. I'm saying that the modern gospel is not only very different from the gospel Jesus and the apostles proclaim prior to His death, but suggests a version of the Judgment totally foreign to what Jesus preaches. You simply cannot read any of the first three gospels and come away believing the gospel is what we are told it is today. You certainly cannot read any of these gospels and Acts (which records the earliest teachings of the apostles as they spread the gospel) and take from them a view on the Judgment that is compatible with what evangelicals teach as the biblical truth.

That Jesus does not publicize His atoning death makes His discussion of the Judgment even harder to swallow if we assume He cares at all for the **lost house of Israel** He came to save. The Jews whom Christ speaks to, having no understanding of Christ's atoning sacrifice or Messiahship, can not help but take Christ's words in a direct fashion. Nor can we brush such concerns under the rug by claiming Jesus speaks in parables precisely because the Jews are not supposed to understand Him. Not all of Jesus' parables are inscrutable; some Jesus explains to the crowds, others the listeners understand without explanation (e.g., *Matthew 21:45*), and many of Jesus' teachings are not in parables at all — as in *Luke 10:25–28*, where Jesus leads the scribe to answer his own question.

Furthermore, one can only push this explanation so far, for Christ claims in *John 18:20*, **I have spoken publicly to the world. I always taught in the synagogues and in the temple courts,... I have said nothing in secret.**

In any event, being "unclear" is very different from inviting people to false conclusions. Furthermore, if Matthew, Mark, and Luke did not intend for their readers to take Christ's teachings as recorded, they certainly could have clarified them. As it is, the explanations captured are hardly the message one expects if the gospel writers were pushing a theology where forgiveness through faith is the prevailing factor at the Judgment.

The original apostles do not take the gospel to the Gentiles until 10 years after Christ's death, and that was only due to divine intervention. A decade after Christ's resurrection, Peter has to be commanded three times *by God* before he so much as enters a Gentile's house, let alone tells him of the Jewish Messiah. It isn't that Peter hates the Gentiles or wants them to go to hell (for hell had nothing to do with the early gospel), but rather that he still sees the Law as a dividing wall between Jews and Gentiles, and he (like all Jewish Christians) keeps the entire Mosaic law.

Whatever our conception of the gospel and salvation are, it has to make sense of these practices by the Lord's apostles. If the heart of Jesus' gospel lives somewhere in the ribcage of **by the works of the law, no flesh is justified**, it's hard to make sense of the (Christian) Jews' continued observation of the Law, to say nothing of their efforts at forcing it upon Gentiles — unless perhaps our interpretation of Paul's admonition is off.

The *DONT WALK* sign had led me on a journey...a journey that left me as bewildered as you might be right now. But with lots of reading and some inadvertent help from a Calvinist pastor, I found a route to a new place — a place where one can make sense of all these puzzling pieces.

To do this you have to throw away the frame most people push Christianity into, for the framework most people are taught from childhood is a very human-centric one. We should be seeking a blueprint that puts God's desires, as made clear throughout scripture, at the center of our theological universe.

Join me as we step into a world where humanity revolves around God rather than the reverse, a world where Jesus means exactly what He says, Paul means exactly what he says, and we allow the Christ to accomplish the work Isaiah, Jeremiah, Ezekiel, and the other prophets said He would.

– II –

JESUS' TEACHING ON THE JUDGMENT

In chapter one I boldly claimed that the interpretation we take from Paul's writing chafes against Jesus' teachings on the Judgment. I gave a couple examples and then broached a whirlwind of related questions and ponderings.

As mentioned earlier, Jesus and His apostles could not have spread a message about how His blood was going to redeem us from our sins — no one, not even His disciples, knew He was going to die. He alluded to this a few times, (which the gospel writers point out because it would have significance for their audience), but this could hardly have been part of His or His disciples' general message to the Jewish crowds if not even John, Peter, and the rest had figured it out. (Just a reminder — there is a deeper discussion on what Jesus did not preach in the appendix beginning on page *177*.) We will investigate Jesus' general message in chapters five and six, but here we focus just on His words concerning the Judgment and why the standard reconciliation between His words and church doctrine simply does not work.

Here I'm not developing an extensive description of the Judgment but merely demonstrating a need for a conversation. Don't draw too many conclusions from the observations in this chapter, observations that might leave you even more bewildered and quizzical than the last chapter. The good news is that in chapter three I start answering some questions instead of just piling more on.

Nor am I looking for a total refutation based on a single passage (though I do believe some of these examples provide that). My point is not *this parable absolutely unmans the modern gospel.* Rather, I'm asking people to look at the collection of teachings the gospel writers included and realize they point unequivocally at conclusions very much in conflict with the evangelical dogma.

The Synoptic Gospels

Matthew, Mark, and Luke are called the Synoptic Gospels because they give a synopsis of Christ's ministry. Since they largely reinforce each other, I will discuss examples in Matthew. As we look at these passages, ask yourself what message Matthew is conveying. How would a 1st-century Jew understand Jesus' teachings (or Matthew's compilation of them)?

Note, there are passages whose relevance to the final Judgment is debateable or that appear to blend this judgment with others. Here I've captured only those passages where it can be certain that heaven-or-hell Judgment is in view.

Matthew 5:22–30

Here, Christ gives several warnings about hell, portraying the dangers of sin rather graphically, saying things like **If your right eye causes you to sin, tear it out and throw it away! It is better to lose one of your members than to have your whole body thrown into hell.**

Now, I don't believe Jesus is advocating actual self-mutilation, but the gist of His message is something along the lines of *Avoid sin at any cost, for sinning puts you in danger of hell, which is worse than anything you might imagine.*

These admonitions strike me as unnatural when put next to the modern gospel. Christ speaks to people who have already sinned. According to the modern gospel, they are *already* "guilty," regardless of whether they sin in the future or not. In *Mark 9:43–49* Jesus directs these warnings to His disciples. Why would His disciples (who began believing in Him back when He turned water into wine: *John 2:11*) be in danger of hell? On top of that, why would they be in danger due to possible future sins?

Christ's words imply that all are in danger of hell due to their sin without necessarily being *already condemned*; that is twice removed from the modern gospel. Evangelicals claim believers are in no danger of hell while non-believers are in total danger. They further claim we all naturally deserve eternal wrath.

Matthew 7:21–23

Jesus crowns the Sermon on the Mount by saying

> **Not everyone who says to me "Lord, Lord" will enter into the kingdom of heaven — only the one who does the will of my Father in heaven. On that day, many will say to me "Lord, Lord, didn't we prophesy in your name, and in your name cast out demons and do many powerful deeds?" Then I will declare to them "I never knew you. Go away from me, you lawbreakers."**

Jesus does not dispute that they have true faith, faith enough to throw out demons. Yet Christ indicates these will be rejected at the Judgment.

Some key on the **I never knew you** snippet, as though that is the cause for rejection. In reality Christ has already given the reason: **only the one who does the will of my Father.** This passage leads into *7:24–26*, contrasting those who adhere to Jesus' commands (**Everyone who hears these words of mine and <u>does</u> them**) with those who ignore the commands comprising His sermon. Comparing the parallel in *Luke 6:47–49* (where Jesus contrasts those who put His commands **into practice** and those who do not) shows that *Matthew 7:21–23* matches up with **Why do you call me 'Lord, Lord' and don't do what I tell you?** (*Luke 6:46*) So we must understand the condemnation in *Matthew 7:21–23* is due to disobedience, not a lack of relationship.

When Jesus says **I never knew you**, He is *disavowing* them, not indicating a lack of familiarity. Like in *Luke 13:27* (**I don't know where you come from**), He is not saying He doesn't know the people — He taught and ate with them. Rather, He is disassociating Himself from those who do not do God's will, just as Peter did when he denied association with Christ (e.g., *Luke 22:55–60*).

This denial should not surprise us. As Paul writes in *2nd Timothy 2:12* to *believers* **if we deny Him, He will also deny us.** His words in *1st Thessalonians 4:3–8* show this rejection cannot be seen as simple unbelief.

Matthew 12:36–37

Jesus tells the Pharisees **I tell you that on the day of Judgment, people will give an account for every worthless word they speak. For by your words you will be justified, and by your words you will be condemned.**

When I asked my evangelical friends about the first of these two verses, I was told, "There will be an accounting, but we will not be condemned by it." That struck me as odd. It does not make much sense given the second verse.

Furthermore, how does the idea of our being **justified** by our own words fit the gospel we are taught?

Matthew 13:24–50

Jesus describes the Judgment in the *Wheat and the Weeds*, a parable recorded in *Matthew 13:24–30* and explained in verses *37–42*. Someone plants wheat in a field and is later told by his slaves that weeds sprouted at the same time as the wheat. The slaves ask him if they should go pull up the weeds now. The owner replies **No, since in gathering the weeds you may uproot the wheat with them. Let both grow together until the harvest.**

At the harvest, The angels pull out the weeds (described as **everything that causes sin as well as all lawbreakers**) and throw them into a **fiery furnace**, leaving the **righteous** to shine in the **kingdom of their Father.**

The most obvious question is, "What would cause the slaves to uproot wheat when pulling out the weeds?" The answer becomes more clear if we understand that Jesus does not mean just any old weed here. He refers to *darnel*, which closely resembles wheat until harvest time. The *fruit* of the wheat plant is very different from the *fruit* of the darnel plant (to put things in the context of *Matthew 12:33*), but otherwise the plants are nearly indistinguishable.

There is no mention of atonement or forgiveness of sins. All plants are judged the same way. The reapers are not told to overlook the bad fruits of certain special plants. While parables are not exhaustive treatments of a subject, we expect some mention of Christ's sacrifice if forgiveness of sins (rather than judgment of fruits) is the prevailing factor at the Judgment.

A few verses after explaining this parable, Jesus gives a very similar one in *Matthew 13:47–50* where fishermen cast nets. The conclusion of that parable reads **It will be this way at the end of the age. Angels will come and separate the evil from the righteous and throw them into the fiery furnace, where there will be weeping and gnashing of teeth.**

Some claim the first parable says nothing about how the Judgment works, but teaches that only good seed can bring forth good fruit. This makes little sense of the whole dialogue between the reapers and the owner. In any event, the second parable contains nothing that would point to this conclusion.

Evangelicals often explain parables like these by saying our works are judged *as proof of our faith.* Another solution Christians propose is "God judges us by our works, but only judges believers by their *good works*," which is the Lutheran position (as described in *Christian Dogmatics*).

These explanations fail to explain why Jesus makes no mention of atonement or forgiveness. A straight-forward reading has Jesus tying the Judgment to repentance, rather than to belief, forgiveness, or redirection of God's wrath. In particular, it is hard to reconcile this parable with the claim that those who never hear of Jesus are simply "out of luck" because God's hands are tied.

Worse, these defenses fail to respect Jesus' point. Christ's words are a call to repent from **everything that causes sin**, which He alludes to before these parables (*Matthew 13:15*). Indeed, Matthew describes the same message of repentance with identical imagery when referring to John's ministry in *3:8*.

This must be an exhortation to repentance rather than something more arcane, for the disciples indicate they understood these parables (*Matthew 13:51*), yet Jesus had not even begun to speak of His later suffering (which occurs in

Matthew 16:21). Matthew gives no commentary here or anywhere else that allows a reader to violently reinterpret this parable as anything other than a call to turn from evil deeds for the sake of the hearer's eternal destiny. If one (unforgiven) sin were just as damning as a trillion, Jesus would be giving His listeners false hope. If repentance toward God is not sufficient to pass the Judgment, then Jesus is criminally misleading His listeners. Jesus does not serve up this call to repentance with a side-order of the modern gospel or anything else that could be construed as "belief in Christ." At this point the general Jewish population had no idea that Jesus was the Christ.

These teachings of Christ really represent two separate problems for the modern gospel. First, Jesus is presenting a Judgment using language that people today would decry as "works-righteousness." Secondly, Jesus' description implicitly disproves the idea that none are "righteous in God's eyes." When Jesus speaks of **the evil** in this parable, He clearly does not mean *everyone that has not been cleansed by My blood*. There is no inkling of that either in the parables or in the commentary by Matthew. No objective person would read this and think the **evil** here refers to every person's default state. If Jesus wants His disciples to change their understanding of *the evil* versus *the righteous*, He would not describe the **evil** people in *Matthew 13:41* as **everyone who causes sin and the ones who practice lawlessness** *just as He did in Matthew 5:19*.

Matthew 16:26–27

Jesus says **For the Son of Man will come with His angels in the glory of His Father, and then He will reward each according to what he has done**.

To explain this verse and similar ones, some strands of Christianity developed "rewards theology." They claim good deeds earn prestige in heaven's society without determining who gains admittance. In other words, they say Christ is talking about icing on the cake here… without discussing the cake.

But Christ is clearly not referring to such "bonus points" here because this passage comes immediately after the warning **For what does it benefit a person if he gains the whole world but forfeits his life? Or what can a person give in exchange for his life?** (The Greek for "life" and "soul" are the same.)

Another reason Jesus cannot be referring to mere rewards here is that the verse He quotes from the Old Testament (*Psalms 62:12*) is the same one Paul uses in *Romans 2:6* when describing who goes to heaven and who goes to hell — exactly what "rewards theology" claims Jesus is not discussing here.

As in *Luke 10:25–28*, Jesus is affirming the Jews' understanding of God's Judgment, not reinterpreting it.

Matthew 25:31–46

Could Jesus be more clear about the Judgment than in His parable of the sheep and goats? ... **inherit the kingdom prepared for you from the foundation of the world. For I was hungry and you gave me food, I was thirsty and you gave me something to drink...** certainly seems clear to me. He goes so far as to call one group **righteous** before contrasting them with the **unrighteous** who ignored those in need and will depart into **eternal punishment.**

Christ calls certain people **righteous** based on charity and stewardship. He makes no reference to Christians being judged any differently than unbelievers. How would a miserly believer fare according to Christ's depiction?

Artificial Righteousness

Some evangelicals preach that nothing we do makes us righteous, even after we believe. They claim that our righteousness, at least for purposes of the Judgment, is an artificial righteousness God gives us. Just as God places our sins on Jesus, Jesus' merit is placed on us. I'll occasionally refer to this notion of "imputed" righteousness throughout the book, but for right now I just wanted to point out we find absolutely nothing like that portrayed in Jesus' teachings.

What about John?

It must be admitted that many passages and verses in John appear at first blush to support the modern gospel, but there are also places, like *John 5:29*, that agree with the repeated teachings of the three synoptic gospels.

The passage of Jewish ideas to Greek manuscripts to English translations has been roughest on John's gospel, which presents many abstract discourses Jesus told Jews that John had to convey to Greeks. The next two chapters are dedicated to understanding John's gospel, but for now I'd like to use a single, extremely famous, example to show how easy it is to misconstrue John's words.

John 3:16 represents to many a clear articulation of the gospel. It has all the ingredients: God's love, the giving of the Son, belief, and eternal life. What happens when we read the passage in context?

The **eternal life** in *John 3:15–16* is linked to the **kingdom of God** described in the earlier conversation John is commenting on (verse *6*). Jesus says **unless a man is born of water and spirit, he cannot enter the kingdom of God.** Reading the longer passage confirms that the **kingdom of God** is a reference to the Spirit received through baptism, not post-Judgment life in heaven. I realize it's odd to say that **eternal life** refers to life in the present rather than life after the Judgment — we will discuss this at length in the next two chapters.

John 3:16–21 does not say that unbelievers are condemned due to a general unrighteousness plaguing all humanity. What is the reason given?

> **Now this is the basis for judging, that the light has come into the world and the people loved the darkness rather than the light, because their deeds were evil. For everyone who does evil hates the light and does not come to the light, so that their deeds will not be exposed.**

The condemnation described is *because the person loves the darkness rather than the light*, which is very different from the reason given by the Church. Imagine a 2nd-century Jew who has never heard of Jesus and is trying to do God's will, living by the commandments given in the Torah. The evangelical viewpoint is that such ignorance is no excuse...but does that Jew fail to believe *because she hates the light?* No. She fails to believe for the same reason that ancient people didn't believe in Elvis sightings.

Now, consider a 21st-century Buddhist who lives out Christ's laws but does not self-label as a Christian because every Christian he ever knew was a judgmental jerk. Did that Buddhist *reject* Christ because he *hates the light?*

No, the passage is not a universal discussion of how the Judgment works; by its own wording it could apply only to those with full knowledge of Jesus. Even if this passage refers to the final Judgment, it would not do evangelicals any favors, for the passage clearly links the condemnation to someone's *disposition*.

In reality, John is referring to the judgment of the Jewish leaders who rejected Christ (*3:19*). This condemnation *has already taken place* (*3:18*), for the Romans came in 70 A.D. and destroyed the temple, an indescribably severe loss for the Jews whose entire culture revolved around it.[1] As we will see in chapters five and six, the Jews reject Christ because He exposed their twisting of God's Law to their own ends, hence the **For everyone who does evil hates the light and does not come to the light, so that their deeds will not be exposed.**

So, John is not discussing the Final Judgment; even if he were, the reason for condemnation here is not the reason given by the modern gospel. John indicates a Judgment of disposition, which is very different from the Judgment claimed by evangelicals. This whole passage makes more sense when you understand John's purpose in writing his gospel, which we will discuss in chapter nine.

---

[1]Indeed, *John 11:48* is an ironic prophecy. It's also a clever wordplay because "take away our temple" could just as easily refer to Christ's crucifixion — the Greek for "take away" is the same word John uses for "crucify," and Jesus' body is God's temple.

Why the Standard Answer Fails

Evangelicals have faced a philosophical problem for centuries. *If we are saved by faith, what stops someone from being a terrible, greedy, selfish person, all the while being assured a place in heaven based on faith in Christ?*

A commonly given response is "true faith produces works." While this addresses the *philosophical* issue described above, it does not solve the *biblical* problems described in chapters one and two.

The philosophical problem "why do believers get to safely do anything they want?" is *not* the same as "if going to heaven is based only on forgiveness through faith, why is that message not found in Jesus' teachings?" I think Christians confuse the two, thinking an answer to the first is a solution to the second.

I've hinted already why "we are judged by our works as evidence of our faith" is not a satisfactory answer. After all, if Jesus thought the Judgment really boiled down to forgiveness through faith, He could have simply said so. If the apostles saw Christ's purpose as delivering people from hell, they would have gone to the Gentiles sooner. They didn't.

Here I'd like to show directly why "true faith causes good deeds" does not resolve the difficulties posed by the teachings of Christ.

In *John 5:29* Jesus describes that He will raise all the dead, . . . **the ones who have done what is good to the resurrection resulting in life, and the ones who have done what is evil to the resurrection resulting in condemnation.** (Incidentally, I asked a trained evangelist about this passage and was told "John doesn't say there *are* any people in the group Jesus says had 'done good.'")

Based on this verse and many similar passages, the *only* way to maintain the evangelical view is to claim *only believers can do good* and *all believers do good.* But evangelicals *do* say only believers in Christ can do deeds that please God. So it does not seem like there's a problem.

But there is a problem — *Someone can be pleasing to God without having faith in Christ or knowing the gospel.* This has been shown throughout scripture by several people in different categories. Similarly, the Bible gives several examples of people having true faith who are still condemned by their deeds, the deeds Jesus claims are the basis for Judging.

We'll look at each side of the *We are judged by our deeds as evidence of our faith because faith in Christ (and only faith in Christ) leads one to do works pleasing to God* defense here. If *either* half failed, it would show the modern gospel is not biblically supportable. It really should not surprise us that neither holds, for "true faith produces works" is far too pat an answer to address why Jesus' portrayal of the Judgment is so different from what most are told.

Claim 1: Does True Faith Always Produce the Righteous Acts Jesus Says Will Be the Basis for Judgment?

This may sound like a stupid question. "If your faith does not produce works, it was not real faith to begin with" sounds like a reasonable claim.

The problem is that it considers the question within a vacuum, naïvely suggesting that our faith or lack thereof is the only thing determining our actions. In the real world, our various beliefs, desires, psychological insecurities, misconceptions, and emotions each play a role. When I chose not to disclose that my Christian faith was one reason I stood waiting for the *WALK* sign (way back at the beginning of chapter 1), it did not retroactively scuttle a lifetime of belief. You could say my faith was weak at that moment or that I was a coward, but you could hardly claim the action was because I didn't have *any* true faith. Yet, Jesus and the authors of the New Testament willingly suffered persecution orders of magnitude greater than whatever I was dodging with Danielle. They would damn me for such craven behavior, and rightfully so! (*Luke 9:26*; *Romans 8:17*; *Hebrews 10:25–36*; and *1st Peter 4:16–17*)

There are plenty of broader examples in scripture. We will note these while taking a closer look at the reasoning used to prop up the "true faith produces works" defense. When investigating this topic, it is critical to observe that only "true faith" can grant someone the present gifts of Christ's work. Hence, we will be looking particularly at places where the Bible refers to someone who has received these blessings. For example, if the Bible says someone has been **sanctified by Christ's blood**, that person *had* to have "true faith."

Defense 1: Faith Produces Works out of Gratitude

One common rationale is that we are so grateful for Christ's work that we naturally desire to do God's will. That sounds good in theory, but claiming this is the motivation for good works paints God as a pretty stupid Supreme Being. The Old Testament shows humans do not act this way. What do we see almost immediately after God rescues the Israelites from Egypt? They don't even get to Sinai before beginning to complain. *Exodus 15:1–19* is their song of triumph; by *16:3*, they'd rather be back as slaves in Egypt!

Similarly, Aaron was singled out as God's mouthpiece and head of the entire priest caste, but he still became envious of Moses in *Numbers 12:1–3*. Saul was elevated by God from nothing to be king of Israel, and yet it did not lead him to do all that the Lord commanded. He certainly performed many works for God, yet God found him wanting. Solomon was graced with more than perhaps any Old Testament king, yet the vast grace shown to him did not keep him faithful.

Defense 2: A New Heart Provokes Good Deeds

The more common reason given is that believers will naturally do good works by virtue of the new heart worked by their conversion. The claim then is that anyone who is not doing good works was never really converted in the first place. As logical as this sounds, it is also contradicted by the Bible. The error here is that the "new heart" spoken of is misunderstood.

It is not that we get brainwashed into doing God's will when earlier we did not desire it. The Old Testament is festooned with people with a heart for God before such a "new heart" was available. Rather, those who already desire to do God's will are given a better understanding of what that will is and a stronger resolve toward doing it. This gets back to *John 3:19–21* and *7:17*; there were *already* people who desired to do God's will. The new heart enhances their ability to do it. Paul speaks of the same thing in *Romans 7:15–25* (before receiving the new heart) and *Romans 8:1–8* (describing the effect of the Spirit after being pulled from the spiritual shackles that our Bibles translate as **condemnation**).

In the New Testament we see examples of people who were freed from sin by genuine belief, yet even the new heart did not provoke the level of righteousness demanded by Christ. He tells John (*Revelation 2:3–5*) to write the church in Ephesus, saying that He is **aware that you have persisted steadfastly, endured much for the sake of my name, and have not grown weary.** In the next breath He says **You have departed from your first love! Therefore, remember from what high state you have fallen and repent! Do the deeds you did at first.** That hardly sounds like the people lacked authentic faith.

The writer of Hebrews describes the same problem in *Hebrews 10:24–31*, speaking to people he says have been **made holy** by Christ's blood. A rather direct rebuttal is given in *2nd Peter 1:8–9*, citing the danger of **becoming ineffective and unproductive in your pursuit of knowing our Lord Jesus Christ more intimately** for someone who has **forgotten about the cleansing of his past sins.** Later in the same epistle we hear about those who have **escaped the filthy things of this world** but are then re-ensnared to them. For these, Peter claims **their last state has become worse for them than their first.** Nor can all this be swept under the carpet of "falling away," as though Peter is talking about loss of faith. Rather, Peter specifically refers to turning **back from the holy commandments that had been delivered to them** (*2nd Peter 2:20–21*).

Add to the above the many exhortations by Paul for people who were already sanctified to live in the way they should. Indeed, that is the entire point of *Romans 6:12–23*, a passage that would be unneeded if a new heart were, by itself, enough to ensure good deeds. Paul spends several chapters blasting the church of Corinth for living sinful lives even though they had been **washed**, **sanctified**, and **justified** already (*1st Corinthians 6:11*).

Jesus describes the situation well in the Parable of the Soils in *Matthew 13:3–23*; *Mark 4:3–20*; and *Luke 8:5–15*. Some people never believe. Some people believe, even **receive the word with joy**, but persecution stops them from holding fast to the Christian hope. Others believe, but the competing lies of the world stop them from being productive. Only some who believe bear fruit.

It is important to note that this second group actually did truly believe. Jesus says so in Luke's account. Their belief just could not stand up against persecution, much like Peter's didn't stand up in *Matthew 26:69–75*. This is the concern the writer of Hebrews is responding to in *Hebrews 10:25*, for some believers had stopped meeting in fellowship for fear of persecution (see *10:32–39*). He is most definitely writing to true believers, believers who have had their **hearts sprinkled clean** according to *10:23*.

Similarly, the focus is not on the death of the third group, but rather that they did not produce anything. The lies of the world (Jesus mentions fear, materialism, and covetousness) make someone unproductive. These people do not lose faith but rather have their faith overrun by provisions of the flesh.

Claim 2: Must one believe in Jesus to do good?

This side is slightly easier to consider because we no longer have to worry about whether a given person's faith counted as "true faith" or not. Instead, we only have to look at people who were genuinely described as pleasing God.

Nineveh — Enemies of God

Jonah's work in Nineveh has to look bizarre to anyone who holds the modern gospel. Jonah's short book poses a significant problem for evangelical claims because a wicked people with no belief in a coming Messiah avoids God's wrath purely through repentance, without any sacrifice or faith in a far-future Christ.

Rahab — Oblivious to the Gospel

Rahab (*Joshua 2:1–3*) is commended for her faith in *Hebrews 11:31* and *James 2:25*. But what did she have faith in? She certainly didn't have faith in Christ, nor in any kind of gospel message. The only thing Rahab knew was that the God of Israel (Whom she knew nothing about!) was real.

That's it. That was all she knew — *the God these other people worship exists and has power.* James' general conception of faith (*James 2:19*) **God is one** is not much more sophisticated than Rahab's. Jesus Himself lumps this with the two great laws when quoting from the Old Testament in *Mark 12:29*: **The most important is: "Listen, Israel, the Lord our God, the Lord is one..."**

If Rahab (a heathen prostitute who had no understanding of the gospel) can be commended for her actions based on faith, we *must* allow that someone can act on a faith *in God* without any knowledge *of Christ*, or *the gospel*. Rahab's faith was not in forgiveness of sins. Rahab's faith was shown in her actions and her belief (*Joshua 2:11*) that **The Lord your God is God in heaven above and on earth below!** One cannot say she put faith in God to protect her, for it was the spies she trusted with regard to her personal security — and her immediate deliverance from death was conditional on her following their instructions exactly. Her faith was in God's power, not in any personal divine intervention on her behalf. Even if one reads into the text that Rahab was saved because she depended on God's mercy, that is hardly a defense of the evangelical position. First, Rahab's action certainly had nothing to do with her *eternal* security. Secondly, one can "rely on God's mercy" without any belief in (or even knowledge of) Christ.

If Rahab can be commended for responding to her primitive understanding of the Living God, why can't others who lack the gospel also do God's will? Rahab's example shows that you can do good *based on whatever understanding of God you have, even if you know no gospel.*

Noah — Before there was a Gospel

God **found favor with Noah** (*Genesis 6:8*) *before* he built the ark. There was no gospel to believe in, no Christ to look forward to. God's promise to Abraham was the foundation of the gospel,[2] and he would not come for another 20 generations. Noah found favor by doing God's will as best he knew it.

---

[2]Some claim there were predictions of Christ earlier than Abraham, suggesting that people from the beginning were told of a coming savior. The Jewish writers of the New Testament, who knew the Old Testament backwards and forwards, don't describe any. Nor do we see remarks stressing the importance of believing in a coming savior *anywhere* in the Old Testament or the concept that the Messiah was to save *individuals* from *hell.* We have no indication *Genesis 3:14–16* was treated by those before Abraham as anything but a "just-so" story explaining why snakes have no legs. Among the dozens of prophecies the gospel writers show Christ fulfilling, not one of them hails from before Abraham's time. When Paul explains why the Gentiles could receive the Holy Spirit, it is because they have become **descendants of Abraham** (*Galatians 3:29*), and the reason Christ gives in *Luke 19:8* for salvation coming to Zaccheus' house is **because he, too, is a son of Abraham.** The writer of Hebrews describes how it is the **descendants of Abraham** God gives help to in *Hebrews 2:16.*

Cornelius — Before Hearing the Gospel

Cornelius' deeds found favor with God (*Acts 10:4*) *before* Peter preaches the gospel to him. In fact, unlike the Jews of the Old Testament, Cornelius was not even looking forward to salvation in the abstract sense. The Jews, including the apostles, solidly believed that the Christ was sent just for them. For example, Paul writes to Gentiles in *Ephesians 2:12*, **you were at that time without Christ, alienated from the citizenship of Israel and strangers to the covenants of promise, having no hope and without God in the world.** Cornelius refused to convert to Judaism, so it can hardly be thought he had faith or hope in *their* Messiah. Based on the description from Acts, there is little reason to believe Cornelius thought of Jesus as anything more than a powerful man of God rumored to be healing people around Judea.

What makes Cornelius, who lived after Christ's coming, wasn't a Jew, and had not heard the gospel, any different from people today who try to do God's will as best they know it?

These examples show what most accept without evidence: people can do godly deeds based on whatever knowledge of God they have. Helping the poor, defending the oppressed, depending on God to provide, and many other virtuous enterprises adorn the Bible from Genesis to Revelation. Can anyone really claim it is impossible to do these without faith in Christ? (I would concur it is impossible to do these things for the right reasons without faith in *God*.)

I'm not saying that people can just ignore Christ or that we should not proclaim the risen King. I'm just showing that the "true faith produces works" idea does not resolve the conflicts I've described so far because non-Christians can do God-pleasing works through whatever faith in God they have. There is a big difference between saying you cannot do good without faith *in God* and saying you cannot do good without faith *in Christ*. Yet evangelicals only allow the latter, for Peter claims **there is salvation in no one else** (*Acts 4:12*).

Some say "If you don't believe in Christ, you can't have faith in the living God, because the living God sent Christ. If you believe in a god that didn't send Christ, you believe in a god that does not exist." This reasoning appeals to dubious logic and is beaten senseless by several biblical examples.

Did Rahab respond to faith in a false god? Was Noah faithful to a false god? Was Cornelius commended for idolatry? None of these knew the gospel of Christ. Paul claims God's plan for all people to have a part in Abraham's blessing had been kept a secret (*Romans 16:25–26*; *Ephesians 3:5–6*; and *Colossians*

1:26). Isn't the logical conclusion that these people were affirmed by direct belief in God's existence and power in the present rather than faith in a gospel of future grace? If the above examples did not convince you that ignorance does not make people idolaters, I refer you to Paul's respect for the Athenians in *Acts 17:23*.

The logic claiming "anyone who does not believe in Jesus cannot have true faith in God" is dangerously close to saying "If you don't believe everything we believe, you're an idolater." Using this reasoning, any Christian sect can claim all others are cults. For example, Lutherans (who believe the bread and wine of communion are more than a mere symbol of Christ's body and blood) could say, "If you believe the bread and wine are a mere symbol of Christ's body and blood, you are an idolater. Your Jesus never existed because the real Jesus (the one *I* believe in) said that the bread **is** His body and the wine **is** His blood."

The above paragraphs show the sort of energy wasted in fighting between factions. We can disagree without cultifying each other. What does Paul say in *1st Corinthians 12:3*? **No one can say, "Jesus is Lord," except by the Holy Spirit.** The same knife that divvies up the church cuts the hearts within it. How can we show Jesus' love to the world if we cannot show it to our brothers and sisters in Christ? The emotional mortar spent firmly maintaining orthodoxy's walls would be better spent mending creation and the lives within it.

The same applies to individuals in a given church. We should be united by our love of God and obedience to Christ, not our catechisms. A "dogma first" mentality may allow a church to win the battle of confessional purity, but risks losing the war — ministering to those for whom Christ died. When Christ healed people, He didn't ask them to affirm 23 articles of faith. When Paul refers to defending **sound doctrine**, he writes of *applied* doctrine regarding behavior **conforming to godliness**, not abstract theories about how God works. Our spiritual roadsides are bedecked by the battered souls of orphans effectively disowned by their local churches, to say nothing of those feeling lost within their congregations. Remember, dogma was likely the reason the priest in the Good Samaritan parable stayed far from the victim, who might have been dead — even accidentally touching a corpse would render him unclean for temple service.

I think many believers grapple with the claim that only those lucky enough to hear about Christ have a chance at heaven. I doubt most evangelicals ever come to complete peace on the matter. Instead, they stop wrestling with these issues because no one presents a satisfactory solution. Our desire for personal security, our preferred conceptions of God, and pressure from the church create a draining tug-of-war in the heart of the believer, and I think many Christians eventually block it off, deciding it isn't worth the emotional turmoil.

Summary and Final Notes

Jesus' version of the Judgment stands in complete conflict with what people are told constitutes "Bible-based Christianity," which depends upon an *interpretation* of Paul.

Jesus' Teaching	Modern Interpretation of Paul
All deeds relevant	Only unforgiven sin relevant
Judgment like an evaluation	Judgment like a court of law
No special treatment for believers	Absolute special treatment
Those who do good are called to life.	Those who believe are justified.
Workers of lawlessness are "in danger of" hell, regardless of their faith.	Non-believers have no hope of justification regardless of their actions.
People are called righteous without mention of faith.	No one is righteous.
Focus on faithfulness to Jesus' commandments	Focus on faith in Christ's sacrifice
Righteousness by adjudication	Righteousness by imputation

You should not jump to conclusions about the Judgment based on the chart above. I'm not laying a foundation for Unitarianism, saying that it doesn't matter what you believe or that all religions are routes to God or anything like that. I am simply investigating the Judgment here.

One can hardly defend the broad chasm between Jesus' teachings and modern dogma on the basis that Jesus was not "showing the full picture" to the Jews. These parables represent not only Jesus' teachings to the Jews but the teachings Matthew, Mark, and Luke chose to capture for their audiences. As demonstrated in this chapter, if the gospel message is *Jesus died for our sins to allow God to excuse believers at the Judgment*, then Matthew does a rather rotten job of transmitting that message. While Jesus does give the disciples extra clarity on some parables, we must also keep in mind Jesus' defense before the Jews in *John 18:20–21*, where claims to have preached His message openly and **said nothing in secret**.

In any event, Jesus' descriptions and admonitions are hardly a "partial picture" of a Judgment resembling that painted by evangelicals. One does not prepare lasagna by beginning with a Graham-cracker pie crust and filling in appropriately.

The last two rows of the chart deserve special consideration. People often speak of "faith in Christ" when they really mean "faith that Christ's blood is sufficient to pay my debt" or "faith that Christ can save me from hell." These understandings of faith are even further removed from Jesus' description of the Judgment. Whatever faith is shown by the works being judged is certainly not a faith in the sufficiency of Christ's sacrifice. It is easy to imagine people having full confidence that Christ's sacrifice has paid their debt, yet living with no respect for Jesus' commands of love toward all and succor to the oppressed. Isn't the conservative church regularly indicted on this very charge?

Similarly, the righteousness of which Christ speaks repeatedly cannot by any reading be seen as righteousness gained by God taking Jesus' righteousness and putting it on believers. There is none of that to be seen in the wheat, fish, sheep, or any other metaphors Christ uses. Nor is it to be found in others' descriptions of the Judgment. For example, *1st Peter 1:13–16* exhorts people to righteousness and then *1st Peter 1:17* reads **If you address as Father the one who impartially judges according to each one's work, live out the time of your temporary residence here in reverence**. *James 2:12–13* is similarly at odds with evangelical thought on this score.

These differences cannot easily be reconciled by saying "It is the will of God to believe in Christ" or "If you believe, you will do the will of God." There are plenty of people (those who came before Jesus, those who never heard of Jesus, those who heard a warped version of the gospel, etc.) who can do God's will and never come to faith in Christ. Furthermore, Christ is just as fervent in warning His disciples about the dangers of sin as He is those who would reject Him.

Such pat answers subordinate Christ to Paul, showing more interest in making Christ comply with our philosophy than allowing Him to simply mean what He says. It is not that His rendering of the Judgment is *incomplete* — His picture is *incompatible* with anything resembling the modern one. To say evangelicals get the Judgment right is to call Jesus a liar. The dogma of the church will pass away, but *The Sheep and the Goats* will remain for any who have ears.

The issue is not that Paul and Christ disagree with each other, but rather that they *appear* to conflict due to the interpretations we are taught and assumptions we bring into our Bible reading. When Paul clearly speaks of the Judgment, his version is in line with Jesus'. We do not need to force one to agree with the other through rhetorical acrobatics, but we will need to put aside our expectations when trying to understand Christ's purpose. And that starts in the next chapter.

– III –

THE FRAME

After Dartmouth, I taught math a private school for a few years, a job I landed mostly by suggesting the *papas y huevos taco* to a random guy at *Lou's Diner* — but that's another story. Sometime during March, the school would send a letter home with each student asking the parents to indicate their plans for the coming year. The letter went something like this:

Dear Parent, as this year draws to a successful close, we at Salisbury are already determining the budget for the next one. To inform this process, we ask that you return the enclosed commitment card indicating your plans for the coming year.

We provided the parent an envelope and a small candy cane.

A student of mine, Marci, brought back an envelope that seemed a bit fatter than the rest. I did not think much of it until the principal called me into her office. Rather than send back the commitment card, Marci's dad had returned a lengthy letter, which lay on the principal's desk. She read it to me, and it went something like this:

During the last year, Salisbury has failed to address even the most prosaic issues we parents brought to its attention last May. We still wait half an hour every afternoon due to Salisbury's inefficient dismissal procedures. We still worry about the lack of an integrated fire alarm system, and the school has failed to install a much-needed security solution to protect our children during the day.

It is therefor [sic] unsurprising that Salisbury failed to address our less mundane concerns as well. Marci is still taught Spanish by a teacher whose English she cannot understand. She still receives inadequate time to complete her work during study hall, forcing her to finish her assignments at home, cutting into family time. Worse, her math teacher [*that would be me*] has relentlessly given exams all year no mere mortal could

37

possibly complete in the time allotted. We cannot in good
conscience put her through another such year.

Were that not enough, Salisbury has also failed to modernize
their computer lab or dismiss uncertified...

The letter went on and on describing the father's gripes, and it ended rather abruptly after three pages of criticism with no indication that he planned to re-enroll Marci. Twice her dad said he could not allow Marci to go through another year like this one. The principal drafted a letter lamenting that Marci's needs were not being met and stating that we wished her well next year at whatever school her parents transferred her to.

Imagine our surprise when we received another note a few days later that essentially said "Oh, we were not planning on changing schools. Marci will stay at Salisbury for next year."

Why is this response so shocking? To put a fine point on things, the original letter is misleading for two reasons:

- It leaves out something of vast importance which is not suggested by the letter as a whole, something we would expect to read if it were true (that the parents were going to re-enroll Marci).

- It includes several particular points (the complaints) that, on their face, indicate a stance the writer does not have, and no efforts are made to stop the reader from misunderstanding these points.

If the gospel message were really what evangelicals indicate, then these same criticisms apply to the gospels of Matthew, Mark, and Luke. If all are bound to hell without Christ's intervention, and only those who believe are saved from the eternal wrath of God, then the gospels written by these three men leave us scratching our heads. Why would they not clearly state this "gospel," and why would they incorporate so many teachings of Christ that consistently lead their readers to other conclusions?

These questions and observations left me bewildered. Christian study materials are not much help. I urge you to consult commentaries and read their explanations of passages like those I've cited so far. I believe you'll find they tend to bend Christ's words to match a theology not found in the text.

Is Paul wrong? I didn't accept that. For whatever reason, Jesus repeatedly speaks of people being **righteous** and a Judgment based on deeds with no reference to believers and non-believers being treated differently, yet Paul appears to stress the opposite: **For by grace you have been saved through faith, and this is not from yourselves — it is the gift of God.**

To summarize these differences:

Favoritism	Paul seems to say believers and non-believers are treated very differently at the Judgment. Jesus never indicates partiality, and many of His teachings would look odd if there were any:

    Forgiveness All are forgiven when they forgive others. No one who fails to forgive is forgiven.

    Judgment All are judged in the same way they judge others.

    Sin All are in danger of condemnation due to their sin, including believers. Indeed, *Mark 9:43–48* is addressed only to His disciples.

Works/Faith Every discussion of the Judgment by Jesus relates to words and deeds, and some believers are rejected by Christ. On the other hand, Paul writes, in *Romans 8:1*, **There is therefore no condemnation for those who are in Christ Jesus.**

Righteousness Jesus calls certain people **righteous** based on their deeds, even those who lived before Him and did not know of a coming savior. He refers to others as **doing what is good**. However, Paul claims that **no one is justified by the works of the law**.

I read and read and pondered and thought, finding no fully satisfactory solution. I couldn't share much of this struggle with others in my fellowships. As I'm sure many of you can appreciate, most churches are not very welcoming of questions about the faith, even from those who are serious believers. Posing questions about the faith is confused with questioning the faith itself.

When I did ask leaders and peers about these issues, the responses suggested they had given little thought to these quandaries. No one seemed to really want to wrestle with what scripture said.

Is Our Frame Crooked?

If Paul and Jesus appear to give conflicting descriptions of the Judgment, perhaps the problem lies in our reading. Maybe our fundamental assumptions cause us to see things that aren't there.

For example, consider the question *what is the purpose of religion?* I think many grow up (as I did) thinking religion's purpose is to secure your spot in the afterlife. We see Christianity as answering *How do I get to heaven?* in the same sense that science answers questions concerning the natural world.

That notion would seem half-baked and misinformed to the Jews. The ruling Jewish sect, the Sadducees, did not believe in the afterlife at all. And those Jews who believed in an afterlife did not focus on it. Some held the coming Messiah had something to do with this afterlife, some didn't. It was simply not a critical part of their beliefs, certainly not the central purpose of God's plan.

The Jews of Jesus' day cherished a connection with God spanning two millennia, back to the promise made to Abraham. Their entire society revolved about the fact that they were God's chosen people. Belief in God impacted their culture as gravity impacts ours. The idea that religion was meant to answer the question "how does one get to heaven?" would make as much sense to them as saying bakers exist to give out free samples. Asking the Jews why they believed in God would be akin to asking a mother why she loves her children.

While we're discussing basic assumptions, consider the question "What is salvation?" We use the term all the time. Those passages where Paul appears to conflict with Jesus describe how we are **saved**. What does the word mean?

To Jews (e.g., Paul), the term *salvation* referred to God's rescuing them from *their oppressors* and elevating them *above other nations*. In *Luke 1:71* Zechariah prophesies that Jesus would bring **Salvation from our enemies and from the hand of all who hate us.** This is a prophet of God speaking God's Word. The disciples show the same understanding in *Luke 24:21* at the end of His ministry: **We had hoped he was the one who was going to redeem Israel.**

Many Christians believe this simply shows Jewish ignorance of God's plan. But where did God describe this plan? Jesus says the prophets spoke of Him and the coming Kingdom. What did they say? The prophets describe a coming age when Israel is elevated above *while coexisting with* other nations (e.g., *Ezekiel 37:27–28*), and none of the prophecies concerning Christ clearly relate to an individual's afterlife.[1] During most of Israel's history, there was no hope placed in life after the grave, as illustrated by *Job 14:10–12*; *Psalms 30:9*; *Ecclesiastes 3:19–20*; and *Isaiah 38:18*. Also, the *wrath* envisioned in the prophecies is not an individualized one at the Judgment, but rather a global one where God *vindicates* Israel by punishing those who were oppressing it.

In conclusion, *the prophets portray a very different understanding of salvation than what is assumed today.*

---

[1] Note that *Daniel 12:2*, the only clear description of the coming resurrection in the Old Testament, does not tie the event to Christ but rather the angel Michael. Resurrection language was sometimes used elsewhere figuratively to describe Judah's return to power.

Salvation Now: The Spirit's Indwelling

While *salvation* is often thought of as "going to heaven," some have a broader view of the term, holding that believers enjoy salvation *already* as a foretaste of heaven-after-Judgment. Depending on what church you attend or the kind of Christians you hang around, the notion that salvation is experienced *now* might sound rather odd. For those not familiar, let me give a crash course.

While the Mosaic covenant was in effect, the Spirit of God resided in the temple. The temple of the new covenant (the covenant instituted by Christ) is a spiritual one built from the souls of believers. To hold the Spirit and consecrate this temple, our souls had to be cleansed and healed, for **no one pours new wine into old wineskins. If he does, the new wine will burst the skins and will be spilled, and the skins will be destroyed.**[2]

Romans 8 explains this at length, but you get the gist in *Ephesians 3:16–17*, where Paul describes his prayers... **He may grant you to be strengthened with power through His Spirit in the inner person, that Christ may dwell in your hearts through faith...**

To grasp the Spirit's purpose, you must understand Israel's 2000-year struggle with God. The Old Testament chronicles the history of Israel and tells the sad tale of a people who could not remain faithful to God. This is **the** recurring problem in the Old Testament. *Jeremiah 31:31–34* shows God's response:

> **A time is coming... when I will make a new covenant with the people of Israel and Judah. It will not be like the covenant that I made with their ancestors when I delivered them from Egypt. For they violated that covenant... I will put my law within them and write it on their hearts... People will no longer need to teach their neighbors and relatives to know me.**

Christians join this covenant by receiving the Holy Spirit. Why does this count as salvation? By nature, we are enslaved to sin, much as a drug addict is enslaved to narcotics. We naturally tend to serve worldly desires rather than God's. The Spirit counsels us to know God's will and strengthens us to do it.

Christ refers to this freedom from sin's domination in *John 8:36* when He says **So if the Son makes you free, you will be free indeed**, and Paul refers to the same in *Acts 13:39*:... **and by this one everyone who believes is freed from all things from which you could not be freed by the Law of Moses.** Peter agrees in *2nd Peter 2:20*. Part of Hebrews is dedicated to this concept as well (see *Hebrews 9:14* and *10:1–2,14*).

---

[2]*Matthew 9:17; Mark 2:22; Luke 5:37; 1st Corinthians 3:16; 6:19; 2nd Corinthians 6:16.* See also *John 7:39; 16:12;,7; Acts 1:4–5; 2:33–39;* and *Hebrews 9:14–17.*

The Two Salvations Contrasted

So, then, we have two kinds of salvation. One salvation, which I'll call *deliverance*, describes what most people consider "the gospel" — being saved from hell. The other salvation, which I'll call *regeneration*, describes the healing and strengthening of a soul. In regeneration, we are transformed by the Holy Spirit from creatures mastered by our weaknesses into people who can overcome selfishness to be faithful to the Living God.

Many Christians only speak of deliverance. Others, especially those who refer to a personal relationship with Christ, consider both salvations as the "package deal" that faith gets you. If both kinds are taught, they are always presented as two sides of the same coin — inseparable.

But this "two sides of the same coin" notion is not supported by the Bible:

They relate to different sets of people: Regeneration occurs only through the covenant enacted by Jesus, so only those who came after Christ are in a position to enjoy it. Deliverance transcends covenant, pertaining to all people, for all will be judged. We know some people who lived before Christ will survive the Judgment, but no one prior to Christ could enjoy regeneration through the Spirit, as noted in *John 7:39* and *Hebrews 11:39*, for the Spirit had not been given. In the Old Testament, the Holy Spirit can be *upon* someone, but not *inside*. The inside had to be cleaned first, as described in *Hebrews 9:14–23.*

They address different effects of sin: Deliverance saves us *from accountability for sin* while regeneration heals us *from the debilitation due to sin.*

They affect the actions of different agents: Deliverance saves us from *God's Judgment*; regeneration saves us from *sin's poisoning of our nature.* In *2nd Timothy 2:25–6*, Paul evinces hope that opponents of the church will be given **. . . knowledge of the truth and they will come to their senses and escape the devil's trap where they are held captive to do his will.**

They speak to different desires: Regeneration speaks to God's desire to have a faithful people. Deliverance speaks to the human desire for immortality.

They undo the consequences of different types of sin: Sacrifices were *never* instituted to *deliver* individuals from the consequences of deliberate defiance, as indicated by *Hebrews 9:7* and *Numbers 15:27–31*. *Hebrews 10:26*, written to believers who (according to *10:29*) have *already* been sanctified, gives a new covenant equivalent: **For if we deliberately keep on sinning after receiving the knowledge of the truth, no further sacrifice for sins is left for us.** (Stay tuned to see why you don't have to be deathly discouraged by this warning.)

Paul and Christ list a raft of sins that appear to disqualify people from deliverance in *1st Corinthians 6:9–11* and *Revelation 21:8* respectively.

Conversely, none of these stops someone from gaining regeneration. *All* people can come to Christ and receive the Spirit. Many in Corinth had a history of practicing exactly the sins Paul warns against. This has a parallel in the Old Testament where the cleansing sacrifice (done to cleanse the temple, not to attain forgiveness for the people) had to cleanse for *all* sins.

One is easier than the other: There are at least six ways given by the Bible to be forgiven of sins (escaping punishment for them), but *Hebrews 9:22* specifies only one way to purify a soul. (We'll take a look at those six in chapter five.)

Only one is prophesied: The Old Testament prophesies speak repeatedly of regeneration by the Spirit's work on the heart in the coming age, but not deliverance from hell. They described Israel being freed *from its enemies*, not from *God's eternal wrath*.[3]

Deliverance	Regeneration
The guilty pardoned	The guilty rehabilitated
Saves us from God's wrath	Saves us from sin's warping of our nature
Serves our desire	Serves God's desire
Transcends covenants	Pertains only to the new covenant
Does not apply to some sins	Applies to all sins
Jesus as ferryman	Jesus as healer
Jesus as scapegoat	Jesus as Passover sacrifice[4]
Allows immortality	Supports faithfulness
Occurs on the final day	Occurs when one receives the Holy Spirit
Many routes to forgiveness	Only one route to cleansing
Not Messiah's purpose	Part of Messianic Kingdom

---

[3] *Luke 1:70–71; Jeremiah 30:7–11; 31:31; Ezekiel 11:19; 34:23–39; 36:26; 37:23–38; Amos 9:11–15; Zechariah 12:9;* and *Joel 2:27–29*

[4] Actually, both atonement and Passover, because part of the atonement sacrifice was to cleanse the temple: *Hebrews 9:21–23*

A Conjecture

I realized that *if* these two ideas, *regeneration* and *deliverance*, were not merely two sides of the same coin, it might solve the apparent conflict between Christ and Paul. Perhaps, I conjectured, when Paul says things like **For by grace you have been saved through faith** (*Ephesians 2:8*) *he was using the term "saved" only in the regeneration sense!* In other words, Paul used "saved" to denote the indwelling of the Holy Spirit and membership in the new covenant, not to refer to *deliverance* from hell.[5]

This goes beyond the question of what Paul means. The real question is "What does Jesus save us *from*." I claim the Bible indicates Jesus saves us from many things, but God's eternal wrath in hell is not one of them![6]

I realize that may sound too preposterous to consider, like hearing the sun does not go around the earth. Given how the church has presented the gospel, the idea that salvation has nothing directly to do with the Judgment might make as much sense to you as putting an elevator in an outhouse.[7]

Keep in mind that the Jews saw the future resurrection in very simple terms — God would raise up the righteous, either to establish the kingdom described in the prophecies or after such a kingdom had been established. They did not have evangelicals around to tell them that we all naturally belong in hell and need Jesus to save us from that fate. Why would Paul use *salvation* to refer to a deliverance no one (in the 1st century) thought was needed? Indeed, the most affluent Jewish class, the Sadducees, did not believe in an afterlife of any kind, yet they looked forward to the Christ bringing salvation to the Jews.

The prophecies that speak of the Christ do not cast *salvation* as "deliverance from God's eternal wrath," a notion that can hardly be found anywhere in the Old Testament. Rather, the prophets of God who spoke of the Savior saw an ordained King leading them out of oppression to serve God. They were not being saved *from God*, they were being saved *for God*. The problem disrupting the kingdom created by the old covenant was not "how can I get these sinners into heaven later." The problem was that God's people were not doing God's will. In addition to idolatry, there was massive injustice and mistreatment of the poor. These were the problems that caused Israel and Judah to be oppressed, and these are the problems Christ came to address. As Peter claims in *Acts 3:26*, **God raised up His servant and sent Him first to you, to bless you by turning each one of you from your iniquities.**

---

[5]Similar remarks hold for **justify**. See chapter ten.

[6]Jesus *did* assuage God's wrath, but not in the way most Christians suggest. That's a topic for chapters nine, ten, and eleven.

[7]a line I stole from *Road House*

Christ strengthens our spirit so we can overcome selfish, ungodly desires, the unfaithfulness that destroyed Israel and leads God to proclaim the need for a new covenant in *Jeremiah 31:31–34*. It is this salvation Paul describes in *Romans 7:14–8:9*, which we will examine in chapter ten. Luckily, Paul puts it in clearer terms in *Romans 6:6* **...our old man was crucified with Him <u>so that</u> the body of sin would no longer dominate us.** Other allusions include *Titus 3:5* and *2nd Thessalonians 2:13*.

This was part of a larger salvation picture, but once again it is the *salvation of the Jews* that is in view. Peter describes the role forgiveness of sins plays in *Acts 3:19–20*. Forgiveness allows for the receipt of the Spirit (the **times of refreshing** in *3:19*, also see *Acts 2:38*) in the present, a gift to tie us over until Christ returns once **all things have been restored**. It was the expectation of this return of Christ and establishment of a new kingdom of God that the early Christians were focused on. Moses freed the sons of Abraham from idolatry and physical slavery to found a kingdom for God based on the old covenant. Jesus is doing the same on a grander scale: freeing people from sin to join a new covenant in the kingdom He is returning to claim.

At present this "freedom from sin" is in the form of the Spirit, which frees us from the *domination* of sin (though we still feel tempted by it and can unwisely choose to indulge in it). After Christ's return, our bodies will be transformed as well, just as Christ's was, and no longer prone to our selfish desires. Thus, salvation is all about repentance, transformed hearts, and transformed bodies, not about God doing accounting tricks to let us into heaven. *The idea that Christ's work is meant to altar the consequences of His own righteous judgment on the last day has absolutely no basis anywhere in scripture.*

I'm not trying to persuade you that I'm right (yet)... just that if I were right it would no longer force Jesus and Paul to conflict. It also unknots a whole mess of other tangles we haven't even discussed yet!

If this present liberation is Paul's focus, the great disconnect between Christ's version of the final Judgment and Paul's discussion of salvation would disappear in a single stroke. There would be no conflict because Paul does not have the final Judgment in mind when he writes of salvation and justification.

We would no longer have to make excuses for Christ (and the gospel writers) because Christ and Paul would be talking about different things.

I realize this probably seems completely alien to you. What would lead me to even consider it? I would later find significant support for this idea within Paul's writing, but it was John's that gave me the first clue.

John and *Eternal Life*

When trying to describe Jesus' teachings to his Greek audience, John uses the term **eternal life**[8] *a lot*, as often as all other New Testament writers combined. I noticed that this **eternal life** is used in a peculiar fashion. In particular, John writes of **eternal life** in a way resembling present *regeneration* through the Spirit rather than future *deliverance.*[9]

Three arrows pointed me to this understanding of **eternal life**:

Arrow 1. Present Tense

Jesus says people have **eternal life** *now,*[10] which should be our first clue that perhaps the term does not mean what we think it means. If we *already* have **eternal life**, and we still die, then the term (as used by John) cannot mean the type of immortality we expect our bodies to have after the resurrection.

Some explain this by saying **eternal life** is a promise of the *real* eternal life we'll have later. A more accurate claim would be that **eternal life** refers to an actual evidence (i.e. the Holy Spirit), rather than merely a doctrinal claim, that proves to us what God is planning in the future. This is how the early Christians saw it. Just as the freedom from captivity was hard evidence to the Israelites that God intended to fulfill the promise made to Abraham, the present spiritual transformation by the Holy Spirit is proof of the physical transformation God intends later. This is proof of God's power and intent, not an individual guarantee. Thousands of Israelites saw God's power in the manna and the exodus, but not all were allowed into the promised land (see *Hebrews 3:11–13*).

Christians defend the idea that "eternal life" can be used in the present to refer to the assured immortality they have later by claiming that once you come to faith you can never fall away. This doctrine is known as "once saved — always saved." I call it OSAS.

Jesus seems to think differently on the matter. He pleads with His disciples in *John 15:4–6* to **remain in me**, an exhortation that would make little sense if it were impossible to fall away. In *Matthew 13:20* Jesus refers to a group of people who believe and **receive the word with great joy**, but ultimately lose faith. *Hebrews 6:4* describes people who have been **partakers of the Holy Spirit** (impossible without genuine faith) falling away, and *2nd Peter 2:20–22* similarly pertains to genuine believers who become re-ensnared to the world.

---

[8] Or the Greek we translate as **eternal life** — more on that later

[9] I was to learn later *why* John uses the term **eternal life** in this way, but that will have to wait for chapter four. At the time I had no understanding of the Jewish context or Greek words behind that phrase.

[10] *John 3:36; 5:24*; and *10:28* are three examples.

Add to this the many passages where Paul and others ask believers to continue in the faith. People who believe in OSAS largely use Paul's letters to defend their views... so one wonders why Paul himself urges his audience so to remain **firm in the faith** and why he worries that his readers had **believed in vain.** *1st Thessalonians 3:7–8* and *Galatians 4:11* (spoken to a community who already **believed**, see *Galatians 3:1*) are particularly difficult for OSAS supporters, as is Paul's cautioning believers not to **destroy** other believers **for whom Christ died** in *Romans 14:15* and his concern for himself in *1st Corinthians 9:27*.

Arrow 2. Life and the Spirit

I found that John uses **eternal life** as others use **Spirit**. I'll give three examples here and then an interesting synthesis. Remember, I'm not proving anything right now. I'm trying to illustrate what clues caused me to *conjecture* that salvation refers to a purely present gift separate from the Judgment.

Observation 1: Both eternal life and the Holy Spirit indwell.

John 4:4	... but the water that I will give him will become in him a well of water springing up to eternal life.
1st John 3:15	Everyone who hates his brother is a murderer; ... no murderer has eternal life abiding in him.
Acts 9:17	... has sent me so that you may regain your sight and be filled with the Holy Spirit.
Romans 8:11	... through His Spirit who dwells in you.
1st Cor 3:16	Do you not know that you are a temple of God and the Spirit of God dwells in you?

Observation 2: Both eternal life and the Holy Spirit are promised.

We will discuss the importance of "The Promise" later. A sampling now.

Luke 24:49	And behold, I am sending on you what my Father promised...
Acts 2:33	... and having received the promise of the Holy Spirit from the Father...
Galatians 3:14	... so that we would receive the promise of the Spirit by faith.
1st John 2:25	This is the promise which He Himself made to us: eternal life.

1st John 1:2   . . . **and proclaim to you the eternal life, which was with the Father and was manifested to us.**

Note the last example says **the eternal life** (it's there in the Greek, too), as though it is an object, being, or force instead of a condition. Similarly for the phrases **with the Father** and now **manifested to us.** *Acts 2:36* describes the sending of the Holy Spirit as *the* blessing promiscd to Abraham. The early Christians saw the Spirit as proof that God was fulfilling the promise to Abraham to found a godly kingdom through which all nations would be blessed.

Observation 3: The life Jesus has sounds like it must be the Spirit.

Several verses refer to Jesus having *life* that would be hard to understand if it didn't mean *indwelling of the Holy Spirit.* For example **In Him was Life, and the Life was the light of mankind** and **For just as the Father has Life in Himself, He has granted the Son to Have Life in Himself.**[11] It's difficult to see how the life that the Father **has granted** Jesus to have could refer to anything other than the Holy Spirit.

Synthesis: Jesus' Anointing

We begin to see the deep cohesion among these observations when we put *1st John 1:2* together with *John 1:1,14.* John takes an abstract term, **the Word**, and declares it was **with God** and then **dwelt among us**, referring to **the Word**'s manifestation as Christ. And then (in *1st John 1:2*) he takes another abstract term **the Eternal Life** and says that it was **with the Father** and now **manifested to us.** Given that John's gospel describes the Spirit as being a guide sent to dwell in the disciples after Christ leaves them (*John 14:16–20*). Christ is **the Word** manifest to us, and the Spirit is **the Eternal Life**, the blessing promised to Abraham, first given to Christ — so important every gospel spells it out: *Matthew 3:16; Mark 1:10; Luke 3:22; John 1:4,32-33* — and then manifest to us (*1st John 1:2*) as an **eternal inheritance** after his death (*Hebrews 9:14–15*).

Arrow 3. The Jewish Notion of Life

In chapter four I'll describe how Jesus' notion of life is linked to being part of God's house. Jesus uses death to refer to those outside God's favor.[12] If the Holy Spirit is the gift of the new, eternal covenant Jesus enacted, then **eternal life** becomes an apt metaphor for its receipt.

---

[11]*John 1:4* and *5:26*
[12]*Matthew 8:22; 23:27*; and, as we will see later, *John 5:25*

Why Is This Important?

You might be feeling a bit lost...wondering *So what?* about all this. *Why does it matter if "eternal life" and "salvation" are things Christians have in the present rather than the future?*

The passages that plainly describe the Judgment or speak of people going to hell describe a Judgment very different from the one espoused by evangelicals. Most of the passages that are used to support the modern gospel use words like **saved** and **eternal life**. But if these refer to the present rather than the future, they are no longer relevant to the Judgment.

If these passages refer to how Jesus teaches us to know the Father rather than how God grades our final exam, then they no longer support the notion that all believers (and *only* believers) survive the Judgment.

Even those passages where **eternal life** appears to refer to the future often deserve a second look. In *John 6:40* Jesus says **...everyone who beholds the Son and believes in Him will have eternal life, and I will raise him up at the last day.** If **eternal life** meant what we might normally think, wouldn't the order be different? Wouldn't Jesus *first* resurrect us and *then* give eternal life?

From hearing most Christians talk, you get the impression that all your sins are presented at the Judgment. Since even one sin makes us unfit for heaven, anyone who is not forgiven is damned, and that forgiveness is given to people who believe in Christ (and no one else).

Problem is, none of that appears in the Bible. *There is not a passage anywhere that refers to forgiveness of sins through faith in Christ playing a role in the Judgment.* That point alone should make you wonder if modern Christians have talked themselves into an understanding of Christ's purpose far afield from the gospel the apostles spread.

Claiming salvation lives in the present has a more personal impact as well. *1st Peter 1:18* says Jesus saves us from an **empty way of life**. We all have felt that. We all know the quiet desperation of living in a world that seduces us to seek that which we cannot attain, a world where our history, our baggage, and others' expectations shackle our spirits. Christ invites us to fulfillment *today* by showing us the one Lord whose opinion matters while conditioning and healing us to meet that Lord's expectations. In Christ, *anyone* can succeed in the only way that counts — if you can love God and your neighbor while renouncing the world's lies, you can serve well and please the only Master who matters.

Summary and Final Notes

All I've done so far is present a conjecture that Christian *salvation* often refers to a purely present-day blessing/condition linked to the new covenant and that it has nothing directly to do with the Judgment. Jesus' work was not to *curb* God's eternal wrath but rather to *cure* Satan's poisoning of our spiritual health which makes us unable to live faithfully. We are being saved from our spiritual weakness, not from accountability. Christ came to lead people out of spiritual captivity to form a kingdom after God's heart, a kingdom Jesus would return to claim visibly later.

In short, *salvation* addresses our sinful natures, the saboteur of the first covenant. This matches the need for, purpose of, and salvation wrought by the coming savior as found in the Later Prophets.

I've shown how the two ideas Christians refer to as "salvation" are not inextricably linked to each other and the Jewish conception of salvation did not include deliverance from God's eternal wrath. It is their conception of salvation we must consider if we are to understand the Bible (which was written by Jews). The Christian church did not begin thinking of salvation primarily as a heaven-and-hell affair until hundreds of years later. Why do we read our Western, modern definition of salvation into words written by 1st-century Jews?

If my conjecture were true, if **salvation** principally refers to the present, Paul and Christ would no longer conflict. We would also be able to give satisfying answers to questions that trouble modern Christianity. Examples: *How can anyone in the Old Testament go to heaven? Why does Jesus talk so much about sin if all that really matters in the end is whether someone believes?*

Maybe this is a *frame* that can hold the puzzle pieces without our jamming them in, a frame that has room for Christ's actual teaching. As a substantial bonus, this distinction allows us to genuinely investigate the Bible's teachings on the *Judgment* without fretting over what our conclusions imply about *salvation*.

John uses the term **eternal life** in a way that supports this idea, except I couldn't find a verse that comes right out and says **eternal life** really means knowing God in the new covenant sense through the Holy Spirit. I searched and searched for such a confirmation and could not find it.

As closely as it would match the description of the new covenant given in *Jeremiah 31:34*, as nicely as it would remove the apparent conflict between Paul and Jesus, as much as it would make sense of all those difficult passages we Christians gloss over, I couldn't really get behind the concept without at least one direct passage confirming what **eternal life** was...and that's where the Calvinist I mentioned earlier comes in.

–IV–

FROM ETERNAL LIFE TO SALVATION

Imagine you are an alien, a member of an extraterrestrial race visiting Earth to study human culture.

I'm sure if this really happened, several observations would bewilder you — men who would rather eat a live frog than admit they are not an expert on every subject, women who ask questions they already know the answers to (or questions they don't want the answers to), and Christians who judge non-Christians when both Jesus and Paul explicitly forbid it. However, pretend your first field study of humanity is a soccer match.

So, picture yourself watching a soccer match for the first time, *but your alien eyes cannot see the ball.*

Imagine how weird the game would look. To your eyes the match seems an unruly, high-intensity dance. Everyone appears to know where to go; groups of players regularly converge, but with no rhyme or reason as to *why*. Occasionally, the goalie dives to the ground, and the crowd screams in unison. It's like watching a complex card game without grasping the rules. You know there is structure behind the apparent chaos, but you cannot determine what it is.

You hit upon an idea. *What if there is a ball that only they can see?* In some sense this is a clever answer to the mystery... but it's not totally satisfactory. It *explains* what you see, but there is no evidence it's true. You have no reason to believe balls exist that humans can see but you cannot, much less that humans would be so discourteous as to use them.

This contrived situation portrays the feelings I had regarding the problem described in the first two chapters and the conjecture I proposed in chapter three.[1] I had hit upon an answer but couldn't find explicit support anywhere in the Bible. At that point I did not know the linguistic and Jewish cultural support for the

---

[1] Richard Feynman described how physicists often worked using this analogy.

idea (which I will get to later in this chapter). I looked and looked for some passage that told me the invisible ball was there, but I just could not find it.

Ironically, the most Calvinistic pastor I've ever met found it for me.

Norm Koop, son of Reagan's Surgeon General, is the pastor of First Congregational, a Calvinist church with an impressive fellowship. His sermon one cold April Sunday treated the "The Real Lord's Prayer" as he called it: *John 17:1–26*. He focused on verse *13*. **This is eternal life — that they know you, the only true God, and Jesus Christ, whom you sent.**

It was like a Volvo slapped me "up side d'head."

Pastor Koop explained how the term **eternal** did not refer to the chronological length of life but its *quality*. For weeks I had searched for this exact idea — that John uses **eternal life** to refer to *present-day* salvation, the *regeneration* I mentioned on page *39*.

The Greek construction John uses here is one he employs elsewhere to give exact descriptions of things, like a dictionary might. One example is *1st John 3:23*. **This is His commandment: that we believe in the name of His Son Jesus Christ and love one another, just as He gave us the commandment.** He uses the same Greek grammar in *John 17:3* to define **eternal life**. (Literally, the Greek is **the** eternal life, like in *1st John 1:2*.)

To illustrate how John uses this language in a "definitional" way, see also *John 1:19*; *3:19*; and *15:12*. They all use the same Greek grammar. As does *1st John 1:5* and *3:11*.

Jewish "Eternal Life": O'lam Ha-Ba

You might be thinking, "Okay, so I see how it is a problem that every description Jesus gives of the Judgment would lead His audience to a conclusion that the modern Church rejects. But isn't it also a problem to believe that **eternal life** doesn't simply mean 'eternal life,' regardless of what *John 17:3* says?"

That's a good question… and I'm glad you asked it. (Or, rather, I'm glad you're willing to let me pretend you did.) We read **eternal life** where Jesus and other Jews are discussing **O'lam Ha-Ba**, a Jewish idea literally meaning "World to Come."

What is **O'lam Ha-Ba**? Well, that itself is a hard question. You won't find it discussed as such in the Bible, but that shouldn't surprise you now that you know the Jews (who built their culture upon the Old Testament) have little focus or clarity on the afterlife. **O'lam Ha-Ba** has multiple meanings. It can refer to the spiritual afterlife immediately after death. It also refers to the age God promises in the Old Testament when the Messiah will unite Israel and Judah in power (like David did) while punishing those nations that have oppressed it. It also refers to the age *after that.*

Various Jewish factions hold different ideas of how the future will unfold. Some think the Messiah will simply come and bless the offspring of Israel, and that is the extent of the **O'lam Ha-Ba.** Rather than focus on heaven and hell, the Hebrews see blessings and curses manifested in the size and position of their progeny and the condition of their death. The blessed are buried in their home-lands and have many prosperous children and grandchildren. The cursed die terrible deaths in disgrace and have their children bear part of their punishment.[2] Thus, it is understandable that many simply look forward to a time where their children or their children's children will be vindicated. That is, after all, what Zechariah prophecies after being **filled with the Holy Spirit** in *Luke 1:67–75.*

> **Blessed be the Lord God of Israel, because he has come to help and has redeemed his people. For he has raised up a horn of salvation for us in the house of his servant David, as he spoke through the mouth of his holy prophets from long ago, that we should be saved from our enemies, and from the hand of all who hate us. He has done this to show mercy to our ancestors, and to remember his holy covenant – the oath that he swore to our ancestor Abraham. This oath grants that we, being rescued from the hand of our enemies, may serve him without fear, in holiness and righteousness before him as long as we live.**

This passage is breathtakingly powerful in portraying salvation as a fulfill-ment of the promise to Abraham while delineating specifically what that promise was. The **as long as we live** part places the blessing squarely in the present. We see the end goal is not our immortality but rather God's glory — not deliverance from God's wrath but protection from anything that hinders our serving God.

Another belief common to Judaism is that a grand resurrection begins the Messianic age. Those resurrected (not all of humanity, just the righteous ones from Israel's past) will help bring about the kingdom described in the prophets. Others think the Messiah will first set things aright and then much later there will be a resurrection of the righteous to live in that blessed kingdom. Those

---

[2]*Genesis 26:24; Numbers 25:13; 1st Samuel 24:21; 2nd Kings 5:27;* and *Proverbs 11:21*

Jews used **O'lam Ha-Ba** to refer to both the coming age of the Messiah and again *separately* to the time after *that* when the righteous are raised.

When Jews ask Jesus about "eternal life" in the Synoptic Gospels, they likely have the afterlife in mind rather than life in the Messianic age. The wording of *Matthew 19:16* suggests they, like most, are more interested in their own future than God's plan. They think Jesus is a rabbi (or perhaps a prophet), so they ask Him questions that are under debate.

But even these Jews do not have immortality in mind so much as "life in the next world" — whether that is the spirit world they will go to after death or a stake in the glorious future kingdom when God finally pays back all the nations that have oppressed Judah. To the Jews, it isn't about immortality; it's about *inclusion*. Salvation isn't about evading wrath; it's about *vindication.*

Some may have believed in the immortality of the soul, and that the righteous who are resurrected may not die again, but there is no consensus. In fact, Maimonides[3] sees the future resurrection as a mere sidelight, after which the resurrected would, quite naturally, die again! The focus was exactly on what the words mean: the "World to Come" — when God vindicates Israel who can then serve God in peace, free from persecution. It's really hard to get our modern, Western, individual-based, immortality-seeking minds around the Jewish understanding of the afterlife.

The linguistic confusion here isn't because the Jews were sloppy with their speech or that Jesus used misleading language. The word translated **eternal** in the gospels does not, in fact, mean "eternal"!

There *is* a Greek word that means eternal, **aidios**. It is just not the one used throughout the gospels. It appears only in *Jude 6* and *Romans 1:20.*

A Quick Greek Lesson

[Nothing here is meant to suggest endless life-after-death does not exist. I'm just describing what the words used by the New Testament writers (and the Jews they were quoting) meant. I do this because many of the passages Christians use to describe the gospel refer to "eternal life," so it is important to understand what was really being discussed.]

The Greek word translated **eternal** in the gospels is always **aiōnios**, an odd term rarely used in Greek literature. The closest thing to a good English translation is "measureless" or "indefinite." It doesn't mean "without end" but rather

---

[3] Also known as "the Rambam," (for Rabbi Moshe ben Maimon). He lived in the 12th century and was easily the most important rabbi of the middle ages and one of the most influential rabbis in the history of all Jewish thought.

"so vast the edge is unseen." The Hebrew equivalent even comes from the word for "unseen." It thus makes a good choice to denote a vastly fulfilling life we can have in Christ (especially to John's Greek audience who might not have had any understanding of the Jewish context). It describes well the opportunity given by a Christ who says in *John 10:10*, **I came that they may have life, and have it abundantly**. Keep in mind that John is transcribing Hebrew or Aramaic dialogue into Greek words. His use of a rare, vague Greek word to describe the life one has with the Holy Spirit is a natural one.

However, it makes a poor choice if you wish to describe "life without end." **Aidios** is the word that conveys that concept clearly.

Aiōnios doesn't mean "eternal" as we use the term, for Paul uses it in *Romans 16:25* to refer to the age before Christ, which had ended.[4] When the Greeks translated the Old Testament, they use **aiōnios** to refer to items that are not eternal, like landmarks (*Proverbs 22:28*) and walls that had already been torn down (*Isaiah 58:12*). The Jews did not even *have* a clear notion of "eternal" in the sense that we use it. Many older cultures simply lacked the idea.[5]

What Did Jesus Mean?

The notion of the **O'lam Ha-Ba**, and in particular a resurrection of the righteous, had incubated during the time between the Old Testament and the New Testament, a four-hundred-year gap when the Jews did not have a prophet from God. We thus expect Jesus to have a clearer and different understanding of the **O'lam Ha-Ba** than the Jews He speaks with.

When Jesus uses the term, especially in John, He means the union with God accomplished through the Spirit. Is that not the most natural meaning of *John 17:22*, where Jesus prays that His disciples **would be one as We are one**. He has declared the Messianic age is imminent, and refers to a special relationship with God available in that age. This conception of **eternal life** shows several times in John, not just in *John 17:3*.

John 1:4

The very first time **life** shows up in John is *John 1:4*: **In Him was life, and the life was the light of mankind.** This describes the Spirit who, according to *John 14:26*, **. . . will teach you all things**.

---

[4] Plato (who appears to have coined the word) *contrasts* **aiōnios** with **aidios**, writing that gods are **aidios** while our souls are merely **aiōnios**.

[5] A good friend of mine spent years in the Philippines as a missionary. They do not have a term for "eternal" even now. The closest he could come to saying "eternal life" was *Buhay na walang hangang* which means "life with no until."

John 5:24–29

I discussed *John 6:40* earlier. Another passage that appears to link faith, **eternal life**, and the Judgment is *John 5:24–29*. A close examination shows this passage speaks against the modern gospel rather than for it.

John 5:24–29 has two chunks. The first explains Jesus' role as Spirit-giver. The second describes Jesus' role as judge and resurrector. His opinion of the Jews He spoke to is shown in *5:38* and *5:42*.

Jesus describes the present and the immediate future in the first section, saying **the dead will hear the voice of the Son of God, and those who hear will live.** That makes sense if **eternal life** means having the Holy Spirit, which transforms the spiritually dead to spiritually alive. Contrast that with the latter part which speaks of a future time where *all* will come out, **the ones who have done what is good to the resurrection resulting in life, and the ones who have done what is evil to the resurrection resulting in condemnation.**

John 5:24–25	John 5:28–29
Time is here now	Time is coming
Only some hear and come out	All hear and come out
Based on "hearing"	Based on doing good versus evil
Based on present faith	Based on past action

At first Jesus appears to be repeating Himself, but when you look at the details, every one of them is different. The first half refers to life obtained by hearing/believing/obeying the message in the present, and the second describes a Judgment based on what those in the tombs *have done* (past tense).

John 17:2

Note the logic in *John 17:2*. **Just as you have given Him authority over all humanity, so that He may give eternal life to everyone you have given Him.** How does Jesus' *authority* over humanity pertain to the "normal" idea of eternal life? To evangelicals, Jesus' *sacrifice* is what allows our eternal life.

However, if you see **eternal life** as the Jewish *O'lam Ha-Ba*, where God has put a son of David in authority to give light to the nations and instruct God's people in righteousness, it makes more sense.[6] *John 16:15* shows this connection between Jesus' authority and the sending of the Spirit directly: **Everything that the Father has is mine; that is why I said the Spirit will receive from me what is mine and will tell it to you.**

---

[6]See *Isaiah 16:5*; *Jeremiah 30:9*; *Ezekiel 34:23*; and *Zechariah 12:10*

Bridging from John to Paul

We've discussed **eternal life** in John at length, but one thing I've left out is "how do you get it?" John is quite clear on that score. Several times belief is given as the direct cause of eternal life, and *John 20:30–31* gives this truth as the purpose of his gospel: ...**so that you may believe that Jesus is the Christ, the Son of God, and that by believing you may have life in his name.**

But isn't belief the basis for **salvation and justification** according to Paul? *Ephesians 2:8* is the most famous example of this: **For by grace you have been saved through faith...**

If John uses **eternal life** to refer to what Jesus gives believers, and Paul emphatically claims that salvation is by faith alone, then it is at least plausible that they refer to the same thing. We should immediately ask two questions:

1. Does Paul link faith and salvation to receiving the Spirit?

2. Are there places where Paul clearly describes the Judgment?

Paul and the Spirit

Paul does link the Spirit to both faith and salvation in a way more direct than we might expect.

Galatians 3:2   ...**did you receive the Spirit by the works of the Law, or by hearing with faith?**

Galatians 3:14   ...**by faith we might receive the promise of the Spirit.**

Titus 3:5   **He saved us ...by the washing of the new birth and re-newing by the Holy Spirit.**

Paul's Teachings on the Judgment

When I began rereading Christ's teachings on the Judgment, they seemed to contradict Paul's. Further study revealed the discrepancy is between *passages that **clearly** refer to the Judgment* and *passages we **assume** are related to the Judgment*. When Paul directly treats the Judgment, he says things very much in line with the teachings of Christ described in chapters one and two.[7]

---

[7]When considering Paul's writings on the Judgment, you have to separate those passages that speak of God's wrath in the present age (in particular the wrath on the entire world that ends this age), and the Judgment of all individuals living and dead that happens after the events of the second coming have run their course.

Romans 2:9–10 **There will be affliction and distress on everyone who does evil, on the Jew first and also the Greek, but glory and honor and peace for everyone who does good...**

1st Cor. 6:9–10 **Or do you not know that the unrighteous will not inherit the kingdom of God? Do not be deceived; the sexually immoral, idolaters, adulterers... and swindlers will not inherit the kingdom of God.**

1st Cor. 9:27 **I subdue my body and make it my slave, so that after preaching to others I myself will not be disqualified.**

2nd Cor. 5:10 **For we must all appear before the judgment seat of Christ, so that each one may be paid back according to what he has done while in the body, whether good or evil.**

I'll stop there, noting *Colossians 3:5–6,24–25* and *Ephesians 5:5*, both written to *believers*, carry a similar message. In particular, Paul's discussion of his own fate in *1st Corinthians 9:24–27* should disabuse anyone of the thought that deliverance from hell is a "free gift" or that the Judgment is one of faith.

Hence Paul, like Christ, paints a Judgment where believers and non-believers are treated the same. There is no mention of God transferring righteousness, no mention of perfection required, no mention of forgiveness being a prevailing factor, and no indication that our good works are judged separately for purposes of "rewards." There are those in both classes (believers and non-believers) who do God's will and examples in both groups who fail to do so. All, believers and unbelievers, who rebel against God's law are in danger of His wrath; why else would Paul repeatedly exhort believers not to fall into sin?

In particular, there is no indication the Judgment is like a court where justice is meted out only for our crimes. Evangelicals push that basic paradigm upon their listeners, but you will have a hard time finding it anywhere in the Bible.

Finally, ponder the following pair of statements (New American Standard Bible translation):

Romans 2:13 **For it is not those who hear the law who are righteous before God, but those who do the law will be justified.**

Romans 3:20 **Because by the works of the Law no flesh is justified.**

At first blush, these appear to conflict. However, this illusion dissolves when we allow that Paul separates salvation (receiving the Spirit) from the Judgment.

These verses demonstrate Paul using the terms "justified" and "law" in two separate ways. The first statement refers to *individual* accountability with respect to the final Judgment, and the **law** refers to God's over-arching law of right and wrong. The second statement refers to God's sending of Christ, personal transformation, receiving the Spirit, and joining the new covenant through faith. The **works of the law** referenced are those holdovers from the Mosaic law (principally circumcision) that some Jewish Christians and those whom they influenced were trying to force upon Gentiles in the early church.[8]

So, Paul and Christ do not disagree about the Judgment when one looks at verses where they clearly describe it, rather than passages we merely assume refer to the Judgment.[9]

Unfortunately passages that clearly refer to the Judgment are hardly ever mentioned in church. Instead we are fed a steady diet of a few other passages that we *are told* refer to heaven and hell, like an automated radio station playing the same five jazz songs repeatedly while claiming it broadcasts classic rock.

Chapter ten is devoted to understanding Paul and his writing. If you want something to ponder in the meantime, consider the two verses:

1st Timothy 4:10 **...we have set our hope on the Living God, who is the Savior of all people, especially of believers.**

Colossians 1:20 **...and through Him to reconcile all things to Himself by making peace through the blood of His cross – through Him, whether things on earth or things in heaven.**

The first of these is odd for obvious reasons. For the second, consider *why* angels in heaven (whom we assume have not transgressed) would need to be reconciled to God? Similarly for other creatures. *Colossians 1:16* indicates a wide scope when interpreting this passage; what would **all things, whether visible or invisible** mean otherwise?

---

[8]To see this, cross-reference the next few verses of this passage with *Romans 4:15* and *5:13*, where Paul explicitly indicates he is referring to the Mosaic law. This is similar to, but not the same as, a perspective on Paul now shared by many scholars, including N.T. Wright and James G.D. Dunn.

[9]Some of these latter refer to the physical wrath God visits upon the earth prior to the Judgment. See chapters eight and ten.

Summary and Final Notes

I've tried to show that verses typically used to support evangelicals' version of the Judgment are actually references to membership in the new covenant because John often refers to the Holy Spirit by using the Greek words translated *eternal life* and Paul appears to use the term *saved* in a similar way. In both cases *regeneration* rather than *deliverance* is in view. Indeed, every practically every NT writer (Matthew, Mark, Luke, John, Paul, Peter, Luke, and the writer of Hebrews) gives a description of the Judgment where no special treatment is afforded to believers.

After hearing Pastor Koop's sermon on *John 17:3*, I spent several years studying the Bible and other sources, trying to get at the heart of the matter. The rest of this book is dedicated to the question of what salvation is and, perhaps as importantly, what it *isn't*.

To Christians concerned for their eternal security, I wish to say up front that there is plenty of encouragement and hope for those who genuinely desire God; why else would Jesus tell ... **everyone who looks on the Son and believes in Him will have eternal life, and I Myself will raise Him up on the last day** and **If you obey My commandments, you will remain in My love; just as I have obeyed My Father's commandments and remain in His love. I have told you these things so that My joy may be in you, and your joy may be complete.** I ask you to bravely venture into some choppy seas that will challenge what you have likely been taught and perhaps taught others, clinging to the assurance that God is a loving (and living!) God.

I'm not suggesting a unitarian theology; I very much agree with Jesus when He says **I am the way, the truth, and the life. No one comes to the Father except through Me.** And yet, I also agree with His very general statement **Whoever does the will of the Father are my mother, my brother, and my sister**, a claim transcending time, covenant, and enlightenment. To see why these viewpoints are not at odds, read on.

My goals so far have been to raise questions, point out some real problems with the perspectives we have been asked to accept, and present a viewpoint that allows Jesus and Paul to each mean what he says. I haven't given in these first four chapters a full picture of what *salvation* is or how the Judgment works. I've merely indicated how the Church's understanding of both conflicts with the Bible.

INTERMISSION

So far, we[1] have been discussing Jesus' and His apostle's teachings about eternal life, salvation, and the Judgment. In the first four chapters I developed a conjecture that *salvation* in general does not refer to escaping hell, but instead describes present spiritual liberation and strengthening. Salvation is thus effected by the indwelling of the Holy Spirit — the new covenant relationship in which God counsels us in righteousness and empowers us to be faithful. This indwelling is what Jesus often means by **eternal life.**

In other words, our salvation addresses the problem God faced throughout the entire Old Testament: *How can I have a faithful people with a heart for Me?* rather than the nowhere-mentioned problem *How can I get people into heaven?*

The immediate (for purposes of reading this book) benefit of entertaining this notion of salvation is that it allows us to discuss Judgment as a separate topic from salvation. We can take a sober, penetrating look at what scripture says about this event without constantly worrying *What does this say about Christ?* or *What does this imply about salvation?*

Much of what we're told about the Judgment comes from our assumptions that tie salvation to it. Once we remove those assumptions, we can bravely affirm truths that earlier might have left us feeling conflicted.

So, as we look into the Bible's teaching on God's Judgment, please try to keep at bay the "what would this mean about..." concerns. The last portion of this book is devoted to addressing those ramifications. I may tear down your mansions, but you will not be left an orphan.

---

[1]And by *we*, I mean *I.*

Preview

The specific content of the next three chapters:

Chapter 5 How does the standard understanding of the Judgment compare to scripture?

Chapter 6 What is a more biblically consistent understanding of the Judgment?

Chapter 7 Jesus promises that those with genuine faith are assured a positive outcome at the Judgment; what does "faith" mean in this context?

If you have not done so already, you may wish to read through the nineteen problems listed in the topical index found on page *173*.

Judgment —
Tearing Down Mansions

_V_

A Chain of Broken Links

Imagine you are Abigail, a Jewish mother in Galilee fifty years before Christ. You keep the Torah and look forward longingly for the Messiah to appear and redeem Israel. You have a daughter, Gomer, when you are 30 and die in 7 BC.

Your daughter also lives as a reverent Jew looking forward to the Messiah. She has a child, Mary, and dies in AD 27 never having heard Jesus teach because He had not begun His ministry. Mary, also a reverent Jew, gives birth to a daughter, Rachel, in AD 10.

Rachel grows up and leaves Jerusalem in AD 29 to wed a Jewish man in another land. She lives until AD 60, but none of the apostles visit her city to share the gospel, so she never hears of Jesus at all.

After Rachel leaves, Mary hears Jesus' answer to the scribe in _Luke 10:25–28_. She takes this to heart and lives her final days loving God and her neighbor as best she can. However, she does not live long enough to find out Jesus is the Christ.

So, we have four Jewish women, none of whom could have faith in Jesus as a savior or any of the other standard beliefs of Christianity. To summarize:

Woman	Situation
Abigail	Right place at wrong time
Gomer	Right place and time, didn't hear message
Mary	Right place and time, only heard Jesus' moral message but obeyed
Rachel	Wrong place, right time

Which of these women pass the Judgment?

"None" would be the simplest answer, except we know from _Luke 13:28–29_ that those who came before Jesus are not so easily dismissed. Once it's clear *some* non-believers are accepted, a whole can of worms explodes in your face, for you have to explain why people in 1st century BC who never heard of Christ might pass the Judgment while those who never heard in 1st century AD cannot.

If "believing in a coming savior" is the criterion, then all the Jews in the last several centuries before Christ make it in (including those who stoned the prophets God sent) while Rahab, Job, and Noah are left in hell.

Jews did not begin believing in a unique savior until after David's reign. And the idea of looking for "a savior to reconcile God and man" shows up nowhere in their history. The Messiah shown in the prophets clearly comes as a military/political leader to vindicate God's people over the nations that oppressed them. The Jews looked forward to a savior who would *turn* Israel back to God, not *reconcile* Israel to God — certainly not one to reconcile *the world* to God. The Jewish mindset about what Jesus came to do *for Israel* is illustrated by Zechariah before Jesus was born (*Luke 1:67–75*), by Jesus while He lived (*Matthew 10:5–6; 15:22–24; Luke 5:32; 19:9–10*), and by the apostles after He died (*Luke 24:21*).

The question of how those who came before Christ can "make it" is one of many problems for evangelicals. This chapter probes the logic behind their dogma, which resembles a chain:

1. God, as an infinitely good and perfect being, cannot tolerate unrighteous creatures in heaven.

2. Any sin is enough to make someone unrighteous in God's eyes, so we have all disqualified ourselves.

3. Jesus gave Himself as a sacrifice so God could transfer/forgive our sin.

4. Those who believe are no longer in danger of condemnation because their sins have been removed/forgiven.

5. Those who do not believe do not receive forgiveness. Sins cannot be forgiven "for free" without compromising God's perfect justice.

6. Those lacking faith cannot repay God for their unforgiven sin. So, they are cast into eternal suffering as objects of God's wrath.

Your church, or the Christians who have preached to you, may have only emphasized some subset of the above or explained some parts differently, but the discussion here is likely applicable to whatever version you've heard.

We'll examine each link to find this chain of logic comes from human philosophy rather than biblical evidence. This chapter is not designed primarily to explain how the Judgment works. Its point is to show how it *doesn't.*

Link 1: No Unrighteousness in God's Presence

There is no passage supporting the idea that unrighteousness cannot exist in God's presence.[1] People just take it as a given based on their understanding of God. That's dangerous reasoning from the start, basing an entire theology about heaven and hell on a principle the Bible never claims.

But the situation is more dire than mere silence. Satan is as *unrighteous* a creature you could hope to find, yet God not only allows him an audience, but Satan stays in heaven with his angels until the resurrection of Christ.

In Job, Satan comes and presents himself to God. The Lord does not come looking for him. When God asks **Where have you come from?** in *Job 1:7*, Satan's answer **From roving about on the earth, and from walking back and forth across it** certainly does not sound like Satan is still on the earth.

Revelation 12:7–12 is even clearer. We are told there is **no longer any place found in heaven for him and his angels**. Satan is accusing people **before God** and is **cast down** to the earth. The timing is definitely upon Christ's resurrection. The angels defeat Satan **by the blood of the lamb**, and only *after* **the ruling authority of His Christ** has come. This ruling authority came when Christ accomplished what God had set before Him to do (*Philippians 2:9–11* and *Hebrews 2:9*). And, obviously, Satan can hardly be accusing **our brothers** in heaven if this is somehow a picture of his pre-creation defeat.

Regardless of our take on Satan, *John 8:44* and *1st John 3:8–10* indicate that the devil can hardly be considered righteous. If Satan is allowed in God's presence, one is hard-pressed to say God is *incapable* of tolerating the unrighteous.

But what counts as *unrighteous* in God's eyes? That's the next link.

Link 2: One Sin Enough — All are Unrighteous

No passage says a single sin destroys our righteousness.[2] Evangelicals make that claim based on their belief about how God should be. This philosophy is applied to a few verses Paul writes that are taken out of context to suggest all people start off condemned to hell.

---

[1] Some give the Garden of Eden as support, but a close reading of *Genesis 3:22* shows God expelled Adam and Eve not by necessity but rather by choice.

[2] In fact, we should probably stop using the term "righteousness" because it has gained a connotation somewhat afield from the meaning of the word. The meaning the word has attained colors our reasoning as we read the Bible.

Lucky for us, the whole Bible portrays the nature of God's Judgment, and it violently opposes the notion that all are unrighteous and belong, by nature, in hell. Of course all have sinned, but the culture Paul addresses does not think absolute, lifelong perfection is required to be righteous and/or have a place in the coming kingdom, nor does the Bible make such a claim. *Ezekiel 18:27* and *33:19* condemn the modern view: **But when the wicked turns from his wickedness and practices justice and righteousness, he will live by them.** This exposes two problems at one stroke. First, the scripture would be meaningless if living righteously before God were impossible. Second, it gives the lie to the idea that a single sin condemns us.

Furthermore, scripture verifies that this righteousness comes from doing God's will. Is that not what *Luke 1:6* says about Elizabeth and Zechariah? **They were both righteous in the sight of God, following all the commandments and ordinances of the Lord blamelessly.** This doesn't mean they are *perfect* as we modern Western Christians would use the term. Then again, Luke is not a modern Westerner. [For an example of this Jewish understanding, consider the question posed to Christ in *Matthew 19:16*, **Teacher, what good thing must I do to gain eternal life?** If the Jews think absolute perfection is required to be righteous and/or have a stake in the **O'lam Ha-Ba**, there would be no debate about how much is "enough."]

We simply *must* get out of our heads the definition of righteousness the modern church has hammered into our skulls if we are to understand the Jewish writers of the New Testament.

It's instructive to look more deeply at these two aspects (Are all unrighteous? Does God judge by a perfect standard?) to see how clear the Bible is. You may also want to look up "righteous" in an online Bible search and see how the modern take would make much of the Bible nonsensical.

All Unrighteous?

King David murdered a man out of adulterous lust, yet for centuries God showed mercy to Judah based solely on David's worth in God's eyes.[3] In *1st Kings 9:4*, God refers to David as one who **walked in uprightness** and had a **heart of integrity.** This example is doubly important because the key passage (*Romans 3:10–18*) Christians take as suggesting all are worthy of hellfire is a quote by David. In reality this quote is a confirmation that the Law had not kept (or made) Israel faithful. Paul is indicting the Jews with their own scripture (the psalms Paul quotes), hence the wordplay in *Romans 3:19* — ... **whatever the**

---

[3] *2nd Chronicles 21:7* is one of many examples.

law (Torah) **says, it says to those under the Law** (the Jews). The Law that had defined Israel's covenant had not produced a faithful nation (even at its height, during David's reign), so how could Jewish Christians possibly think to force circumcision and other aspects of the Mosaic law on Gentile believers? Having begun in the Spirit, how could they believe the Law of Moses was the way to continue their journey into Christ's righteousness? (*Galatians 3:3*)

According to *Genesis 6:9*, **Noah was a godly man; he was blameless among his generations. He walked with God.** Does that mean Noah never sinned? No. It just means perfection is not the baseline for judgment by God, who tells him in *Genesis 7:1*, **I consider you godly among this generation.**

Enoch and Elijah, who were taken directly to God, represent a significant problem for evangelical theology. (The Reformed Presbyterian Church's official stance is that these two were taken to the edge of heaven but had to wait outside!) Daniel, Noah, and Job are called righteous in *Ezekiel 14:14*.

Jesus references **righteous** people from Old Testament times in *Matthew 13:17*, and Cornelius (who was not a Jew and did not believe in Christ) finds favor with God in *Acts 10:3–4*. In *2nd Peter 2:9*, after a long discussion of exclusively Old Testament personages who were not even in Abraham's covenant, Peter refers to God separating the **godly** from the **unrighteous**.[4]

Matthew 25:37 is particularly hard to dismiss, for not only does Jesus call people **righteous**, but it is clearly based on their own actions. Is Jesus a liar? Or does He just not know of what He speaks?

One Sin Enough? How does God Judge?

Furthermore, God repeatedly shows a Judgment that is relative to the enlightenment one is given, not an absolute one. The support for this is truly massive. Throughout the Bible, God judges based on five factors:

- Judgment by Comparison: God judges based on what other humans did. (E.g., *Matthew 11:21–24; 23:29–33; Luke 11:31–32;* and *Romans 2:27*)

- Judgment by Enlightenment: The more understanding of God you have, the more is expected. *Matthew 23:29–33* is an interesting illustration, where Jesus places the guilt of past generations on the Pharisees, who should have learned from their mistakes. *John 15:22–24; Isaiah 65:12;*

---

[4]Other verses you might like to investigate in this regard: *Genesis 15:6; 26:4–5; 2nd Samuel 22:20–27; 1st Kings 15:3,14; Isaiah 1:21; 3:10; Jeremiah 2:2; 11:16; Jeremiah 24:5; Ezekiel 18:5–13; 19:20; Micah 7:2; Malachi 2:6; Luke 1:6; Luke 2:25; 1st Peter 2:19;* and *James 5:16*.

Jeremiah 36:31; and *1st Samuel 3:13* are other cases. The book of Zephaniah appears devoted to this idea. *James 3:1* gives a post-resurrection example demonstrating not all people will be judged by the same standard.

- Judgment by Conscience: *Genesis 20:5–6*; *Romans 1:18–19*; *1st Corinthians 8:10*; and *James 4:17* illustrate how people are judged (or not) based on their own understanding of right and wrong.

- Judgment of Hypocrisy: People are judged by the same judgment they use for others. *Luke 6:37* casts this in very general terms — **Do not judge, and you will not be judged; do not condemn, and you will not be condemned; forgive and you will be forgiven.** Other examples are *James 2:13*; *5:9*; *Matthew 7:2*; *John 9:41*; and *Romans 2:1*.

- Judgment by Depravity: Occasionally God judges people for being so depraved that they have lost their understanding of right and wrong. (E.g., *Jeremiah 6:15*)

The "one sin makes you unrighteous" axiom is doomed for two separate reasons. First, God's Word and Christ both call many people **righteous**, though they were guilty of sin. Secondly, the "one sin equals unrighteousness" philosophy claims God holds all to the same standard. Scripture utterly rejects that.

Paul's letters often contain long arguments meant to address very specific issues. We cannot rip short snippets from their larger context without respect for the particular purposes Paul had in mind and apply them as universal truths, especially when they conflict with acres of scripture.

Link 3: Christ's Sacrifice and God's Justice

Christ was definitely a sacrifice, just not in the way (or for the reason) indicated by evangelicals. They use a very small set of verses to claim the core of the gospel involves Jesus as a sacrifice in response to God's need for justice at the Judgment, but the was far from the focus or claims of the first several centuries of Christianity. There are only two verses in the New Testament that even *use* the Greek word for atonement, so it's a tough case to make this the nucleus of the gospel.

Chapter 11 elaborates on how Christ was a sacrifice and the relationship between that and God's mercy. It also engages several verses used to support the modern gospel. For right now, I'll just point out two major flaws:

- Very few descriptions of the Judgment include any notion of forgiveness of sins, let alone suggest this is the prevailing issue.

- The legalistic transfer of sin from believers to Christ is generally supported by an analogy Paul uses in *Romans 4*. However, there is no discussion whatsoever of *sin* or *guilt* being transferred or forgiven. The foundational example Paul uses is Abram from *Genesis 15:6*, yet in the whole story of God affirming Abram based on faith, there is no transferral of punishment, *nor any place to transfer it*. If justification is through transfer of sin, then how could God justify Abram without any sacrifice or mention of forgiveness? Paul uses the same argument in *Galatians 3:6*, and once again gives no hint of sin, guilt, or punishment being transferred or forgiven. If Abraham's justification was based on the blotting out of his past iniquity, you'd never know it from any account by Paul or Moses.

Link 4: Persistent Forgiveness for Believers

Hebrews 10:24–27 indicates that Jesus' sacrifice does not deal with deliberate sin done after one receives enlightenment. Christians are challenged by this passage, and many turn it into a warning against "falling away." (Though if you don't think losing faith is possible, that presents an altogether different problem.)

But this passage is not about unbelief — not in the sense most people would use the term. It would be pretty surprising if this refers to falling away when the author quotes the Old Testament in *Hebrews 10:30*, saying **The Lord will judge His people.** (They aren't *His* if they've fallen away.) Rather, the author is rebuking certain Christians for hiding their Christianity due to fear of persecution. That isn't unbelief by most standards. When I chose not to tell Danielle (you remember, the Danielle from the first page of chapter one) that I was a Christian, it wasn't because for 15 seconds I no longer believed in Christ — at least not in the way we normally use the term — I was just a coward.

We have to read the text for what it says. It commands people to continue meeting publicly, even in the face of persecution (*10:25*) and encourages them to spur each other to righteous living (*10:24*) because Christ's sacrifice does not work forgiveness for deliberate sins of believers (*10:26*). It must refer to believers, for the writer speaks (*10:29*) to those who have been **made holy**.

This does not mean that those who deliberately sin are hopelessly damned. Recall the whole notion of perfection (of one sort or another) being necessary to escape hell is a crock. That is, after all, the point of this chapter.

This example is not unique. I've already given several passages where Jesus and Paul indicate believers are just as endangered by sin as non-believers are. A particularly potent example is *Matthew 7:23*, where believers who had enough faith to exorcize demons do not escape the consequences of their sin on the day of Judgment. But other, less obvious problems arise when the Bible is read attentively. Consider *James 5:15*. Why on earth is a believer needing forgiveness of sins? And if he is not a believer, how can the prayers of others save him?

Link 5: No Forgiveness Outside the Cross

Those who claim only belief in Christ grants forgiveness would have better luck finding support from the back of a Cracker Jack™ box than from scripture.

It is true that faith in Christ is the *only* way for someone to achieve *regeneration* through the Spirit, but the Bible gives several other means of forgiveness:

- By forgiving others (*Matthew 6:14*)

- By repenting (*2nd Chronicles 7:14*; *Isaiah 55:7*; *Jeremiah 36:3*; *Ezekiel 18:27*; *33:14–16*; and *Luke 3:3*)

- By the Church's intervention (*Matthew 16:19*; *18:18*; *John 20:23*; and *2nd Corinthians 2:10*)[5]

- By having someone else pray for us (*Numbers 14:20*; *2nd Chronicles 30:18–20*; *Acts 7:60*; and *1st John 5:16*)

- By confessing our sin (*1st John 1:9*)

The point is that God is the One who *chooses* to forgive sins. There are things we can do to provoke this forgiveness, but in the end God will forgive whomever God wishes for whatever reason God wishes, and it really isn't any of our business! If the Lord chooses to forgive someone who rejected Christ, so be it. As we'll discuss later, the question of what really constitutes rejection of Christ is rather a fuzzy one in any event.

A common explanation of the above is that Christ's sacrifice is really the only way God has the ability to forgive sins, and the examples listed are not sufficient for forgiveness themselves but merely "opportunities" for God to grant the forgiveness Christ secured. The problem with this reasoning (other than obviously reading into a raft of scripture a message found nowhere) is the same

---

[5]These must be taken with a grain of salt. In particular, the first three use a verb tense whose meaning, quite frankly, we simply are not sure of.

as the problem I presented in chapter 2. *Anyone* who believes in God can repent. It requires no knowledge of Jesus, the gospel, or anything else to repent. *Anyone* can be prayed for. *Anyone* can forgive others. The evangelical claim is that only those who believe in Christ have access to forgiveness, yet we see Stephen praying for the Jews who are stoning him after rejecting the gospel.

To claim these promises of forgiveness are valid only for believers contradicts scripture and calls Jesus a liar. If faith in Christ were required to receive forgiveness, one has to wonder how Moses' intercessions for the Israelites (who were busy worshipping a golden calf because their faith had run out!) succeeded (*Exodus 32:9–14*) and God's forgiving of Abimelech (who obviously had no gospel to look forward to, not even being a son of Abraham) in *Genesis 20:17* would be quite puzzling indeed.

Throughout the Old Testament we see several examples where forgiveness, mercy, pardon, or aversion of wrath are accomplished, prophesied, or offered for reasons having nothing to do with sacrifice, often to people who could have nothing akin to *faith in Christ*. In addition to the examples in Exodus and Genesis described above, I would cite *Genesis 18:24–32*; *Numbers 14:19–20*; *16:46–47*; *1st Kings 8:47*; *2nd Kings 5:18–19*; *8:19*; *2nd Chronicles 30:18–20*; *32:25–26*; *Jonah 3:10*, and *Jeremiah 5:1*. The reasons given for this forgiveness/atonement/mercy/pardon are rather diverse, as are the situations. The example of Naaman in *2nd Kings 5* is particularly interesting. He was not a Jew, had no understanding of the gospel, had barely any understanding of God, and asked for forgiveness for a sin *he had not even done yet*.

When I have discussed these examples with evangelicals, their last-ditch defense has been that forgiveness of one or two sins is not going to save someone from hell — only forgiveness of every sin can do that. Thus, these isolated cases are irrelevant. This effort at diversion fails for three different reasons (at least):

- If forgiving a single sin really makes no difference in the end, one has to wonder why Stephen went to the trouble of praying for those who were stoning him.

- The entire conservative evangelical view on salvation is based on God's inability to forgive *any* sin except by appeal to Christ's blood. Obviously, these examples show that to be a false claim unless believers and non-believers alike have access to forgiveness through Christ's blood, which would similarly break the standard reasoning here.

- Two of the means (general repentance and forgiveness of others) do not refer to forgiveness on a sin-by-sin basis anyway.

Christians often cite *John 14:6* (**No one comes to the Father except through me**) and *John 8:24* (**For unless you believe that I am He, you will die in your sins**) to support exclusivity. These refer to regeneration rather than deliverance, both being tied to Jesus' cryptic remark **Where I am going you cannot come**. See chapter eleven for a discussion.

Link 6: No Way to Repay

Evangelicals assume eternal suffering is the only way for God to justly punish us. They do not accept purgatory because it has no basis in their Bible.

Why can't we bear the punishment for our sins during our own lives? This does not mean those actions disappear from the books. We can still be *judged* based on our actions, even if we have paid for them (much as an employer might consider an ex-convict's previous crimes when deciding employment).

The Bible claims that God's wrath is indeed exhausted or spent by suffering in the present. Examples include *Judges 1:7*; *2nd Kings 9:26*; *Isaiah 10:25*; *Lamentations 4:11*; *Jeremiah 51:6,56*; and *Ezekiel 5:13*; *6:12*; *7:8*; *13:15*; *20:8,21*. The two Hebrew terms used in most of these passages highlight the idea of God's wrath not merely being manifest but actually being exhausted or "used up" in these passages. One of those words is the word **shalom**, generally meaning peace, and the other term (**kalah**) is actually the word for ending, ceasing, finishing, completing, or being consumed.

This idea of people bearing the punishment for their sin in their present lifetime is a recurring theme on an individual basis as well. It is, in fact, what is meant by Jesus' words to the Pharisees in *John 8:21* when He warns them **you...die in your sin**. This phrase, meaning to die as the punishment for sin, is found in *Numbers 27:3* and *Ezekiel 3:20*. Other examples of people bearing the punishment of their sin in the present are *Leviticus 20:20*; *22:9*; *Numbers 18:22;32*; *2nd Samuel 12:13*; and *Ezekiel 18:24*.

Thus, since God is able to repay people in their own lifetimes for their sin, the idea that God *must* send all sinners to hell because of "unpaid debt" is lacking in any biblical support.

Silent Assumptions

In addition to errors in these explicit links, there are silent assumptions in evangelical logic that should be exposed.

First, they assume the Judgment bears the likeness of a courtroom where only our guilt for crimes is being investigated. That isn't the picture of the Judgment we see in the Bible. A simple reading of the passages discussing the Judgment shows all our deeds, not just our failures, are considered.

If the Judgment is like a courthouse, it's a rather odd one. The penal code is so strict that all are guilty, the punishment is worse than death and the same for all convicts, but full pardon is given to those who believed a message proffered by a political institution with a history of corruption, hypocrisy, and terror.

Second, while there are passages linking sins to the Judgment, it appears God is concerned not with our individual sins but rather the disposition they suggest. When Jesus says in *Revelation 21:8* that **cowards, unbelievers, the detestable, murderers, the sexually immoral, sorcerers, idolaters, and liars** will have a place in the **lake that burns with fire and brimstone**, He does not mean "those who have ever been cowards," "those who have ever murdered," etc. David murdered, Moses murdered, Peter was a coward, Rahab was sexually immoral, Abraham lied, and Joseph practiced divination.

This same point is found in *John 3:16–21*; *7:16–17*; and *8:42–44*. John describes that some people naturally walk toward the light and others naturally shy away. Our faith, like our deeds, demonstrates who we really are. If we genuinely want to do God's will, Jesus' commands make sense to us, and we follow them. If we do not, we find a reason not to follow Christ. The condemnation in these verses is based on the logic that our faith or lack thereof in Christ speaks to our desire to be faithful to God. No mention is found of an artificial righteousness, where God merely "declares" us to be safe by putting our sins on Jesus.

The third silent assumption is that the Judgment is best seen as the last act of this era. Based on the Jews' understanding of the end times (and *Revelation*, for that matter), it is just as appropriate (if not more so) to see the Judgment as commencing the next era, or rather a bridge to it.

The finale of our present era is better seen as the devastation prophesied at its end. I mean here the physical *wrath* that Paul and others frequently refer to, the global wrath we see depicted luridly in the Old Testament prophets and the New Testament apocalypse.

Summary and Final Notes

If even one of these links were disproved, standard evangelical dogma would be defeated. In fact, we find none have clear support, and most have little else backing them while being refuted by multiple passages.

We have manufactured a Judgment that suits our psychological needs rather than God's attributes and designs. We have our eyes so much on immortality that we've made the Judgment the end of the game. We see it as a wrap-up session where God's sense of justice (or, rather, *our* understanding of that justice) must be served. But the Judgment and its aftermath are not God's opportunity to balance a budget of wrath at the end of the fiscal year.

We've turned the Judgment into a courtroom scene where the purpose is for God to balance accounts, as though every sin is a debt that comes due on the final day. That's not at all the version shown in the Bible, so it is unsurprising that the logic used by evangelicals runs into problems.

Modern doctrine appeals to believers because it gives us a sense of security and superiority. It also effectively prompts evangelism. After all, who would not want to save others from hellfire, especially when the solution is so simple?

It's worthwhile to point out that the Jews for many centuries were *confident* in God's love for them and had faith in the coming Messiah to save them. And it was exactly this confidence that made them ignore and stone the prophets who told them that they really did need to turn from evil and do good or else they, God's beloved, would face the wrath of the Almighty.

God's covenant with them, and even the special love given to David, did not preserve them when they failed to bear fruit. Paul's warns Gentile *believers* to take a lesson from this very act in *Romans 11:20–22*:

> **Granted! They were broken off because of their unbelief, but you stand by faith. Do not be arrogant, but fear! For if God did not spare the natural branches, perhaps He will not spare you. Notice therefore the kindness and harshness of God — harshness toward those who have fallen, but God's kindness toward you, provided you continue in His kindness, otherwise you also will be cut off.**

A longer reading of this passage and the prophets shows that the "unbelief" here, while manifested in the Jews' general (but not total) rejection of Christ, was actually due to their previous history of wickedness. (c.f. *Matthew 13:13*).

–VI–

WHAT JUDGMENT *Can* WE EXPECT?

I spent 8 months in Budapest, learning mathematics while realizing how blithely ignorant most Americans are to their own privilege. I overheard three men while enjoying some *Rántott Czirke*[1] at the *Kék Rózsa* one Saturday.

Evidently, they were all artists who ran orphanages for artistically talented children. The tradition is that any student who paints a picture worthy of a spot on the wall is assured room and board as long as he or she chooses to live there. Given the difficult economy, those who run orphanages have to be mindful of their budgets. The three men were discussing who got the spots on the wall and who eventually was told they could no longer have a place at the table. My Magyar is not particularly good, but here is how I translated their discussion.

György Szabó, a semi-famous still-life artist, spoke first:

"Sadly, none of them paint as well as I do, and I stopped hoping for that years ago. Now I just tell all of them that if they do chores around the house and come to lessons every day for five years, they earn a spot on the wall. I make the agreement with every one, and some fulfill their end. After they serve five years, I put one of their pieces up. I suppose if someone did paint a picture as good as my work, I would accept it outright, but that has never occurred."

Csaba Petruska mocked this solution and offered his own:

"Don't the paintings you put on the wall disgust you? I could not stand to live around all those catastrophes. Here is how I have chosen to deal with the problem. My son, who is as good a painter as I, comes into the orphanage once a year. He offers to paint a picture for anyone who wishes and even allows them to sign their own name to it. I put all those on the wall and reject the rest. Oddly enough, few choose to take advantage of the offer. They tender their own work

---

[1]Essentially "chicken fried chicken," which, as anyone bred in the southwest can tell you, is nothing like "fried chicken."

instead, which of course I reject. This way I can be merciful to those who realize their shortcomings, and I do not have to live around a bunch of ugly paintings."

Hermann Tóth practically exploded at this point: "What type of fools[2] you are! Why on earth would you expect these kids to paint as well as we do? They have had neither the years nor the upbringing that we have. Only an idiot would expect a four-year-old to paint like Monet![3] You two have the brains of mashed-up yams."

Csaba and Győrgy were shocked but could hardly utter much in their own defense, so they asked Hermann what he did. He answered:

"I do the only thing a reasonable person would. I give lessons as I can when I'm at the house. My son eventually moved in and now is available to everyone for guidance. Though he is patient with those who desire guidance, not all his students took his teaching to heart and the unsightly results have, quite sadly, caused others to go it alone. In the end I consider what guidance each has had and what potential the painting shows. If I think the child will end up contributing to the goals of my house, I put the painting up. If not, I don't."

The first man clearly allowed orphans to earn their way onto the wall. If an orphan worked for five years and then was denied, that young artist would have a justifiable complaint. The second person gave away spots on the wall as a free gift. But what about the third?

It cannot be said that Hermann required people to *earn* their way since he was the final arbiter of quality, and no agreement was in place. He took what pleased him. It is not like an employee earning a paycheck. Nor did Hermann use a system based on grace, though clearly he showed it in considering the background and potential of each artist rather than only the painting itself.

Hermann's system resembles a mother who buys her 2nd grade daughter an ice-cream cone when she brings home a pleasing report card. The mother is happy with the report card even though she could have done better herself. Further, she is not under any obligation to get the ice cream for her daughter, but graciously chooses to because of her daughter's work. Her daughter didn't "earn" the ice cream — her mother was under no obligation to buy the treat for her. Yet, her daughter's actions were certainly the instigating factor, conspiring with the mother's natural love for her daughter.

---

[2] Actually, the exact expression he used does not fit the timbre of this book, so we'll pretend he said "fools." This pretense should not be difficult, for the entire conversation is a complete fabrication. The restaurant really does exist though, behind a massive synagogue. If you go there, order the *Rántott Czirke* (it isn't on the menu) and give Esther my regards.

[3] Had this conversation really occurred, I suppose someone might have interrupted them, pointing out that Monet did, in fact, paint like a four-year-old.

I bring up Hermann and the mother to illustrate that the question "Do you believe you earn your way into heaven, or is it by grace?" represents a false dichotomy.[4] I'm not claiming Hermann's method is exactly the same as God's, but it is far more *consistent* with scripture than Csaba's.[5]

Before giving my "two-line answer" to the question posed as the title of this book, I want to give some commentary on issues pertaining to how different types of people may be judged.

Those Who Came Before Christ

The question of how those who came before Christ are judged is not of practical concern, for we can do nothing for them. However, our understanding of the Judgment has to be applicable to them as well.

Clearly Enoch made it onto the wall. One would think the same of Noah and Job, who are called **godly men**. Yet, none of these hoped for a savior.[6] God's grace clearly extends to those who have never (and will never[7]) hear any kind of gospel, as shown by Jonah being sent to Nineveh.

Given the number of people explicitly commended or called righteous who were outside Abraham's covenant (e.g., Abel, Enoch, Noah, Melchizedek, Rahab, Job, the Queen of the South), one should assume that all peoples (those who knew of the Promise and those who did not) have some chance of being placed in the category Jesus describes in *John 5:29* as **those who did what was good**.

---

[4]I would further claim that a study of what Paul was calling **grace** would show it generally referred to God's sending of the Spirit.

[5]Quite possibly Christ's work opened heaven in a general sense. One could argue that had Jesus never come no one would be allowed in because, at the very least, the proceedings shown in Revelation could not occur. However, this does not pertain to individual deliverance.

[6]*Job 19:25* should not be construed as an indication that Job looked forward to a savior. The word translated **redeemer** is the word for an avenger or vindicator. The NET commentator puts it accurately: **The word "redeemer" evokes the wrong connotation for people familiar with the NT alone; a translation of "Vindicator" would capture the idea more.** Job is saying that God will vindicate him to those who have **turned away** from him (see *Job 19:19*. It is further worthwhile to note that the Hebrew behind *Job 19:26* is so inscrutable that H.H. Rowley says **The text of this verse is so difficult, and any convincing reconstruction unlikely, that it seems best not to attempt it.** In any event, Hebrew history knows no indication of hope for deliverance from the grave until 1500 years after Job is thought to have lived, and this is shown in the Bible by Job's own remarks in *Job 14:10–12* as well as David in *Psalms 30:9*, Solomon in *Ecclesiastes 3:19–20* and King Hezekiah in *Isaiah 38:18*.

[7]Some believe Jesus preached to those who had died before His coming based on a reading of *1st Peter 3:19*. While an interesting possibility, the Reformed church rejects this interpretation.

One would think these people are judged based on all the things Jesus indicates. They will be judged as they judged others. They will be forgiven commensurate with their forgiveness of others. *Luke 12:48* indicates people will be judged by the light they have been given.

Those Who Never Heard the Gospel

People who came after Jesus but never heard of Him are generally considered a separate category from those who came before, though it is hard to see why a Jew born 300 years before Christ is judged differently than a Native American born 300 years afterward.

There are passages in the Bible that touch on this subject, but they do not portray some magical division in time after which no one receives forgiveness except believers in Christ. Rather, passages like *Acts 17:30* indicate that God is now calling all people to **repent**. When one takes into consideration how radically monotheistic the Jews were (see *James 2:18–19*), Paul's proclamation indicates the Father no longer tolerates idolatry and desires that all people (rather than just the physical sons of Jacob) come into covenant with the Living God. Jesus is not mentioned by name.

So, it seems the difference between those living before Jesus and those living later is that worship of idols and pantheons leads to greater condemnation. After all, Rachel's theft of the household gods (*Genesis 31:34*) is recounted without a hint of judgment, and men practiced idolatry before Noah, but the only sin given as a reason for the flood is **violence** (*Genesis 6:11–14*).

Those Who Reject Christ

Even though it goes against the idea that salvation is only through **faith in Christ**, many hold out hope for those who never hear "the gospel." But it's harder to find serious Christians who believe that those who actively reject Christ can still survive the Judgment. There is certainly some basis for this:

Matthew 10:33 **If you deny Me before men, I will deny you before My Father**

John 12:48 **The one who rejects Me and does not accept My words has one who judges him; the word I spoke is what will judge him at the last day**

On the other hand, we also have scripture such as *1st Corinthians 7:14*, **For the unbelieving husband is sanctified through his wife. . .**

Furthermore, the Jews who stoned Stephen (*Acts 7:59–60*) are at the top of the list among those who reject Christ, yet what does Stephen say? **Lord, do not hold this sin against them!** It seems odd for Stephen to be concerned with this particular sin if those who were stoning him had *absolutely* no hope.

Let's temporarily put these verses to the side and ponder the notion of *rejecting Christ*. What does that mean?

Imagine a 13-year-old girl in an unreligious family. Let's call her Anita. Anita is home alone and a group of Muslims come by to tell her of Islam. If she closes the door on the Muslims, did she reject Christ? Most would say "no."

Now, imagine a group of Christian Scientists or Jehovah's Witnesses come by, and Anita remains uncompelled after listening to them. Did she reject Christ in doing so? Most conservative Christians would say "no" to that as well because these two groups are often considered outside the group of "true Christians."

Let's say a liberal Episcopalian friend invites Anita to a church get-together. The pastor sees Anita and tells her of Jesus' love. The conversation has little impact on her. Many (most?) conservative Christians would not consider this rejecting Christ either.

The question is, *how accurate a gospel do you have to reject before it counting as rejecting Christ?* If a disillusioned Catholic disavows and never hears the Protestant version, did she reject Christ?

If I'm correct and Christians today are not proclaiming an accurate gospel, is anyone really rejecting it?

The issue becomes even murkier when we realize that a person's acceptance or non-acceptance of Christ as Lord is not a single decision made at a particular time — we also have to consider the messages the unchurched get when they *are not being evangelized*. Christians are representatives of Christ. If our lack of love towards others, our pitiful record at modeling Christ, or a history rife with hypocrisy and corruption in the church cause people to reject Christ, I would say they no more rejected Christ than when Anita was visited by the Muslims. They were not shown Christ, so how could they reject Him?

John 3:18–20 says evildoers hate the Light because they don't want their deeds to be exposed. Is *that* the reason people reject Christianity? Or is it because our poor efforts to model Christ fail to compel them?

Consider the parable found in *Luke 12:42–48*, which discusses people God places in spiritual leadership positions. In this parable, an unrighteous steward treats the household unjustly and does not teach them to do their duties. When the master returns, we find that all are punished, for none were doing what they should have been doing. However, Jesus says of those who received no guidance **But the one who did not know his master's will and did things worthy of punishment will receive a light beating.** Compare this to the servant who was put in charge and did not do as he was told: **the master will cut him in two and assign him a place with the unfaithful.**

The odd thing here, other than the obvious judgment by works, is that one wonders what **a light beating** means. It hardly sounds like a description of heaven… but at the same time we do not get the feeling from the Bible that there are nicer shades of hell. Of further interest is that the servant **was assigned a place with the unfaithful.** This suggests a punishment altogether different and worse than those who were ignorant.

It's possible, of course, that the present-age application of this parable only refers to those in the church. Christ's original targets here were the priests who **have taken away the key to knowledge. You did not go in yourselves, and you hindered those who were going in.**[8] But if we are the salt of the Earth and a lamp on a hill with a duty to disciple all nations, then I could easily believe that the present-day application of this parable views the entire world as the household. Then one would argue that there is hope for those who reject Christ due to the behavior and poor ministrations of Christians. *John 12:48*, generally given as proof that those who reject Christ are condemned, actually works against that philosophy in this regard. If people reject Christ due to the corruption of the church, then they can hardly be said to have rejected *Christ's Word* (which we'll discuss more in chapter nine).

One final nitpick to consider is Christ's warning regarding blasphemy of the Holy Spirit in *Matthew 12:31*. Jesus has more than present-day forgiveness in mind — **whoever speaks against the Holy Spirit will not be forgiven, either in this age, or the age to come.** Since Jesus says that those who **utter blasphemies** or **speak a word against the Son of Man** *can* be forgiven, it suggests rejecting Christ need not constitute an *unforgivable* sin. Otherwise, why state at length that words against the Son are forgivable while those against the Spirit are not only unforgivable now, but also in the age to come?

The above notwithstanding, there *is* the major point that Jesus' teachings have been transmitted through the ages. Anyone with access can read and decide, as Jesus describes in *John 7:17*, **whether it is from God or whether I speak from myself.** Part of those teachings involve Christ's own Lordship and uniqueness. It is a very real problem to say you agree with Christ on a moral level but then reject His words about Himself. If we simply take from Christ

---

[8]*Luke 11:52*

what we already agree with, we have learned nothing. That's like only attending class on days when you already know the material. Submission to Christ is seen when we logically realize that if He has so much wisdom concerning things we already partially understand, then He also has enlightenment in areas we cannot understand due to our self-absorption.

There are teachings of Christ that we do not wish to believe, or more pointedly do not wish to obey. But the cost of favoring *our* desires is to claim that Jesus is a liar or insane. *We either believe Jesus has an understanding of God that far eclipses our own, or we do not.* If the former, we have no reasonable conclusion other than that Jesus really is the Christ, given rulership over all Creation.

Of course, we could claim, as some have tried, that Jesus never said all those things about Himself. But to do this is much harder than it might seem. Most of us are now far removed from the torture, persecutions, and martyrdom faced by early Christians, including many of the apostles. To deny Christ's position and uniqueness is to suggest a mass insanity wherein scores of people would rather be tortured over many years or publicly (and painfully!) executed than deny Jesus as risen Lord who showed power through the Spirit among His disciples.

Furthermore, to deny this uniqueness of Christ, you are more or less forced to deny His resurrection. It would be odd indeed for God to raise Jesus from the dead if He were merely a prophet or teacher. **To deny the resurrection is to deny all Christianity**. To accept the resurrection puts one in a difficult place if one does not want to also accept Christ as a unique figure in spiritual cosmology, the only path to God. While some of the New Testament's authorship is in doubt, there is certainly enough text that even the most liberal scholars agree were written by apostles to clearly affirm that Christ's position as Lord is an essential belief for any follower of Christ.

What's my point here? I am saying most people today lack excuse for not following Christ and accepting Him as Lord over heaven and earth. Anyone interested can read Jesus' teachings and consider their ramifications. However, those who do not choose to do such investigation may well receive clemency, for the church has not given them good reason to do such research. If non-believers do not see the good wrought in Christians by the Holy Spirit through faith in Christ, can we blame them for not pondering Jesus' Word? Why should people look into what Christ actually preached if we Christians seem to care so little for it ourselves?

Those Who Believe in Christ

The fate of those who believe in Christ depends on what one means by *believe*. People who have been **enlightened** by Christ, as *Hebrews 6:4* puts it, have lost whatever clemency ignorance may have afforded them.[9] Those who receive the most enlightenment are held to the highest standard. Even Paul says that he has to be careful for his own sake in *Acts 24:16*, and James warns in *James 3:1*, **Not many of you should become teachers, my brothers and sisters, because you know that we will be judged more strictly.**

None of the above should surprise us. As Christ says in *Luke 12:48*, **from those who have been given much, much will be required.** He reiterates the difficulty and danger of discipleship in *Luke 14:26–35*. That we are enlightened and freed from bondage to sin obligates us all the more to obey God's commands. This is Paul's point in *Romans 6*, but *James 2:12* captures it more succinctly, **Speak and act as those who will be judged by a law of freedom.** James' language in *2:9* makes it impossible to put a spin of grace on this.

The above warnings should not discourage us from sharing Christ. In addition to being commanded to tell others of Jesus, we should see evangelism as an opportunity to help others be the creatures they were meant to be. Also, believers are the only people who are assured of a positive fate if they stand firm, obeying Christ's commands, as Paul describes in *Romans 2:7*. The next chapter is devoted to a more thorough discussion of what this faith looks like.

My Answer

When *Revelations* describes life after the Judgment, John speaks of a new creation — a new heaven and a new earth. Those chosen by Jesus enjoy life within a vast, blessed city called **New Jerusalem** that God places on the new earth. If we see the Judgment as a beginning rather than an end, as the advent of a new blessed kingdom in this new creation, an answer to the question *Who really goes to hell?* presents itself. We can conjecture a rule that not only respects God's desires but also matches the scriptures's portrayals of the Judgment:

Jesus chooses citizens for New Jerusalem whose history demonstrates they will contribute to its purpose. All others are left outside (in hell).

God has indicated a desire for a righteous nation from ancient times. Should we not expect that eternal desire to inform the Judgment?

---

[9] c.f. *John 9:41*; *15:22–23*; *Romans 5:13*; and *James 4:17*

Summary and Final Notes

Most details concerning the Judgment and the life thereafter remain unknown to us.

A biblically consistent answer is to say Jesus chooses for life in the hereafter those whose history indicates they will contribute to God's goals for the kingdom of the new era. This matches perfectly well with my view on Christ's purpose. *Titus 2:14* puts it well:

> **He gave Himself for us to set us free from every kind of lawlessness and to purify for Himself a people who are truly His, who are eager to do good.**

It also explains the particular condemnation given to those who cause others to sin (e.g., *Matthew 5:19*; *13:41*; and *18:6*). Obviously, this type of character is not what New Jerusalem needs.

We can say without fear of contradiction that people are judged by the light they have been given. Thus those who have been enlightened by Christ, freed from bondage to sin, are held to a higher accountability than others. However, such people are the only ones who have a promise to hold onto. Jesus assures us that an authentic faith will see all His followers through. In the next chapter we investigate what kind of faith He means.

I have placed online some thoughts on life and death after the Judgment.

–VII–

FAITH ... AND FAITHFULNESS

Jesus promises that those who believe in Him are assured life after the resurrection. What kind of faith does He mean?

Saving Faith

Saving faith is a common catchphrase, born from evangelicals' need to condemn the "My sins are forgiven, so I can do whatever I want" idea that can easily be taken from a reading of their beliefs. At the same time, they don't wish to suggest our deeds themselves have merit, so the distinction of *saving faith* as opposed to *dead faith* (à la *James 2:20*) became a popular one. Evangelicals often characterize *dead faith* as a merely academic affirmation of Christ.

This works pretty well for most serious Christians, who are certain their faith counts as the "saving" variety. The problem is that almost any faith will produce *some* works. The faith of the people described in *Matthew 7:22* produced many works, and see where it got them! I think a reflective Christian must eventually come to the conclusion that the dichotomy between "dead faith" and "saving faith" is a false one — a contrivance to make theology go down more easily.

Let's say a Christian wins the lottery — 100 million dollars. Now, if this Christian gave 20 million dollars (completely anonymously) to charity purely due to love for Christ and then used the rest to live lavishly in a mansion,[1] is that "saving faith"? It certainly accomplished genuinely good works. But is that person living faithfully?

---

[1] Putting aside for the moment that in the U.S. we call mansions "homes"

Living by Faith

Paul and the writer of Hebrews give us a clue as to the relationship between faith and works when they quote Habakkuk: **The righteous will live by faith**.[2] Real faith changes the way we live because it *changes the way we see the world*. It causes us to change our ways because our understanding of God makes us see the futility and stupidity of certain actions.

It is not that our heart has been reprogrammed. Indeed, until we receive a transformed body after the resurrection, Paul sees our flesh still pulling us against faithful living. Rather, the Spirit counsels us regarding God and gives us the *potential* to overcome the lies of this world when we see they conflict our understanding of the Almighty.

Many of Christ's teachings boil down to this idea. He mocks the Pharisees by explaining how their actions make no sense in light of their supposed beliefs about God. He describes *incongruities* between what they do and what they claim to believe. He points out it is incompatible for them to worry about what they will eat tomorrow if they believe God is loving, knows their plight, and cares for them. Rather than store up savings against unseen future calamity, they should be aiding those in need *today*. He notes the hypocrisy of expecting forgiveness from God when they do not forgive others, decries the vanity of long, loud prayers to a God who already knows their needs, and exposes the foolishness of neglecting to utilize God's gifts for good.[3]

Jesus refers to this foolishness in *Luke 16:8*, describing how God's people do a poor job of being wise (relative to their beliefs) as compared to those who live by the principles of the world. We who believe so often act as though we do not, like people sticking their hands in water they know is boiling. No wonder Jesus asks, **Why do you call Me "Lord, Lord" and don't do what I tell you?**

Jesus calls for a faith that provokes godly actions not merely out of gratitude of new disposition, but out of wisdom. We know it is unwise to hoard money, we know it is unwise to focus on material possessions, we know it is unwise to hold grudges, and we know it is unwise to sit in complicity while the weak are oppressed. We are not only serving God, but acting according to our understanding of how the world works. Just as a cartographer who believes the world to be round will draw a different map than one who believes the world to be flat, we should sketch out our lives in a way different from someone who believes there is no God.

---

[2] *Habakkuk 2:4; Romans 1:17; Galatians 3:11*; and *Hebrews 10:38*
[3] *Matthew 6:5–8,19–34; 18:33–35; 19:21; Mark 10:21; 11:25; Luke 12:16–34; 18:22;* and *19:20-24*

Faith affects choices because *our decisions are based on what type of qualities we believe God has.* The Bible describes God as

- caring *about* us and having the power to care *for* us.
- caring about people, and by extension caring about how we treat them.
- showing particular concern for the poor, the orphaned, and the widowed.
- forgiving us and expecting us to do the same.
- rewarding those who seek righteousness while punishing those who dishonor the Almighty.

In short, we are to love *and depend on* God while zealously addressing the needs of others, especially those least able to help themselves.

I cannot stress enough the importance of depending on God. A beautiful and underappreciated verse, *Isaiah 30:15*, comes on the heels of Judah's seeking support from external, pagan allies rather than trusting in God: **For thus the Lord God . . . has said, "In repentance and rest you will be saved, In quietness and trust is your strength." But you were not willing.**

Relying on things of this world enslaves us to them. If we are slaves to our money, our house, our fence, or our retirement accounts, our actions and decisions will be guided by those masters rather than God's desires. Jesus' admonition, **no one can serve two masters**, is a timeless one.

The same goes for non-material baggage. If we are slaves to our vanity, our insecurity, our grudges, or anything else that stops us from being a light to others, we must recognize those shackles before they can be dealt with. Jesus did not intend us to be enslaved by these forces of ego.

Christian Charity

The above demonstrates how withholding aid to others is a double violation of God's will. It not only shows us to be *disobedient* (by ignoring the ten-fold repeated exhortation to provide for people's physical needs), but it shows a direct lack of *faith* as well. We hoard for ourselves possessions either to remind us of our "success" or to hedge against future calamity. How is this not like Judah putting its faith in Egypt to provide for their needs rather than trusting in God?

Breathtaking are the number and ardor of exhortations to help those in need. God's ire with those who ignored the poor is more ancient than people realize. Consider the message to Ezekiel describing Sodom. **See here — this was the guilt of your sister Sodom: She and her daughters had majesty, abundance of food, and enjoyed carefree ease, but they did not help the poor** and needy.... God's reproach of King Jehoiakim and extolling of Josiah reads **He upheld the cause of the poor and needy. So things went well for Judah.... this is a good example of what it means to know Me.** Jesus counsels a rich man, **If you wish to be perfect, go sell your possessions and give the money to the poor, and you will have treasure in heaven. Then come, follow me.** Note the treasure in heaven comes upon the charity, as in *Matthew 6:20* and *Luke 12:33*, which appear to be general commands still applicable today. Cornelius' **acts of charity** apparently instigates God's grace toward him.[4]

The Jerusalem Church's only request of Paul is that he **remember the poor,** and James declares, **Pure and undefiled religion before God the Father is this: to care for orphans and widows in their misfortune and to keep oneself unstained by the world** before deriding those who claim to have faith without helping their fellows — **If a brother or sister is poorly clothed and lacks daily food, and one of you says to them, "Go in peace, keep warm and eat well," but you do not give them what the body needs, what good is it?**[5] These are but a sample of passages regarding the importance of helping the poor. I would recommend just doing a quick Bible search online to see the torrent of verses showing God's interest in those who have limited means.

I believe evangelicals have played down this aspect of Christian instruction for several political reasons:

- Charity is too universal. Since anyone can give to others, it does not have the flavor of hard-edge Christianity that other works possess — as though any service that could be done by a non-Christian is a second-class act.

- Conservative Christians tend to extol *prudence*, and are often more interested in being financially smart than spiritually wise.

- Though the Bible decries it, Christians have not earned their judgmental reputation for nothing. Many of those who need assistance have made poor choices in the past (which, as far as I know, is part of being human). Somehow helping them today is seen as subsidizing their past behavior. We would rather sit in judgment over others than meet their needs.

- We have had it hammered into us for so long that we cannot *earn our way into heaven* that any service activity that does not include the gospel almost seems suspect.

---

[4]*Ezekiel 16:49; Jeremiah 22:16; Matthew 19:21;* and *Acts 10:4*
[5]*Galatians 2:10* and *James 1:27; 2:15.*

Creating the Kingdom

The fellowship described in *Acts 2:42–47* demonstrates how faith, hope, and charity can drive the creation of God's kingdom right here and right now. It's a small, bright patch showing the effect Christians should create in the world. This interest in creating the kingdom fell by the wayside due to persecutions, which used to be purely political — now they are socio-political and ideological. The church is assailed on all sides and has hunkered down in defense.

I would suggest this trenched-in mentality has not ultimately met the godly goals of the church. It neither contributes to the church's moral goals of working toward everyone's physical and emotional welfare, nor has it called the nations to glorify God or know the Almighty. Instead, as Paul states in *Romans 2:24* (quoting Isaiah), **The name of God is being blasphemed among the Gentiles because of** us.

Given the state of today's world, I can only assume that our methods and choices as believers have not provoked God's full support. The world today looks very different from what the later prophets proclaimed. The reasonable conclusion is that the prophesied kingdom has not come about because we choose not to engage the world as God desires. A recurring theme of the Old Testament is that God's will is delayed when God's people are unfaithful.

All the abominations God decries through the prophets are still here today. The powerful still take bribes to help the rich. The poor are still oppressed and not given justice. We have 850,000,000 people without sufficient food, and war still ravishes creation. Perhaps this is what delays the second coming of Christ. In a passage quoted by Jesus, Peter, and the writer of Hebrews, God speaks to Jesus saying **And the Lord (God) said to my Lord (Jesus) "Sit at my right hand, until I make your enemies a footstool for your feet."**

How does God make these enemies footstools? Should we stand idly by assuming nothing is expected of us? *Perhaps* God waits for us to defeat these enemies (injustice, oppression, poverty, immorality), or at least show a desire to play our part. *2nd Peter 3:12* may refer to this.

We will continue failing to conquer these enemies of Christ so long as the church focuses its energy on division and conversion rather than discipling. *The Pharisees did exactly that, and Christ excoriates them.* In *Matthew 23:15*, part of a litany of denouncements describing how the Jewish leaders neither taught people how to properly honor God nor did so themselves, He exclaims:

> **Woe to you scribes and Pharisees, hypocrites! You cross land and sea to make one convert, and when he becomes one, you make him twice as much a child of hell as yourselves!**

Summary and Final Notes

The simplest way to understand how we should live is to read Jesus' words very carefully. We don't read enough of Jesus in church today...and we certainly do not dwell on the harder passages. I find Christ's clarity inspirational, just as the Jews marveled, for **He spoke as one having authority.** As the officer in *John 7:46* cried out to the hostile Pharisees, **Never has a man spoken the way this man speaks.**

In addition to Christ, the Old Testament reveals a great deal about God's character. In the Mosaic law, you can find several things described as **an abomination unto God** — things that are not merely forbidden to the Israelites (like pork) but wickedness that God detests in absolute terms. The prophets reveal a raw image of what God found so wrong in the world 2500 years ago, and there is absolutely no reason to suspect things deemed ungodly then are not judged the same way now.

A surefire method of working toward creating the kingdom God desires is to work with the world rather than against it. We can help those who do not know God without subsidizing their ignorance. The unchurched's perceptions of Christians are a mirror, albeit an imperfect one, declaring a need for church reform. Jesus asks His dissenters in *John 8:46* **Who among you can prove me guilty of any sin?** Though we cannot model Christ perfectly, we should still be mindful of the charges made against us. God is not glorified when the nations slander the church.

The leaven of the Pharisees, which Jesus identifies as hypocrisy, thoroughly prevented them from doing God's will. We must transform the church to **silence the ignorance of foolish people by doing good**, as described in *1st Peter 2:15*. Indeed, 1st Peter in general is a good place to start if we want to know where the church needs to go.

INTERMISSION

I asked you earlier to separate, at least for a while, Judgment from salvation so that we could look closely at what scripture says about the former. How you use the rest of this book is rather dependent on your disposition toward what you've read so far.

I believe that the Bible solidly supports the understanding of salvation I put forth in the first few chapters of this book. The Old Testament law, the writings of the prophets who described Christ and His kingdom, the message of Jesus before He died, the gospel spread by His apostles afterward, and the epistles to Jewish and Gentile churches all point to the same conclusion. In these last four chapters, I'd like to prove that to you.

So, if your world has been turned upside down by finding out that Christianity really isn't about untying God's hands to allow our admittance to heaven, then these chapters will piece Christianity back together, showing exactly what Jesus *did* do and why **no one comes to the Father except through** Him.

If, instead, your mind is abuzz with questions like "If all this is true, then what about (*fill in the blank*)?" then these chapters will answer some of those questions.

You can also use them as primers for your own Bible study, choosing which chapter you read based on what books of the Bible you are reading. I hope you will find they broach issues that might not be obvious at first glance.

In any event, you should not feel that you have to read all these immediately, as though I am "building up" to something. I am, rather, "fleshing out." The level you read to should be based on your own needs.

Preview

The content of these chapters:

Chapter 8 Investigates the gospel to the Jews. It focuses on the gospels and Acts. It answers questions like "What did Jesus accomplish through His death?" and "What did Jesus preach as the gospel?"

Chapter 9 Investigates the gospel to the Gentiles. It focuses on the book of John, some critical parables in Luke, and a few key verses describing how Paul saw the "good news."

Chapter 10 Gives four keys to understanding Paul's letters. It shows Paul's priorities, how he saw salvation, his understanding of justification, what he means by "works of the Law," and what kind of wrath he describes believers as being protected from.

Chapter 11 Describes a theory of atonement consistent with the understanding of salvation described here. It portrays the Jewish context and need for a Messiah and answers questions like "How was Christ a sacrifice?" It also demonstrates the critical importance of all stages of Christ's life, which is something the standard gospel does not.

These chapters become more and more demanding as you go forward.

Salvation —
Building up the Gospel

– VIII –

WHAT IS *The Gospel* ANYWAY?

In *Matthew 11:5*, Jesus tells John's disciples He is preaching **the gospel** to the poor. But what is the gospel?

The modern gospel is a very *internal* one. We have to *understand* that we cannot get into heaven on our own. We have to *believe* that Jesus is God. We have to *accept* Jesus as our personal Savior. We have to *have faith* that Jesus can save us from hell. We have to *surrender* ourselves to Christ.

The external consequences of these internal choices are considered "the icing on the cake." I'm not saying the church doesn't care that we practice Christlike behavior, but it is undeniable that the importance of internal resolutions and doctrinal beliefs (as opposed to *belief* in Christ) within evangelical circles is now comparable to the primacy of tradition within Catholicism.

Is the gospel really such an internal one? And are these beliefs of modern Christianity really the core of Christ's message?

The Pre-Resurrection Gospel

An investigation of Jesus', John's, and the apostles' message prior to Christ's death and resurrection quite illuminates the matter. The crowds thought Jesus was a teacher or prophet, did not know He was going to die, did not know He was going to be resurrected, and most definitely couldn't grasp any notion of His being a sacrifice.

As N.T. Wright describes in *Surprised by Hope*, the whole idea that the Messiah would die and be resurrected individually before everyone else was completely new. This is well illustrated by the disciples' taking Christ's death as a sign that He was not the Messiah. How could He redeem Israel if He were dead? *John 12:34* shows the Jews did not realize the Christ would die.

97

One then has to wonder what *Mark 1:14* — **After John was imprisoned, Jesus went into Galilee and proclaimed the gospel of God** — means. This is one of a dozen instances in the gospels where the **gospel** is described as a message to the people. What gospel can Christ and His apostles preach if Jesus forbids them to tell anyone He was the Christ, and His disciples do not realize He is going to die even after He tells them in private?

This is important. Ponder that last question for a moment. Take a walk and consider it. The book will be here when you get back.

The gospel narratives detail the teachings of Jesus. It can be hard to see the forest for the trees, but there are plenty of places where the *essence* of the message has been distilled for us. Let's take a quick journey through those passages to get a handle on what this **gospel** thing is.

Matthew 3:1–2 **In those days John the Baptist came into the wilderness of Judea proclaiming, "Repent, for the kingdom of heaven is near."**

Matthew 4:17 **From that time Jesus began to preach this message: "Repent, for the kingdom of heaven is near."**

Mark 1:15 **Jesus went into Galilee and proclaimed the gospel of God. He said, "The time is fulfilled, and the kingdom of God is near; repent and believe the gospel."**

Matthew 10:7 **As you go, preach, this message: "The kingdom of heaven is near!"**

Luke 10:9 **say to them, "The kingdom of God has come upon you."**

A common theme is **the kingdom of God** or **the kingdom of heaven**.[1] One has to assume that this kingdom, which is **near** and which later is **in your midst**, cannot refer to post-Judgment bliss. This means that these general statements indicate the gospel has *nothing* to do with the Judgment. (Though clearly there are consequences to rejecting Christ's message. We'll discuss that in the next chapter.) Rather, Jesus is proclaiming the "good news" that God has not forgotten Israel. The coming kingdom pronounced in the prophets, a kingdom where peace and justice rule, is imminent. The new covenant is at hand! To the Jews, it is the most natural message in the world. This is yet another reason people

---

[1]By the 1st century, the Jews were so concerned about using the name of God in vain that they often substituted other words for God. "Heaven" was a common example. So "kingdom of heaven" is a more respectful way of saying "kingdom of God."

think Jesus may be Elijah. Elijah is supposed to come right before the Christ as the **messenger of the covenant** (*Malachi 4:5–6*), and Jesus is proclaiming the covenant prophesied in *Jeremiah 31:31*.

Note the emphasis on *repentance* and the strong indication that it comes in **preparation** of receiving the kingdom of God. Today, some people describe repentance as "being sorry for your sins." That is a tragically incomplete understanding of the term. Repentance involves a *change in attitude* and a change in behavior as well. It is not mere contrition. It is not looking at your feet in humiliation; it is turning around and walking the other way. *Luke 3:8–17* is a clear indication of this. Repentance is not abjection — it's rejection.

Even worse—some have taken repentance and twisted it to mean *realizing we need a savior*. The term occurs several times in the Old Testament, and it never means "I know I need a savior." For example, in *Ezekiel 18:30* we read **"Therefore I will judge each person according to his conduct, O house of Israel," declares the sovereign Lord. Repent and turn away from all your wickedness; then it will not be an obstacle leading to iniquity.** And in *Jeremiah 15:7* we see **In every town in the land I will purge them like straw blown away by the wind. I will destroy my people. I will kill off their children. I will do so because they did not change their behavior.** This message pervades the Old Testament: a discouraged God desiring a faithful people. There's nothing abstract or metaphysical here, no complicated logic about what God can and cannot do regarding the afterlife, just a loving husband longing after an unfaithful wife.

The **gospel** we find in the gospel narratives is not a message stressing the importance of *faith* relative to our position in the *eternal* kingdom of God. Rather, it stresses the importance of *repentance* relative to our position in the *imminent* kingdom of God, the kingdom Christ ushered in. These **gospel** proclamations come before Christ even **began** to tell His disciples of anything that would happen to Him (e.g., *Mark 8:31*).

This should not be surprising. Can you find one Old Testament prophet who does not exhort God's people to repent? Rather, they relate repentance to the receipt of God's deliverance repeatedly. In *Jeremiah 25:9–12* we read that the Babylonians were to rule over God's people for 70 years before Israel's redemption. However, Daniel knows that Israel has not repented during that time and hence risks the loss of this deliverance, so he prays on their behalf.[2]

---

[2]*Daniel 9:2–27*. Incidentally, the prophecy Daniel receives provides amazing support for Jesus as the Christ, for it spells out nearly exactly when the Messiah would come 500 years prior to His birth. See *The Coming Prince* by Sir Robert Anderson. Why do we not use this more when sharing the gospel? It is ludicrous that we prefer to evangelize through fear than through truth.

The Post-Resurrection Gospel of Acts

I've shown that the general message Jesus and His disciples preached before His resurrection had nothing to do with His death, but what about afterward?

It turns out that question is easy to answer. There happens to be a book of the Bible documenting the teachings of the apostles to those they evangelized. Acts is the **only** repository of explicit post-resurrection *evangelism* (that is, preaching of the gospel to unbelievers). So any attempt to uncover Christianity's core beliefs should begin there. It provides a snapshot of what Paul, Peter, Stephen, and others thought *made a Christian a Christian.* When it comes to irony, the lack of respect we give Acts is only eclipsed by our prizing the epistles of Paul more than the epistles of Christ. (See *Revelation 2:1–3:22.*)

To show the clarity of the message in Acts, I have organized all the preaching described there and classified its content.[3]

	Jesus is Messiah	Jesus arose	Jesus is Lord	Repent	Jesus will judge all	Believers go to heaven	Others go to hell
2:14–41	X	X	X	X			
3:12–26	X	X	X	X			
4:8–12	X	X					
5:30–32	X	X	X				
5:42	X						
7:1–53	X						
9:22	X						
10:34–43	X	X	X		X		
13:16–41	X	X	X	X			
14:14–17					X		
17:2–4	X	X					
17:18–31		X		X	X		
18:5	X						
18:28	X						
20:20–22			X	X			
22:1–21	X	X					
26:1–29	X	X					

The complete omission of hell is pretty damning[4] to the traditional understanding of the gospel. Those few times when the Judgment is in view, the message does not do the Church any favors.

---

[3]The Greek word translated "Lord" can mean anything from "Sir" (as a greeting) to "God." In the table it means "Lord over heaven and earth." (But that wouldn't fit the column.)

[4]Heh! Seriously, the Greek word for hell doesn't show up anywhere in the book... not once. The word in *Acts 2:27* is *not* **hell** (see chapter nine), though it would hardly matter if it were. How can the gospel have anything to do with Judgment if hell fails to appear *once* in all the evangelism of Acts?

In *Acts 24:1–16*, Paul says he is careful to maintain a clear conscience because both the righteous and unrighteous will be resurrected. The message in *17:30–31* to the Athenians, who had little understanding of Judaism, was **Therefore, although God has overlooked such times of ignorance, He now commands all people everywhere to repent because He has set a day on which He is going to judge the world in righteousness, by a man he designated having provided proof to everyone by raising Him from the dead**.

Due to these examples and the overwhelming evidence in the chart, one can hardly claim that the apostles' gospel is widely preached today. In fact, we have a pretty good understanding of what message the early church taught; pastors just don't publicize it much. The teachings of the ancient church, known as the **Kerygma**, were extremely basic:

- God has fulfilled the promise made to Abraham by sending Jesus, who is the Christ.

- Jesus was crucified and raised from the dead.

- Jesus has been made Lord over heaven and earth.

- Jesus sends the Spirit to believers.

- Jesus will come again and judge the world.

- All should repent and be baptized.

I want to highlight some key parts of this message.

The Power of the Resurrection

I think most people who believe in a divine Being (especially those who read the Bible) take for granted that there will be a Judgment of sorts. The question people care about is how that Judgment works. Things were different in 1st century AD. Part of the message, particularly Paul's, was that there will be a Judgment and a resurrection *at all*. Other mythologies did not call for a Judgment at the end of the era, and the idea that everyone would be given new, uncorrupted bodies was completely foreign to any belief system outside Judaism, and it was not a fundamental or universal belief even for them. Jesus' resurrection is not only a sign that He is the Christ, but also an indication of what God will do to all later.[5] A close reading shows that this is the bulk of Paul's evangelism in Acts.[6]

---

[5]*Acts 4:2* and others, in particular *1st Corinthians 15:12*.

[6]It also takes center stage in the summary of Peter's gospel to the Gentiles in *Acts 10:42*. (For a discussion of the other half of Peter's gospel, given in the next verse, see chapter eleven.)

The Athenians response (*Acts 17:32*) shows this — **When they heard of the resurrection of the dead, some began to sneer, but others said "We shall hear you again concerning this."** Paul's trials in Acts revolve about his supporting the resurrection, a doctrine the Sadducees (the ruling sect of Judaism) disavowed: **. . . I am on trial for the hope and resurrection of the dead!**[7]

Many, though not all, Jews think there is going to be a resurrection at the end of the world — far in the future, as opposed to the near-future hope in a Messiah to deliver them from their oppressors. The idea that the Messiah would die and arise early, *before everyone else*, comes out of nowhere. The idea of physical resurrection is foreign to Greeks, Romans, and most other cultures, so Jesus' is proof that the God of Israel lived. Bodily resurrection is the **hope** of the new covenant. Jews who believe in a general resurrection and Judgment at the end of all days think all will be judged by their deeds (though perhaps the Jews hope Moses will intercede for them). Evangelism in Acts confirms this view, just as Jesus' teachings do.

This **hope** is critical to the early Jewish Christians because they actually see our resurrected bodies as the total fulfillment of Abraham's blessing. Christ was resurrected as the first to receive this body, and everyone who believes in Christ gain the same inheritance Christ has received. See *Romans 8:24*.

The Foolish Path to Kingship

Jesus' resurrection vindicates the God of Abraham, but it also causes division among Jews. The hope of a Messiah was so central to the Jews of Jesus' day that disagreement about the Messiah's identity would obviously create factions in their culture. But the polarization due to Jesus' claim transcended politics.

The Jews look for a king like David to save them from their oppressors. The Jews see physical death as the outcome of sin, and shameful deaths are the punishment for particularly sinful behavior. Conversely, to survive battles and live a long life suggests one lived righteously (*Leviticus 18:5*; *Nehemiah 9:29*; and *Ezekiel 33:19*). Thus, *the idea that the rightful King of Israel would die before saving God's people made absolutely no sense.*

How can a king free his people if he dies? And why would a righteous man, who the Christ certainly would be, die early? It just makes no sense. This is why Christ's crucifixion is **a stumbling block to the Jews and foolishness to the Gentiles**, as described by Paul in *1st Corinthians 1:23*. Paul uses this term, **foolishness**, several times in letters to the Corinthians. It is not a commentary on *why* Jesus died, but rather one on *that* Jesus died. The idea that one could

---

[7]*Acts 23:6*. See also *Luke 20:27–39*; *Acts 24:21*; and *Acts 26:8*.

become a king by shamefully dying with outlaws, apparently crushed by Caesar and rejected by your own people makes no sense at all to those who do not believe that God raises the dead.

For this reason the apostle's claim that Jesus is the Christ causes far more than political strife. It is a blow to the Jews' collective cultural understanding of God's deliverance. As Paul casts the message in *1st Corinthians 15:36*, **What you sow will not come to life until it dies**, is not an easy one to hear. And Jesus' ascendancy through suffering causes jealousy among those Jews who could not accept it (*Acts 17:5*).

The Holy Spirit in Acts — Promise and Gift

While the Judgment gets little play in Acts (other than Jesus being said to be the Judge), *the Holy Spirit* is a major theme of the apostles' ministry. Christ, Peter, Paul, and the writer of Hebrews refer to the Holy Spirit as the **Promise**,[8] inherited after Christ's death. The disciples give it to those who believe,[9] but here *believe* has the notion of *obey*, as shown in *Acts 5:32*: **...the Holy Spirit, whom God has given to those who obey Him.** The Spirit was the mark of membership in God's new covenant, so it makes sense that only those willing to repent of ungodliness and obey Christ's commandments receive it.

The Holy Spirit is also the **gift** described by many apostles. Peter uses this language in *Acts 2:38*; *8:20*; and *11:17*. Luke does so in *Acts 10:45*, and the writer of Hebrews in *Hebrews 6:4*. Paul refers to the Holy Spirit bestowed upon Timothy in the same way twice (*1st Timothy 4:14* and *2nd Timothy 1:6*).

The apostles saw our transformed, raised bodies as the full inheritance available to God's people, but prior to receiving that treasure we have the Holy Spirit. This gift is proof that God is fulfilling the promise to Abraham, just as the Israelites were given proof. They had the manna and God's appearance at Sinai. Christians have the Spirit and its revelation to prove they are heirs of a great inheritance. A whole generation of Israelites died in the desert due to disobedience, failing to collect their inheritance; believers are at the same risk.[10]

Anyone who desires to be part of the coming kingdom is invited to repent of ungodliness and join the new covenant, receiving freedom from the domination of sin. This is the theme of *Romans 5–8*. Paul is not referring to accountability or God's wrath. He is referring to sin's mastery of our weak flesh — the inability of humans to overcome their selfish desires to serve God faithfully. The

---

[8]*Luke 24:49*; *Acts 2:33*; *13:33*; and *Hebrews 9:15*
[9]*Acts 2:38*; *8:14–16*
[10]*Acts 3:23* and *Hebrews 4:5–13* describe this forfeiture of inheritance.

nation of Israel exemplified this predilection toward unfaithfulness, and it fell as a consequence. We will discuss Romans 5–8 more in chapter ten.

Acts turns the modern gospel on its head. We don't see belief causing forgiveness of sins to save us from hell in the future. Instead we find repentance allowing belief, and both bringing forgiveness of sins. This permits receipt of the Holy Spirit, freeing us from bondage to sin *in the present*:

Modern Gospel: Belief → Forgiveness of sins → Deliverance from hell

Gospel of Acts: Repentance → Faith + repentance → Forgiveness of sins → Baptism (receipt of Spirit) → Freedom from bondage to sin

Acts 2:38; 15:9; and *26:20* all describe this, but *3:19,26* is particularly beautiful and comprehensive: **Therefore repent and turn back so that your sins may be wiped out, so that times of refreshing may come from the presence of the Lord...God raised up His servant and sent Him first to you, to bless you by turning each one of you from your iniquities.**

How is Christ to bless us? *What* is the benefit?**...by turning each one of you from your iniquities.** (Note that Peter is describing not just any blessing but *the* blessing promised to Abraham, the covenant anchoring salvation.)

It makes sense for repentance to come first. After all, John the Baptist is sent to **make the roads straight** for Christ by exhorting people to quit their evil deeds, as described in *Matthew 3:3*. Paul's explanation in *2nd Timothy 2:26* describes our captivity to Satan as one of present spiritual weakness. It has nothing to do with God's justice.

The apostles in Acts are not out to save souls *from hell*. They are out to free people from our natural slavery to unfaithfulness, **from everything the Law could not.**[11] This liberation for service to God is worked by the Holy Spirit. The Judgment also factors into their teaching, but as a prompt to *repentance* rather than to faith. The apostles in Acts are not trying to convince people *they need a Savior.* They are displaying Jesus as Lord and explaining the ramifications of His resurrection. You hardly see any mention of "atonement" or "sacrifice" in the whole book. It is the resurrection, not the death, that takes center stage.

Conclusion — Salvation

The repeated teachings of Jesus and His apostles in the gospels and Acts point to one conclusion. *The salvation Christ wrought consists of freeing believers to faithfulness rather than freeing God to mercy.*

---

[11]*Acts 13:39.* We will discuss the Jewish context of this statement in chapter ten.

Jesus' Message — The Rest of the Story

We have looked at the "good news" preached by Jesus — that God has not forgotten Israel and that people everywhere should repent. However, if that were all Jesus preached, the Pharisees would not have hated Him so.

Jesus' message bears a nature strikingly similar to John the Baptist's in *Matthew 3:1–12* and *Luke 3:3–14*. They have the same four components:

- Declaration of the coming kingdom
- Exhortation to repent
- Rebukes to those who had warped God's law to their own benefit
- Specific commandments

We have described the first two already. Just as the Mosaic era began with the Law given on Mount Sinai, the era of Christ began with God's law. Why else would Matthew spend so long (*5:1–7:28*) recording the *Sermon on the Mount*.

Christ gives God's law on earth and continues to do so later through the Spirit. It should not surprise us that Christ's message largely comprises commandments from God. After all, the Jews think He is a teacher or a prophet — teachers interpret the Law, and prophets give God's commandments. When He sends the disciples out in *Matthew 28:19–20*, He tells them **. . . teaching them to obey everything I have commanded you. . .** John's writing is full of references to Jesus' Word as commandments.[12]

Seeing the bulk of Jesus' message in this way is critical, for otherwise we can miss a major point. In today's culture we tend to see rejecting Christ as a matter of unbelief: The person doesn't think Jesus is [fill in all things your church requires]. The standard reasons that someone rejects Christ today are:

- They don't think they believe in God.
- They don't like the idea that God sends people to hell.
- They don't have any reason to believe the Bible.
- They think many paths can lead to God, so the exclusivity of Christianity shows it's invalid.
- The historical behavior of Christians has not compelled them.

None of the above relate to the Jews of the 1st century! They are God's people and cherish God's law. They have far more reason to believe in Christ

---

[12]*John 12:50; 14:15,21; 15:10; 1st John 2:3–4; 3:22,24; 5:3*, and *2nd John 1:6* use the word **commandments**. *John 8:31* refers to **continuing** in Jesus' Word as evidence of being a disciple, *John 8:51–52* describes the **keeping** of the Word, as does *14:23–24* and *15:20*. *1st John 2:7* appears to directly equate the **word** with the commandments of God.

than we do. He raises the dead, cures the blind, and I bet He can even make American cheese taste good.

The reason the Pharisees reject Christ is simple — they don't like what He told them! They do not want to serve God the way He says they have to, as indicated in *John 12:47–48.* They don't appreciate Jesus' criticism in *Matthew 23:23* that they have failed God by not teaching others the **weightier provisions of the law: justice, mercy, and faithfulness**. The Jews reject Jesus for the same reason they killed all the prophets God sent before Him. They do not stumble by lack of faith but rather disinterest in obedience (*1st Peter 2:8*).

Conversely, the *reason* Jesus wants us to believe in Him is explicitly because we find value in His commands. In *John 14:10–12,* Jesus declares He wants people to believe in Him because of His words, but He has done signs so that those of hard heart might believe as well. In *John 7:17* He describes how those who desire righteousness will know that His commands are from God: **If anyone wants to do God's will, he will know about My teaching, whether it is from God or whether I speak from my own authority.** Indeed, *John 7:17* is really a clearer version of *John 3:19–20,* describing how those who desire to serve God find truth in Christ's commands. The Pharisees had no ear for Christ because they did not, down deep, **want to do God's will.** *John 8:37–47* is a critique of the Pharisees on this topic.

What Did Christ Do?

We began this chapter investigating *salvation* by answering the question *What did Christ do?* So far we've looked at the message preached by Christ and His apostles. Other passages indicate more directly Christ's purpose:

Luke 5:32 **I have not come to call the righteous, but sinners to repentance.**

John 16:7 **If I do not go away the Advocate will not come, but if I go I will send Him to you.**

Acts 3:26 **God raised up His Servant and sent Him first to you, to bless you by turning each of you from your iniquities.**

Romans 6:6 **We know that our old man was crucified with him <u>so that</u> the body of sin would no longer dominate us.**

Titus 2:14 **He gave Himself for us to free us from every kind of lawlessness and to purify for Himself a people who are truly His, who are eager to do good.**

1 Peter 2:24 **He Himself bore our sins in His body on the tree, <u>so that</u> we may leave sin behind and live in righteousness. By His wounds you were healed.**

The above is a mere sample.[13]

Jesus comes to do in power what all other prophets had done in supplication: ***turn Israel back to God***. He calls humanity to be the creatures they were intended to be and strengthens them to do so by sending the Spirit.

The difference between the new covenant and the old is not that one gets you into heaven and the other does not. In the old covenant, Israel received God's Word on slabs of stone and through the mouths of prophets, whereas in the new covenant God's commands come through Jesus Christ and the Holy Spirit, who empowers us to faithfulness.[14] The weakness of the old covenant was simple: the external Law did not compel Israel to faithfulness. Any reading of the Old Testament reveals this as *the* recurring problem.

Have We Learned Nothing? Pharisees Redux

Because Christ's coming is written throughout scripture, Christ chides the Jews in *John 5:46* for not recognizing Him. The natural question to ask is "What does the Old Testament say about the Christ?"

I strongly suggest that you read all the prophets of the Old Testament with open eyes. You should find the prophecies center on two points:

- The institution of righteousness by elevating and purifying God's people

- The unifying of multiple peoples under the umbrella of God

Several passages detail *how* God will accomplish the above.[15] In every case the goal is to remove ungodliness from God's people, not to somehow untie God's hands to allow mercy at the Final Judgment. God is not trying to subsidize sin but to end it. And not just to remove it from the accounting books God supposedly keeps — God is not turning a blind eye but rather opening ours.

What you won't find in the Prophets is any focus on immortality or believers being in heaven and everyone else in hell. That would be an odd thing to leave

---

[13]Check out *Luke 13:6–9; John 7:39; 8:34–36; 15:1–8; Romans 6:4; Galatians 5:1; Hebrews 9:14; 1st Peter 1:18–19; 2nd Peter 1:4–5; 1st John 3:4–5,8–9;* and Jesus' seminal prophecy reading found in *Luke 4:17–21.* Notice how many of these verses specify the reason for Christ's work. If this does not convince you of Christ's real purpose, I don't know what to say. I have left out one aspect of Christ's work, which will be discussed in the next chapter.

[14]*Hebrews 8:7–13.* There are, of course, other differences between the covenants. We will compare and contrast these in chapter 11.

[15]*Isaiah 59:20–21; Jeremiah 31:31–34; Ezekiel 11:17–20; 36:24–28,* and *Zechariah 12:10–14* all describe the coming Spirit and its effects; many use covenant language.

out if it were part of the Messiah's purpose. If Christ was meant to solve the problem *How do I get people into heaven without compromising My need for justice?*, the prophets are thunderously silent on the matter. They describe many issues the Messiah would address, but that was not one of them.

Anyone who claims that Jesus' purpose is our individual deliverance from hell has to explain why hundreds of prophetic pages describing what the Messiah would accomplish say nothing about it.[16] The only passage in the Old Testament clearly describing the resurrection is *Daniel 12:1–4*, which associates the Judgment and resurrection to the Archangel Michael rather than the Christ.

Instead you see a repeated call for Israel to return to God. *That* is the problem for which Jesus was the solution. What does Jesus say in *Matthew 23:37*?

> **O Jerusalem, Jerusalem, you who kill the prophets and stone those who are sent to you! How often I longed to gather your children together as a hen gathers her chicks under her wings, and you were unwilling.**

The Gospel

I have already alluded to it, but I want to reiterate a certain framework that explains well the writings of the New Testament.

The gospel message is that the new covenant described in the prophets is at hand. This announcement shares many things in common with the Mosaic covenant. There is a freeing of captives, proofs of God's power, intermittent struggle, an inheritance to be claimed, and a godly kingdom to be formed.

In the case of the new covenant, the freedom is deliverance from sin's domination, the proofs of God's power are Christ's resurrection and the sending of the Spirit. The struggle is our current life we live with a transformed spirit and a selfish flesh. The inheritance is our transformed, resurrected bodies and a place in the kingdom Christ is coming back to claim. While anyone who has faith is an heir to that Kingdom just as Abraham became heir through his faith, that inheritance can also be lost due to personal disobedience.

This is the gospel of the kingdom the Jewish writers of the New Testament understood, rooted in the salvation depicted by the Later Prophets. We will discuss the links between Moses' deliverance and Christ's more in chapter eleven.

---

[16]I do not take space to explain why *Job 19:25* says nothing about life after death. I'll just say that anyone who believes Job (who was neither Hebrew nor prophet) refers to deliverance from hell has a hard time explaining *Job 7:9*.

Summary and Final Notes

Matthew, Mark, Luke, John, Paul, and Peter all concur that Jesus' message was a call for repentance and Jesus' purpose was **to bless you by turning each of you from your iniquities to purify for Himself a people who are truly His, who are eager to do good.**[17]

The "Good News" is that God has not abandoned Israel and that the Promise of the Spirit has come upon them. The further **hope** we find is that since God resurrected Christ, we can have faith that we can also **attain to the resurrection from the dead.**[18] Indeed, the original Jewish Christians saw our resurrected bodies as the "promised land" of the new covenant. Jesus got their first, and we will follow later. Until then, we wander in the desert with the Holy Spirit as our pledge from God that there is an inheritance for those who obey, unlike the generation of Israelites who did not and died in the wilderness, their inheritance forsaken.

Jesus brings God's commandments and rebuke to Israel. They respond in the same way they have responded to the prophets sent before, as described in parable of the vineyard in *Matthew 21:33–43*, which also warns that God's patience with the Jewish leaders has run out. Jesus tells the Jewish leaders what they did not want to hear — His commands and teachings expose how the traditions and requirements the Pharisees are imposing go against the Law they claim to uphold.

This is what *John 3:13–21* is all about. John uses somewhat indirect language to describe how the Jewish rulers had rejected Christ because His words exposed their failures as shepherds — **This is the basis for judging: that the light has come into the world and people loved the darkness rather than the light, because their deeds were evil. For everyone who does evil deeds hates the light and does not come to the light, so that their deeds will not be exposed.** John, writing after the temple was destroyed in AD 70, speaks of the Jews who did not believe as **condemned already** in *John 3:18*. John's passage makes it sound like he is talking in generalities by saying things like **…people loved the darkness rather than the light....** But of course it wasn't *people* in general who rejected Christ, but the Jewish rulers. Jesus only went to the **lost sheep of the house of Israel** (*Matthew 15:24*).

But of course *John 3:13–21* does have general applicability as well. Jesus is *already* acting as judge! His commandments judge us, as they judged the Jewish rulers, because our willingness to follow His commands indicates whether

---

[17]*Acts 3:26; Titus 2:14*
[18]*Philippians 3:11*

we want to do God's will or not.[19] The point of this passage is not that Jesus washes away our sins by His sacrifice, saving us from God's eternal wrath. Rather, Christ's commands are like litmus paper. Our accepting/keeping them (or failing/refusing to) says something about our disposition toward God.

While parts of the apostles' message refers to the future, they are not in line with the gospel preached by the Church:

- Jesus' will resurrect all on the final day by His power, both the righteous and unrighteous.

- Jesus will Judge all, for God has vested that authority in Him. The gospel describes *that* this will occur, not *how*. In the 20 or so times the apostles shared the *gospel* with unbelievers in Acts, the word *hell* cannot be found.

Every description of Jesus' message and purpose, both in the Old Testament and the New Testament, points to a salvation consisting of *regeneration* coming from *repentance* with the goal of a people eager to do God's will.

The idea that Jesus came to save us from God's eternal wrath so that we could go to heaven was not taught by Christ. Nor was it taught by His apostles after His death. Nor was it taught by the early Church prior to the Gentiles' rise to dominance. As we will find out later, it was not even taught by the first several hundred years of the Gentile Catholic church. To believe that this teaching is the true gospel message requires us to pretend Christ willfully withheld such enlightenment from all the apostles who were spreading the message and the Spirit in the first century. In any event, finding this message in the Bible is akin to noting words within the floating chaos of alphabet soup.

There is one part of the gospel message we have not answered yet. Why can John say the **gospel message** is to **love your neighbor as yourself**? While we may agree with the requirement, it's not at all clear why it constitutes "good news."

And that's where the missing link between Jesus' gospel to the Jews and Paul's gospel to the Gentiles comes in...

---

[19]*John 7:17*

–IX–

GOD SURPRISES EVERYONE

Christians have an uneasy relationship with the Old Testament. On one hand, we have to admit that the Living God revealed in Jesus was the God of Israel, the God of the Old Testament. On the other hand, we don't relish being reminded that God had a chosen people. Nor do the aspects of God revealed by the Old Testament sit well with all. So, we pillage it for things that serve our needs, leaving the rest behind. It is scary how little the Old Testament is actively read. We rationalize this by saying the "Christian part" gives a clearer picture of God.

The whole affair resembles how most see American history. We don't think much about precolonial America. Few care about the rich history of Native American tribes, and we have successfully shrugged off as a nation any real guilt over our country being established via genocide of the American Indian.

We use bits and pieces of Native American culture as they suit our needs, much like how Christians take parts of the Old Testament. And we cannot help but think that the land is rightfully ours now.

That's how we perceive the changeover from Judaism to Christianity as well. We see Christianity as rightfully belonging to the Gentiles because the Jews refused Christ. It's a convenient perspective for us, just as it was expedient for 19th-century Americans to feel God had given them the land from coast to coast.

Thing is, that's not how it went down.

Jesus preaches almost exclusively (and rather emphatically) to Jews (*Matthew 15:23–27*). He instructs His disciples to do the same in *Matthew 10:5*. When He speaks to anyone else, it is generally to chastise the Jews (*Luke 7:9*). After Jesus' resurrection, His apostles initially only evangelize other Jews. ***For its first several years, the Christian Church is completely Jewish!*** (Of course, this provokes the question "what happened to all the Jewish Christians?" That is itself an interesting topic, but sadly not one for this book.)

And it is not as though these Christians are just ethnically Jewish. They still keep the Mosaic law. In *Acts 11:7–10*, Peter has a vision where he initially believes that God is commanding him to eat pork, and he refuses! Surely this cannot be explained by saying the disciples (so full of the Spirit they can cast it at will on others) simply totally misunderstood Christ's purpose.

Things become more understandable if you see Jesus through the eyes of His disciples. Jesus comes to redeem Israel; He preaches a gospel to Jews telling them that God has not forgotten them. The gospel He preaches, and the gospel His disciples preach, is totally compatible with their policy of engaging only Jews.

Jesus proves God is keeping the promises made to Abraham; so it makes perfect sense that only his heirs receive the Spirit, the gift given to the prophesied remnant of Judah to build the kingdom of the new Covenant.

But then everything changes.

The change is hard for us to see. We ignore that the original Christians were Jews evangelizing only other Jews. We cannot grasp their shock upon finding in *Acts 11:17–18* that the Gentiles can receive the promised Spirit.

Now, imagine the challenge to a gospel writer. The gospel would, of course, be woefully incomplete if it did not illuminate that God's nation now has open borders. Yet, Christ only proclaimed to Jews the coming kingdom (prophesied by Jews) and never indicated directly that the Gentiles were going to be allowed in! After all, if Jesus had Himself explicitly proclaimed that the Gentiles would join God's people, the apostles would not have waited a decade before taking the message to them, would not have required so much prodding by God, and would not have been so amazed by Peter's testimony. The earliest Christians certainly did not have the view of the Law modern conservatives place on Paul.

To accurately interpret the New Testament, we must understand the relevancy of this message to its original readers. We see it in the Synoptic Gospels and Paul's epistles, but the first place we will study is John's gospel, a book written to the Greeks trying to explain how Jesus opened God's kingdom to them.

Word of God

Gentiles are invited to join God's house, but how does that happen?

Jewish culture is built on the Torah, the first five books of the Bible. Israel is blessed with God's Word and cherishes it in a way we can not comprehend. If modern Christians loved God's Word as deeply as the 1st-century Jews do, every 10-year-old in church would have the entire New Testament memorized.

But what is God's Word to the Jews? The Torah is also called the Law, and the Jews focus on the 613 requirements it contains. Obeying the Torah separates the Jews from everyone who has not been blessed with it, the nations that were not God's people.

Christians marginalize these laws because we, quite frankly, don't like being told what to do and feel we deserve more from God than a list of rules. Furthermore, there is an unfounded idea that the revelation of God in the Old Testament is somehow no longer applicable.

Faithful Jews do not see God's law as a burden, and neither should we. Rather it is a blessing. Parents give rules to children for their own good, rules that might not make much sense to those who receive them. How much wiser are God's commandments, and how much more beneficial for those who keep them? We may not like being treated as children, but what does Christ say in *Luke 18:17*? This does not mean we have to *stay* children with little clarity as to why the commandments are to our own benefit... it just indicates why it might be hard for us to see those benefits before "growing up."

Christians often suggest the Jews erred by focusing on the Law. But the problem was not that the Jews were too focused on the Law. (It is hard to say what else they could have focused on!) The problem was that their leaders abused scripture to give themselves political power. They warped the Torah to their own devices by selectively picking which scripture to emphasize and which interpretation they liked — the Christian church arising afterward did the same.

We underestimate the Torah. Jesus' command to **love your neighbor as yourself** is not new. It is in the Law (*Leviticus 19:18*). There are also requirements to aid the poor (*Deuteronomy 15:7*) and be compassionate to widows and orphans (*Deuteronomy 24:20*); they just were not faithfully obeyed. The wisdom and mercy of the Lord in forbidding any Israelite to lend money at interest to a countryman, or to lend money at high interest to *anyone*, should speak to millions today. Jesus does not attack the Pharisees for being "legalistic"; He derides them for abusing the Law, as in *Matthew 23:23*.

The Law says to **love your neighbor as yourself**, but doesn't say who the "neighbor" is, so the Jews choose an interpretation that serves their needs. The Law says to **honor your father and mother**, but the Jewish leaders are ignoring that in their dealings with those who have made a vow to the temple (*Mark 7:10*).

God's Word separates those who are God's people from those who are, as described by Jesus Himself, **dogs**. The Law forms the covenant relationship God has with the Jews. Not accepting it places one, *ipso facto*, outside that relationship.

Jesus as the Word

John thus presents Jesus as a superior version of God's Word, made available to *everyone*. To have God's Word is to be a member of God's people. John calls Jesus the Word (*John 1:1*) made flesh (*1:14*) from the very beginning. In *1:4–5*, he says **In Him was life, and the life was the light of mankind.** He echoes this in *1:9*. *Psalms 119:105* uses the same language to refer to God's Word.

To make clear Jesus' role, John needed to show two things. First, that Jesus is superior to Moses. Second, Jesus and Moses must be on the same team, or else the gospel is not about uniting Jew and Gentile as a single flock.

This first goal is addressed in *John 3:13*, where John remarks **No one has ascended into heaven except the one who descended from heaven — the Son of Man.** Why did John put that there? What's the point?

The Jews believed Moses had ascended to heaven to receive the Torah directly from God. John not only disagrees but shows Jesus is greater than Moses because He *did* descend from heaven (as the Word). John also limits Moses in *John 7:22*, saying he did not create the Law but only brought it to Israel.[1]

We also see in John a clear indication that Jesus is not rebelling against Israel. Jesus does not attack Moses but claims a higher glory. *John 3:14–15; 5:45–46;* and *7:19* illustrate Christ's alignment with Moses. Moses brought God's Word to the Jews, and Jesus is bringing a clearer understanding of God's Word to everyone, and (through the Spirit) the ability to be faithful — truth and grace.

Bread of Life (Optional)

Based on Christ's Word as the new Law, rejected by the Jewish leaders and now available as a blessing to all, an interesting observation can be made.

In *John 6:32* and *6:48* Jesus calls Himself the **bread of life**. What does He mean? I think most Christians see it as a vague picture of Jesus as sufficient. We often do this with things we don't understand — we take them as vague or make them say what we want. We use fuzzy terms (like "salvation," "believe in Christ," and "gospel") to cope with a system that does not smile on conflict.

Christian groups do not like doctrinal tension because it suggests Christianity is not a mapped-out, logical belief system. If people disagree on an important topic, it means something isn't clear. But if we use vague words, then no one is disagreeing with anyone and we can all pretend we are saying the same thing.

---

[1]To see other examples of Jesus as similar to, but surpassing, Moses as revealer of God's Word, compare *John 5:39; 6:68;* and *12:50*.

Rather than being so frightened of internal friction, we should be more wary of what is lost by stifling debate and undervaluing precision. Attempting to resolve a fuzzy topic, like "salvation," can lead to a greater grasp of many things.

With that in mind, I believe I can put a fine point on what Jesus means when He says **I am the Bread of Life**.

Bread of Life = God's Word = New Covenant's Law

Don't act so surprised.

There are four separate ideas pointing to this claim.

1. John describes Jesus as **the Word made flesh**, and Jesus identifies the bread and wine of communion with His body.

2. Jesus says He is the true bread from heaven, contrasted with the manna sent to the Israelites in *Exodus 16:31–35*. This manna was itself a symbol of God's word as described in *Deuteronomy 8:3*.

3. When Satan tempts Jesus to turn a rock into bread, Christ's reply in *Matthew 4:4* confirms the manna as a symbol for God's word.

4. In *Matthew 16:6*, Jesus tells the disciples to **beware the leaven of the Pharisees**. In *16:12* we find out He is referring to **false teaching** and in *Luke 12:1* it is described as **hypocrisy**, suggesting they have contaminated the Law, leaving it inadequate to keep people in God's covenant, just as the leavening of bread makes it unfit for use in the Jewish rituals prescribed by the covenant. See *Luke 11:52*.

If bread is a symbol for God's word, many verses in John's gospel gain clearer meaning. For example, *John 6:32* conveys the same ideas as *3:13* and *7:22*, emphasizing that Moses did not create the Law but only brought it.

In *John 6:48*, Jesus contrasts Himself with the manna the ancient Israelites received: **Your fathers ate the manna in the wilderness, and they died. This is the bread which comes down from heaven, so that one may eat of it and not die.** This is a false comparison if you take *die* in the normal sense. We die just as the Israelites did.

However, after receiving the manna and the Law, what happens? A year later they are worshiping the golden calf. Half a year after that they lose faith while on the verge of entering the promised land. The word translated **perish** is the same word (in both Greek and Hebrew) used to convey that someone is **lost** in the sense of wandering away. So Jesus could be describing how the Israelites could not stay faithful.

Another interesting verse is *John 3:14*. Why would John bring up the story from *Numbers 21:5–9*? There are other examples (such as Moses' intercession after the people worshipped the golden calf in *Exodus 32:31–32*) Jesus could have alluded to if the point was to show His intercession for us. Why mention the snakes?

One reason might be that Jesus' death heals our spirits from the poison of Satan. But there is also the point that the snakes were sent when Israel detested the bread they had been given. *Numbers 21:5* says **our souls detest this worthless food.** Perhaps John, commenting to his readers, chose to reference a story where the Israelites detested the bread they had been given just as the Jews had rejected Christ, a point John states explicitly in *John 1:11*.

The depiction of eating Jesus' flesh (*John 6:53*) and the symbolism in communion attain greater meaning when we see Jesus giving us the bread we eat — the Word of God internalized = the Holy Spirit. Compare this to Jesus' statement against the Pharisees in *John 5:38* and *8:37*. I will describe another way to understand Christ's words at the Last Supper in chapter 11.

This linkage also gives extra meaning to Christ's retort when His disciples come to Him in *Matthew 14:16* asking him to send the masses away so they could get food: **They do not need to go away; you give them something to eat.** These disciples would later give the Holy Spirit, and hence God's Word, to those who believe.

Misreading Parables

John captures Jesus' teachings in abstract dialogues. In Matthew, Mark, and Luke, homages to the expansion of God's kingdom are seen in Jesus' parables.

We'll talk later how we 21st-century types pillage the Old Testament prophecies, taking those we like while leaving unrespected the treasure trove lying between Isaiah and Malachi. We perpetrate the same crime with Christ's parables. We read them as though Christ is talking directly to us Western, modern Christians and rip away what we want. This philosophy essentially assumes Jesus did not care about the 1st-century Jews He spoke to. We simply cannot read the words Jesus spoke to the Jews and interpret them within the framework of a Christian philosophy 1900 years in the making. Jesus came to save **the lost sheep of the house of Israel**, and His disciples only ministered to Judah for nearly a decade after His death. Any interpretation of His parables that does not consider His Jewish audience shows an arrogance beyond simple ethnocentrism.

I'll give four examples of misconstrued parables from the book of Luke. Others can be found in Matthew and Mark. Keep in mind the context — the Jews were God's people. Christ is heralding not only the reunification of Judah and Israel as foretold in the prophets (e.g., *Jeremiah 3:18*; *Ezekiel 37:19*; and *Hosea 1:11*), but the inclusion of all people into God's nation (e.g., *Isaiah 11:10–12*).

Modern Christians understandably have a hard time reading the gospels in this context because the idea of God's Word and special grace being available to only one nation seems foreign. However, it certainly wasn't foreign to the Jews. Their entire culture was based on being God's special people, blessed with the Law that separated them from the Gentiles.

There were two problems with this arrangement. First, God wanted the whole world to have the blessing of the Word. The second is that the Jews had not done much with the gifts they had been given. They had failed to be a light to the nations. Instead of the nations looking upon them and deciding the Living God was worth following, Judah's hypocrisy and backsliding had caused them to become a **curse among the nations**, as described in *Zechariah 13:8*.

The Lost Sheep, Coin, and Son

Luke 15 contains three parables about the lost. In the first a shepherd goes looking for one sheep even though it means leaving 99 others behind. In the second a woman turns her house upside down looking for a lost coin without paying any mind to the nine she has in safe keeping. In the third a son asks for his inheritance early and leaves home. He squanders his wealth and ends up serving foreigners in another land. Coming to his senses, he returns home, whereupon the father throws him a party. The son's older brother is upset with his father because he has worked obediently without reward for years.

Keep in mind that these parables all teach the same thing, as indicated by the concluding lines of each (see verses *7, 10*, and *32* of *Luke 15*).

Common Interpretations

Christians take all sorts of things from these parables. Most people take away things they want to hear. The teachings that are read into the stories are not necessarily incorrect; they just have little to do with the parables' intent.

For example, these parables are not about how God pursues us — the younger son was not pursued. Nor are they about how God "will always take you back" — the lost coin and the lost sheep did nothing to be found.

When you put a modern gospel spin on them, it gets worse. Things go haywire when you try to make The Prodigal Son a parable meant to teach salvation by grace. I've read commentators make a huge deal about how the son wanted to come back and work for his father, but his father wouldn't let him, as though Jesus' point is that you cannot work for what God wants to give. This interpretation should be dismissed out of hand as it expands one fragment to dominate the rest. In addition, there are four more explicit problems:

- This nuance would be meaningless to the Jews and Luke's readers, and he makes no effort to emphasize the point.
- This teaching does not show up in the other two parables.
- The between the father and the older son does not support this message. The father does not dismiss his son's toil: **everything I have is yours.**
- Such a teaching rather violently opposes other scripture (e.g., *John 6:27*).

Another issue is Jesus' total focus on repentance. That is the moral given at the end of the first two parables ... **there will be more joy in heaven over one sinner who repents than over ninety-nine righteous people who have no need to repent.** There is no mention of faith, sacrifice, or Judgment.

It should be obvious that this parable is not a direct call to prodigal sons if we look at the moral again. Jesus says the point of the parable is that God is pleased when people repent. Why would people who hate God care about that? If you are the type of person who is compelled to do something purely because it pleases God, chances are you not a lost sheep!

There's a more direct reason why we know these parables are not about bringing prodigal sons home. Interpretations that focus on how God takes back anyone often fail to explain the emphasis placed on the dialogue between the father and the older son. This is a grievous error because generally the concluding content of a parable is the most important. Any interpretation of the prodigal son parable that focuses on the younger son is doomed from the beginning.

More Accurate Interpretation

If we fully take into consideration Jesus' Jewish audience, it's much easier to identify what these parables are getting at.

Let's take a deeper look at the prodigal son. He is an ungrateful son who essentially desires his father dead. The younger son wants nothing to do with his father except to have his inheritance. The rebellious youth shows no interest in abiding by his father's rules. His dissolute living causes him to lose everything he had been given, things he had not worked for himself, and he ends up serving foreigners in another land because of it. Jesus specifies he tended **pigs**, indicating that the boy served the Gentiles after losing everything.

This is all a neon sign pointing to one conclusion: *The younger son is Israel!*

David united all 12 original tribes of Israel. When Solomon (his son) sinned, God ripped the 10 northern tribes from him. These 10 tribes became known as Israel while the land of the lower 2 tribes was known as Judah.

Israel fell away when their rulers forced idolatry upon them. God had given them all the land they had, and they began worshipping golden statues. Soon they were overtaken and enslaved by Assyria. They intermingled with Assyrians and other races. Their descendants were the Samaritans the Jews despised. They were worse than mere Gentiles. They were viewed as traitors (*as were the tax collectors in the preamble to these parables: Luke 15:1–2!*).

Thus, Israel matches up strikingly with the younger son. They had been given everything by God, refused to follow the Law, lost everything due to their ungodly behavior, and eventually were enslaved by Gentiles. Repeatedly Israel's unfaithfulness is referred to as **harlotry**,[2] and how does the older son refer to the younger? He says he has **devoured your assets with prostitutes.** Samaritans were hated by Jews who saw themselves as the righteous people in God's house and had no interest in reaching out to their fellow sons of Jacob.[3]

This parable is a slap in the face to the Pharisees who felt entitled to hate their sinful brothers. Jesus is describing how a son who truly desired the joy of his father would heartily welcome the son back. The Jews should not begrudge their foolish brother reentry into God's household, which this parable foreshadows. (Israel later came to symbolize all Gentile nations.)

Jesus is extending the point He made in the Parable of the Good Samaritan, where He said the Jews had to consider even the Samaritans as their neighbors.

The Rich Man and Lazarus

The parable of the Rich Man and Lazarus (*Luke 16:19–31*) tells the story of a rich man and Lazarus, a beggar, who both die. The rich man is taken to Hades and Lazarus is taken to **Abraham's bosom**. The rich man looks up from Hades, sees Abraham, and asks him to send Lazarus to **dip the tip of his finger in water and cool my tongue, because I am in great pain in this fire.**

---

[2]*Jeremiah 3:8–9* is but one example of this.
[3]Speaking of sons of Jacob, there is yet another parallel between the sons in the parable and the kingdoms of Israel and Judah when we consider Jacob's literal sons, but it takes a bit to explain.

Abraham tells him this is impossible because a **great chasm has been fixed between us** and mentions how earlier in his life the rich man had the **good things** while Lazarus had the **bad things**. The rich man then asks Abraham to send Lazarus to his **father's house** to warn them **so they do not come into this place of torment.** Abraham tells him it will do no good because his five brothers would not believe him.

Common Interpretations

Modern Christians immediately turn this into a discussion of faith in Christ, as it foreshadows Christ's own rising from the dead and the Jews' response. While there is certainly something to this, the "faith in Christ" indicated by this parable would not be the kind of faith or belief we normally think of.

Christians also use this parable to emphasize the torments of hell and how they can happen immediately after death. Conversely, they claim people can go immediately to paradise with God after death.[4]

The problem is that none of the above makes any sense when you understand Christ's point here. If you take this parable as a discussion of heaven and hell, you might as well also say that people go to heaven if they are poor and all rich people go to hell. As L. Ray Smith[5] has pointed out, the parable does not say one good thing about Lazarus at all. It certainly does not claim he had any faith.

Indeed, nothing in the parable refers to belief in Christ. When the rich man speaks of sending Lazarus to his brothers, he does not want them to "believe." He asks Lazarus to tell them to **repent**. The discussion of belief in *Luke 16:31* refers to convincing the brothers of the danger to those who do not do God's will.

Hades and Hell

The final reason we cannot take this parable as having anything to do with heaven and hell is that it *isn't about hell*. The word used is Hades. It is just the place of the dead. Linguistically the word means "unseen."

It is the Greek equivalent of sheol, the Hebrew word for where *all* people were assumed to go when they die. For example, the prophet Samuel is raised *up* from the pit in *1st Samuel 28:3–15*. Samuel was a righteous prophet of God,

---

[4]Even Jesus did not ascend immediately to the Father, as shown in *John 20:17*. Whether *Luke 23:43* argues differently depends on what word order and punctuation you use.

[5]I don't agree with much of what Smith says, but he must be given credit for relentlessly seeking biblical truth. I am indebted to him for much of the material in this section.

yet he was still in Hades. Peter makes the same remark about David still being there in *Acts 2:29*.

The Jews' theology regarding the afterlife had changed greatly over the years. One popular idea was (and still is) that people are purified through fire for a time after death. After the soul is smelted, it can move on.

When Jesus wants to talk about eternal torment, He doesn't use the word Hades. He uses the word Gehenna, which is properly translated as hell in most Bibles. Hades is a symbol for separation from the land of the living. Christ Himself was in Hades for a time while dead. That is why we read in *Acts 2:27–31* of His soul not being allowed to **remain** in Hades.

Hades and Death are themselves thrown into **the lake of fire** in *Revelation 20:14 after* the souls of the dead have been taken from them, symbolizing the defeat of Death (see *1st Corinthians 15:26*).

More Accurate Interpretation

This parable is not about the Judgment at all. The parable foreshadows the transfer of God's grace from the Jews to the Gentiles.

The rich man represents Judah. They have enjoyed God's blessings, the Word, the Bread of Life, but they have not done much to help other nations. He has **five brothers** (Judah had 5 brothers). Abraham calls him **child**, and we are told they **have Moses and the prophets**. Jesus goes out of His way to say he wore fine **purple** clothing, which symbolized royalty. Judah was considered the ruling tribe for all Israel (see *Genesis 49:10*).

Lazarus represents the Gentiles. He is begging with the **dogs**, a common epithet for the Gentiles (*Mark 7:27–28*). The beggar's name must be important; in what other parable is such information given? The Hebrew version of "Lazarus" is Eliezer, the name of Abraham's steward (*Genesis 15:2*) who was to inherit everything Abraham had, but ended up getting nothing after Isaac's birth.

Notice where Lazarus is: at the rich man's **gate**. Gentiles who held the central doctrine of Judaism — God is One — and kept the seven Noahide Laws were called **Geirei toshav**: Proselytes at the gate. They were not Jews and had refused circumcision, but they were considered more righteous than those Gentiles who had not abandoned idolatry. They did not have to keep the entire Law, and *the Jewish leaders were not required to give them financial aid* (unlike full proselytes who were qualified for such support). They could worship in the courts of the Gentiles, but could not cross the *gate* between that court and the temple. Speaking of which, the clothing the rich man wore was fine linen, the same type of material specified for Judah's priests.

The **good things** discussed here do not refer to eternal life or bliss. These men represent whole nations, and the **good things** Abraham speaks of refers to what Jesus' Jewish listeners thought of as good — God's favor and providence. Notably, the text of *Luke 11:13* places **the Holy Spirit** in parallel to **good gifts**.

Jesus speaks of a cosmic switch where Abraham's natural children find themselves on the wrong side of the Jordan, the river separating the promised land from the godless nations. The Greek word in the last part of *Luke 16:26* is the word for crossing water. It's no accident that just before this parable, Jesus says:

> **The law and the prophets were in force until John, since then the good news of the kingdom of God has been proclaimed, and everyone is urged to enter it** (*Luke 16:16*).

This gives us a better idea of what aspect of the gospel Luke wanted to emphasize. Paul's gospel revolved about the removal of the Mosaic law as a barrier to the Gentiles. Luke was a protegé of Paul, so we are not surprised to find Luke emphasizing that feature. Jesus is saying that up until John the Baptist, the Law was a dividing wall between Israel and those who were not part of God's people. But now the removal of this partition is declared, and all people are urged to know God and be known to God.

Of course, I cannot stop myself from pointing out that Jesus immediately (*Luke 16:17*) clarifies that God's commandments are in no way abrogated by the removal of this division — **But it is easier for heaven and earth to pass away than for one tittle of the law to become void.**

The Gospel of Paul

No treatment of the Gentile's advent into the kingdom is complete without a discussion of Paul. The next chapter is devoted to him, but here I want to stress simply how much he saw the entry of the Gentiles *as* the gospel. We 21st-century Gentiles can hardly understand the importance this message had to Paul, a conservative Jew who was **entrusted with the gospel to the uncircumcised just as Peter was to the circumcised** (*Galatians 2:7*).

Imagine you have a place of command in Judaism, a religion whose adherents hold themselves as God's chosen people and use the term "unrighteous" to refer to anyone outside the covenant. You're attacking the disciples of a heretical Rabbi causing trouble within the religion, and all of a sudden you receive a vision that turns your world upside down. The heretic whose followers you are persecuting not only turns out to be righteous, but is in fact the Messiah. That

Messiah, the rightful King of Israel, desires to call unrighteous Gentiles to Him, and *you* are going to be His method of doing so!

Paul's evangelism centers upon the unification of all creation under Christ, and in particular the inclusion of Gentiles as equal heirs to Christ's kingdom. **Christ redeemed us from the curse of the Law**, Paul says in *Galatians 3:13–14* . . . **in order that in Christ Jesus the blessing of Abraham would come to the Gentiles.** In addition to showing Gentile inclusion as Paul's focus, a careful reading of *Galatians 3:16–18* allows us to deduce two important points:

- The Spirit is proof that God is fulfilling the Promise to Abraham.[6]

- This promise is the inheritance Paul declares comes from faith in Christ rather than from keeping the old covenant.

The emphasis Paul gives to this message of unification in Christ through the Spirit is staggering. Paul's gospel is not one of grace overcoming God's wrath on an individual, eschatological basis so we can go to heaven. Paul's gospel describes how God, through grace, has **opened a door of faith** for the Gentiles, allowing them to join the Jews in obedience to the Living God. The Gentile nations had done nothing for God, and Israel had utterly failed to keep its covenant with the Almighty. However, grace upon grace, God *still* sends Jesus to unite all people through the Spirit. That is Paul's gospel:

Romans 15:18 **For I will not dare to speak of anything except what Christ had accomplished through me <u>in order to</u> bring about the obedience of the Gentiles, by word and deed. . .**

Galatians 3:8 **And the scripture, foreseeing that God would justify the Gentiles by faith, proclaimed the gospel to Abraham ahead of time. . .**

Ephesians 3:6 **. . . through the <u>gospel</u> the Gentiles are fellow heirs, fellow members of the body, and fellow partakers of the promise in Christ Jesus.**

Ephesians 2:14–16 is particularly striking. Why did Jesus nullify the law? **. . . to create in His flesh one new man out of two. . .** What was the hostility Jesus' sacrifice was neutralizing? **. . . the middle wall of partition.**

This passage also illustrates Paul's point in *Colossians 2:13–15*, which uses similar language and yet is used to support a different theology. The New International Version, for example, translates *Colossians 2:14* as **. . . having canceled the written code, with its regulations, that was against us and that stood opposed to us; he took it away, nailing it to the cross.** This is a perfectly

---

[6]Peter's discussion of the promise to Abraham (*Acts 3:25–26*) being fulfilled by the Holy Spirit's work supports this understanding as well.

fine translation. What is insane is when people suggest Paul refers to Christ's sacrifice canceling the debt we owe to God by transgressing this **written code**.

The Gentiles whom Paul addressed didn't have a written code (the Mosaic law)! How can Paul be suggesting that the Gentiles owe God due to sinning against a Law they were never given?

Paul's point in *Colossians 2:13–15*, as in the Ephesians passage, is that the **written code** with its **ordinances** (like circumcision, observations of special days, and dietary laws — *exactly the things referred to two verses later in 2:16*) was opposed to Gentiles because it separated them from God's people — a division that had become more severe as Gentiles oppressed the Jews and the Jews saw all Gentiles as sinners (for they did not have or follow God's Law).

Paul describes how God has dealt with this hostility from both sides. No longer does the Mosaic law keep Gentiles out of God's kingdom, and at the same time God has forgiven the Gentile's past sins, allowing peace between the two nations . Notably, **peace** occurs three times in *Ephesians 2:14–17* and is the purpose given for Christ's death: **He did this to create in himself one new man out of two, thus making peace, and to reconcile them both in one body to God through the cross, by which the hostility has been killed.** Recall the "hostility" here is not between God and humanity but between those who have the Law and those who do not, see *Ephesians 2:14*. All four times the underlying Greek word (*phragmos*) for partition is used in the New Testament, it refers to a division between God's people and everyone else.

Paul is certainly not suggesting Christ's death frees us from the very real danger of sin, or else *Colossians 3:5–6* would look pretty stupid. In case that wasn't clear enough, Paul reiterates the point in *3:25*. Paul's exhortation is that we follow Christ's commands rather than those of the world.

Christ's destruction of this wall between Jew and Gentile had tremendous practical importance, for Paul was the chief apostle to Gentiles. However, the removal of this wall was part of a grander unification of all things in Christ. There is an undeniable horizontal component to Paul's gospel, and he uses the word **peace** over forty times. Six times he calls the Almighty the **God of peace**, and his desire for peace within the church is a principal reason he warns Timothy and Titus of controversy caused by doctrine. Paul demands we be mindful of the spiritual welfare of fellow believers and desires us to all have peace within ourselves as well, urging us to be content with what we have and find fulfillment in Christ.[7]

---

[7] *Romans 15:33; 16:20; 1st Corinthians 14:33; 2nd Corinthians 13:11; Philippians 4:9–13; 1st Thessalonians 5:23; 1st Timothy 6:4–8; and Titus 1:11*

Summary and Final Notes

God's nation was opened to the Gentiles by God's Word being sent to them, first by Christ and later by the Holy Spirit. Jesus is a new Torah written on the hearts of believers. Just as it says in *Jeremiah 31:33*:

> **But this is the covenant I will make...I will put my law in them and on their heart I will write it. I will be their God, and they shall be My people.**

This chapter described how Gentiles were added to God's people by receiving the Word, and in chapter eleven I'll discuss the other half of the ingress — being received into God's *house*, the temple.

The opening of God's house and the transfer of God's favor from Judah to all who follow Christ represent key ideas in Christ's preaching. I've described how a few of His parables predict these events. The parables of the tenants (*Mark 12:1–11*; *Luke 20:9–19*; and *Matthew 21:33–41*) and the fig tree (*Matthew 21:19*; *Mark 11:12–21*; and *Luke 21:29–33*) are of this type.

These clear parables are not hard to interpret because they predict only the passing of the kingdom due to Judah's failure to do God's work. The problem occurs when the return of Christ in Judgment is mixed in. Recall that *everyone* thought Jesus was coming back very soon. The generation that heard Christ saw themselves as the **firstfruits of the feast to come,**[8] a type of transition phase before Christ returned to usher in the New Jerusalem.[9] Many of His parables appear to blend these two ideas, seeing the Judgment not as an ending but as a new beginning where God's people could do God's work. Jesus clearly laments that the Jews will be cut off from His light, but it is not always clear if that happens at the Judgment or earlier. Passages like *Matthew 23:37–39* suggest it occurred when the Jews rejected Him. Other passages describing the transfer of the kingdom mix the idea of the transfer or enlargement of the kingdom with Christ's return (e.g., the parables of the talents [*Matthew 25:14–30*], the minas [*Luke 19:11–27*], the harvest [*Matthew 20:1–16*], the great supper [*Luke 14:15–24*], and the wedding feast [*Matthew 22:1–14*]). This last one is particularly hard for "free gift"ers to put a modern spin on given that the concluding remark is **...for many are called but few are chosen.**

These parables were particularly important to record in the gospels due to the importance of making peace between Gentiles and Christian Jews in the

---

[8] *James 1:18*
[9] *Revelation 14:4; 21:2*

early church. In particular, they served to discourage Christian Jews from requiring Gentiles to follow the Jewish cultural laws. If we try to read these teachings without considering the context and political situation of their audience, we cannot hope to understand Jesus' message.

It is this destruction of the dividing walls between Gentile and Jew that Paul describes as God's will all along, kept secret through ages past. As apostle to the Gentiles (*Galatians 2:7*), Paul's letters focused on interactions between Gentiles and Jews in the early church. He portrays as a principal part of the gospel the unification of all under Christ.

He calls the justification of the Gentiles **the gospel** in *Galatians 3:8*, says the reason Jesus came was to remove the hostility between Jew and Gentile in *Ephesians 2:14–16*, declares the Gentiles **fellow heirs** through **the gospel** in *Ephesians 3:6*, and says the receipt of the Holy Spirit was the reason Christ **became a curse for us** in *Galatians 3:13–14*.

–X–

MAKING SENSE OF PAUL

Pick any whole number. I recommend picking a number less than 13. Now, if you picked 4, add up the first 4 odd numbers: 1+3+5+7. If your number was 7, add up the first 7 odd numbers: 1+3+5+7+9+11+13. You will find this sum is just the square of your original number. For example 1+3+5+7 = 16, which is 4 squared (4 x 4 = 16).

Now, the above description is worthwhile at some level because it works. You could add up the first 55 odd numbers (1+3+...+107+109) and find that their sum is 55 x 55 = 3025. On the other hand, it is not completely satisfying if it isn't clear to you *why* it works.

You might find my position regarding Paul's use of *saved* similar. In the last section of chapter four, I gave evidence that Paul did not have eternal Judgment in mind when he spoke of being **saved** or **justified**. There I cited passages indicating four reasons:

- Paul, like Christ, warns that sinners are in danger of hell, including those who already believe.
- Paul, like Christ, indicates that all are judged in the same way, with no partiality shown toward believers.
- Paul uses the phrase **received the Spirit** in the same way that he uses the term **saved**.
- Several verses would contradict each other if Paul viewed present salvation as intimately linked to deliverance from hell.

While you may well be happy accepting my position (it does, after all, adhere to the understanding of salvation shared by the Jewish writers of the New Testament and has Orthodoxy beaten hands down in the biblical-consistency department), you might feel a bit like a typical male in a wallpaper store. When someone asks you what color you want, you know the correct answer (i.e., what-

ever your wife told you)... but you don't know *why* it's the best match for your
~~shartroose chartruse~~ ... greenish-yellow couch.

Paul is hard to understand. It doesn't help that Romans, which everyone
quotes, has some of the Bible's most inscrutable language. Nor does it help that
Paul, in the educated style of his day, uses as few words as possible to get across
his point, expecting the reader to fill in the gaps as necessary. The real problem,
though, is that not everyone appreciates the setting of Paul's evangelism. I will
discuss four keys to understanding how his writing's context should influence
our interpretation. Since huge tomes have been written on Paul, you'll forgive
me if I stick mainly to those items pertaining most directly to salvation.

Key 1: Understanding *Works of the Law*

Paul uses the phrase **Works of the Law** *a lot*. What does he mean?

What He Does Not Mean

The clause **no one is justified by the works of the Law** (*Galatians 2:16* and
Romans 3:20,28) has for centuries been used to attack "works-righteousness."
The church has taken **no one is justified by the works of the Law** and turned
it into, "You cannot pass the Judgment through good deeds because God requires
perfection, which none of us attains."

We look at three reasons why this extrapolation makes no sense:

1. Paul is not talking about perfection.
2. Paul is not talking about the Judgment.
3. Paul is not talking about good deeds!

Perfection

Paul cannot refer to the impossibility of perfection. To the 1st-century Jewish
mind, it was, in fact, possible to be blameless. Their understanding of "blameless" and ours are very different. Paul calls himself blameless (with respect to the
Jewish law) in *Philippians 3:6* and Luke writes the same thing about Elizabeth
and Zechariah in *Luke 1:6*. There's no talk anywhere of perfection or how a
single sin makes an individual unrighteous.

Final Judgment

Paul is not speaking of the Final Judgment in these passages. Even the Pharisees did not universally claim that only Jews "made it" through God's Judgment. This was a point of great debate, and some sects believed non-Jews had a stake in the World to Come. A couple centuries after Christ, this would become the official belief of Rabbinical Judaism. The Talmud, the collection of rabbinic discussions that became central to Judaism after the temple was destroyed in A.D. 70, decrees that all monotheists who keep the seven Noahide Laws have a place in the *O'lam Ha-Ba*.

You won't find Paul speaking of the Judgment anywhere around these verses. When Paul alludes to items in the past, they all relate to God's eternal plan to bless the world by exalting Christ. When discussing the present, he refers to the spiritual transformation of those in Christ.

Paul is concerned about the spiritual enslavement of people caused by rebellion against God and about the spiritual freedom to righteousness given to those who believe in Christ. In Paul's theology, the Law causes spiritual death because someone who knows God's commands and breaks them is actively rebelling against God, which enslaves him or her to sin. Christ breaks believers free of this enslavement and protects them from re-enslavement.

When Paul writes of the Judgment, his take is very different. *Romans 2:5–16* presents a version of the Judgment so different from how people interpret *Romans 3:10–26* that some commentators have claimed the text in Romans 2 presents Paul's hypothetical picture of the Judgment had Christ never come!

What Deeds are These?

The most interesting point, though, is that Paul is not referring to doing good deeds. He is referring to the Mosaic law. In particular, he means *those aspects of the Mosaic law that are not part of the Spiritual law of the new covenant.* Paul's point, generally speaking, is that Gentile believers are bound to a law written on their hearts and have nothing to gain (but everything to lose!) by following any additional ordinance. This means that the object of Paul's attack is as far away from "good deeds" as one could imagine, for the spiritual Law (which believers *are* bound to: *Romans 7:6*; *1st Corinthians 9:21*; and *Galatians 6:2*) is all about doing good.

Just look at the examples Paul uses. When describing the **works of the Law** he is attacking, he never refers to anything that we would consider a "good deed." He refers mostly to circumcision, and in other verses to Jewish dietary restrictions, observance of special festival days, Sabbaths, and other items of the

Mosaic law whose purpose was to separate Jew and Gentiles.[1] In other words, he is attacking the very things that built the **wall of partition** (*Ephesians 2:14*) between Jews and Gentiles: the **decrees opposed to us** from *Colossians 2:14*.

Romans 3:28–29 puts to rest any thought that Paul has good works in mind when saying people should not put their confidence in **works of the Law**:

> **For we consider a person is declared righteous by faith apart from works of the Law. Or is God the God of the Jews only? Is He not also the God of the Gentiles?**

If Paul had "good deeds" in mind, this statement makes no sense — Jews and Gentiles alike can do good deeds. But if Paul refers to those items of the Mosaic law that separated the Jews as God's special people, then this passage makes complete sense. Another verse that crystalizes this is *1st Corinthians 7:19* — **Circumcision is nothing and uncircumcision is nothing. Instead, keeping God's commandments is what counts.** How is it possible to read that as attacking legalism?

Paul's point is that God's grace does not depend on race or previous covenants. To understand why this is so important, you need to know some church history.

The Jerusalem Council

Originally the Christian church is entirely Jewish. After Peter and Paul have their visions, Gentiles are evangelized, but the Jewish church leadership does not know what to do with them. (We see Judaism today as a separate religion. To the original believers, Christianity was simply *authentic Judaism* — Christ was the *Jewish* Messiah, after all. Paul calls believers members of the **true circumcision** in *Philippians 3:3*.) Friction arises between the "old Jews" and the "new Jews" (Gentile believers). Gentiles are seen as grafted-on branches, and many Jewish Christians try to force the "new Jews" to keep the Mosaic law.

Paul disagrees with those who think Gentiles must follow the cultural provisions of the Law. He spends great energy fighting them, even publicly opposing Peter in *Galatians 2:11*. The apostles hold a council to consider the situation and ultimately choose to enforce only three Jewish laws upon the Gentiles:

- They should not eat meat sacrificed to idols.
- They should not drink blood or eat anything strangled.
- They should adhere to the sexual code of the Mosaic law.

---

[1]*Romans 2:25; 3:1; 14:5; 1st Corinthians 7:19; Galatians 2:11–13; 4:10; 5:2–6,11; 6:15; 1st Corinthians 8:8;* and *Colossians 2:16–23*

Acts 15 describes the proceedings in detail: the events leading up to convocation, the purpose of the council, and the outcome. *Acts 15* is foundational to understanding the context Paul wrote within, and I urge you to read it carefully.

The apostles only discuss the Mosaic law (*Acts 15:1*), not the general idea of "doing God's will." Certainly other requirements would join these were the council dictating a complete code of conduct. The apostles see these three rules as extending to all believers, even if they are not readily apparent parts of God's *natural* law. Peter's wording in verse 15 has a double meaning, for the term **yoke** refers to the restrictions a rabbi would set as his interpretation of the Mosaic law. The Mosaic law says **honor the Sabbath,** but the rabbis told people the specific requirements. Some might say you could walk up to 2000 cubits on the Sabbath, others might say 1000 cubits, etc.

Not Under the Law?

I often hear people claim they are "not under the law, but under grace," as though Paul is saying we no longer have to worry about our eternal security. I hope the above sections make it clear that Paul is not saying we are exempt from God's commandments. Paul quite clearly refers to the *Mosaic* law the Judaizers were pressing on Gentiles, and only those parts that are not in the Spiritual law, which Paul sums up as **love your neighbor** in *Galatians 5:14*.

Any notion that disobedience no longer carries danger should be vanquished by Paul's concern for sinning believers in *1st Corinthians 6:8–11* and *Ephesians 5:4–5*. They mirror warnings conveyed in *Hebrews 2:2–3* and *10:26–27*. In each case the author writes to genuine believers. The readers in Corinth have already been **washed, sanctified** and **justified**. In Ephesians he writes to people God has forgiven through Christ (*4:32*). The writer of Hebrews engages those who have **received the knowledge of the truth** and have **hearts sprinkled clean**. Paul's caution that believers who go against their conscience do so toward their own **destruction** in *1st Corinthians 8:11* and *Romans 14:15* should give anyone pause, as should Jesus' words to His followers in *Mark 9:43–50*.

Further, there's no indication in *2nd Corinthians 5:10*; *Romans 2:6–16*; or *Colossians 3:25* that God judges believers any differently than non-believers, which brings Paul's version of the Judgment in line with how Jesus repeatedly portrayed it. Strikingly, Paul shows some concern for his own fate in these matters (*1st Corinthians 9:27* and *Acts 24:15–16*).

Separate from these, there is the danger that those who do not obey the law of the Spirit will lose it, as indicated in *Romans 6:12–16*; *Romans 8:12–13*; *2nd Peter 2:20–21*; and Jesus' exhortation to the disciples in *John 15:10*.

Key 2: Salvation — Being in Christ

Paul depicts salvation history both as a drawn-out plan to bless humanity (*Romans 9:1-11:36*) and a long-foreknown plan *to bless Christ* (*Galatians 3:16*).

1st Timothy 2:5 describes Christ as the *only* mediator of the new covenant, so all people must come to God the same way. But to Paul, Jesus was not merely reconciling sinners to God, but rather all things in the world to each other. Humans, angels, animals, heaven, and earth were all being reconciled because they were all being brought under a single Master. Christ, that Master, would later subordinate Himself and all things to God so that God can be **all in all**.[2]

Spiritual Salvation

All things have been given unto Christ due to His obedience, and through Him those who die to the world to live in Him are blessed by His calling us out of desolate unbelief — just as Moses brought the Israelites out of slavery and idolatry. The Holy Spirit is the celebrated proof and preserver of this calling.[3] To a faithful Jew like Paul, who knew the history of his people, the transformation wrought by the Spirit was the perfect gift from God. Israel's history was a study in the weakness of human flesh, the tendency for selfish desires to dominate us.

Paul's agony as a faithful Jew before coming to faith is nearly palpable in *Romans 7:13–25*. He describes how this condition, this spiritual death, arose through Adam's rebellion against God. This weakness passed down to all, even to those who had no specific law to rebel against (*Romans 5:13–14*). The Mosaic law, which might have curbed sin had our flesh been stronger, made the situation all the worse. Israel, in failing to keep the Law, multiplied the rebellion that had caused their weakness in the first place.

Paul uses a special word, ***katákrima***, to refer to humanity's abject condition after Adam's sin, dominated by self. Most Bibles translate it the same way they do the more common term ***krima*** — **condemnation**. The difference is that ***katákrima*** has in mind not only the verdict but the consequences. **Condemnation** in this sense suggests one is *already* "serving time." It is thus a good word to refer to the spiritually imprisoned state of humanity after Adam's rebellion, the same way the term is used twice in *Romans 5:16–18*.

This last example (*8:1*) is often misunderstood. Paul says **there is therefore now no condemnation for those who are in Christ Jesus** and unpacks it like a *matryoshka* doll through the next several verses, ending at *8:7–8*.

---

[2] *Romans 5:8; Galatians 3:8; Ephesians 1:10; 2:12–20; Colossians 1:15–20; 3:11; 1st Corinthians 8:6; 1st Corinthians 15:24–28*

[3] *Galatians 3:22; 4:6; and Romans 8:14–16*

Those who are not in Christ are still in bondage, unable to subject themselves to God's rule. It is the same message as in *Romans 6:6–8*, which shows why baptism is crucial to Paul, for it joins us to Christ in His death. Jesus wore the same weak flesh we do, and in His resurrection this flesh was transformed. We, by sharing in Christ's death, attain a likeness of His resurrected state as our flesh, while still weak, no longer dominates us. This model where Jesus' *resurrection* causes our genuine righteousness allows *Romans 4:25*[4] to make sense as written. Modern dogma, where Jesus' *sacrifice* is the key to everything, trips over this verse, causing commentators to say Paul is just being poetic there.

Paul's perspective makes perfect sense given his own Jewish heritage. Ancient Jewish rabbis claimed that we have two masters while alive — God and our evil inclinations. Ancient Jews thought that when we die we are no longer enslaved to evil inclinations, so we are free to serve only God. Jesus' teaching that we can not **serve two masters** in *Luke 16:13* would have extra meaning to His Jewish audience. Through Christ's death (and the work of the Holy Spirit) we are free to serve as one who has already died.[5] Indeed, this is how Paul repeatedly calls us to see ourselves; for example, see *Romans 6:13*. In other words, *the life we live in Christ is an opportunity to live the life of the next era today.*

Imperial Salvation

But Christ's reign does not begin in the next era. Christ is already King, and saying **Jesus is Lord** for a 1st-century citizen of the Roman Empire was a good deal different than saying it today. While we can grasp at the political persecution saying "Jesus is Lord (and Caesar is not)" might invite, we have a harder time understanding its full meaning.

The emperor of Rome was not only the political leader; he was also a type of god (with his own religion) and a source of providence in an era when self-empowerment and independence did not flourish. People put their confidence in Caesar to meet their needs and defend them. Paul's depiction of Jesus as King is not merely a reference to authority or the requirement that we do His will. It is also an indication of *where we put our confidence.* To rely on Jesus, when others relied on the empire or the temple, required a courage we have a hard time understanding today. Perhaps Paul would tell modern Christians not to put their confidence in their jobs, politics, mortgaged homes, or retirement accounts.

---

[4] **He was given over because of our transgressions and was raised for the sake of our justification.**

[5] Dr. R. Moseley claims a similar lesson in Paul's marriage metaphor (*Romans 7:1–7*). I am indebted to his citing of ancient Hebrew expert David Flusser on this topic.

Seeking theological rigor by asking *Confidence of what?* misses the point. This is not *confidence my sins are forgiven* or *confidence that He can save me from hell.* Such philosophies treat Christ as an expedient rather than a King. The confidence is *if I serve Him, things will be okay.* It is the confidence children have in their parents. We follow Christ because He is the risen Lord; we find our security in knowing His love for mankind and His power to bless.

This is one reason Paul reacts so violently against those who press the Law upon Gentiles. He sees this as putting confidence in the Mosaic covenant rather than in Jesus. Instead of trying to **perfect** ourselves via the Mosaic law, Paul writes in *Galatians 3:3*, we should put our confidence in Christ's transforming work. We **work out our salvation**, as Paul writes in *Philippians 2:2*, by following Christ's commands. Christ is conditioning us progressively into His image — and sometimes there are bumps in that program. In *Philippians 1:10; 2:12–15; 1st Corinthians 1:8;* and *Colossians 1:22–24* we are presented as **blameless** when our **love abounds**, when we **decide what is best, obey...doing everything without grumbling, remain firm** and have God **strengthen [our] hearts**.

We are not presented as **blameless** due to the faith that initially brings us into Christ, as though on the day of Judgment faith in Jesus is some magic soap that works retroactively. Christ is *working* creation into a blameless whole to present to God. There is no metaphysical transaction that removes our sins *on Judgment day*, for that was not the purpose of the atonement.[6] Nor was there any need for this because Paul, like other early Christians, had no interest in decreeing to God how the Judgment *must* work.

Freedom and Slavery in Christ

I've already discussed how in Christ we are *free from sin* in that we are no longer dominated by our flesh, unable to naturally walk with God. We are free in another key way as well. Prior to Christ, God's people had 613 laws. These laws and their interpretations restricted and codified Jewish life in a way Americans, awash in religious liberty, can hardly understand. Rather than the priests and rabbis dictating our behavior, Christians are free to follow God based on Christ's counsel via the Spirit. As Matthew states in *Matthew 23:8*, **Do not be called Rabbi, for One is your teacher, and you are all brothers.**

In this way we are *freed from the Law*. We now have one master, one teacher, and one judge. This is the **freedom** Paul references in *Galatians 5:13*, **Do not use your freedom as an opportunity to indulge your flesh.** He certainly does not mean "you are free from having to worry about your sin, but

---

[6] *1st Corinthians 6:9–10; Ephesians 5:5;* and *Colossians 3:5–6*

you should still not sin." He refers to the idea that each believer is responsible for her own conscience, decisions, and actions. This idea runs through much of Paul's writings: see *1st Corinthians 8:9–11*; *10:29*; *Romans 7:6*; *14:5*; and *1st Timothy 1:9*.

The slaveries of the new covenant come from the freedoms. We have been freed from slavery to self to be enslaved to Christ. We live as a new creation in Christ. We crucified our old self to gain the new creation we walk in today. This not only means that Christ is our new master, but that our service is not a choice. This service is not optional — we do not *choose* to do God's work. Rather it is the natural outworking of a new creation. As Paul describes in *1st Corinthians 9:16*, we are **compelled** to serve. Our service is not "above and beyond" our calling. We cannot boast in our service because it is nothing more than what is expected and reasonable as slaves to Christ. We have nothing to boast in for God has given us everything — even the freedom we have to serve.

But this slavery should not be taken as a suggestion that we have nothing to lose by failing to serve. Nor does it imply that God ignores our actions when evaluating us. Any reading of the longer passage from which *1st Corinthians 9:16* is taken should dismiss these notions, especially verses *23–27*.

Key 3: God's Wrath

Most Christians do not think about the end times, and those who do generally focus on them a bit too much. 2000 years of waiting has thrust the end-time wrath, God's wrath *before* the Judgment, to the back burner.

Early Christians certainly see things differently. They, as the Jews before, eagerly look forward to the coming **Day of the Lord**, when those who are persecuting them will suffer God's justice. Second Thessalonians is written mostly to assure readers that *the day* has not yet come — they have not missed out. Paul also cautions them that *the day* may not be immediate, for some have simply stopped working and are waiting around idly.

Early Christians think their generation is a type of transition period. Jesus is coming soon to finish the transformation the Spirit began. This is why we read **the time is short** in *1st Corinthians 7:29* and **the culmination of all things is near** in *1st Peter 4:7*. Christ will return with God's physical wrath on the earth. It is this global wrath 1st-century believers are looking toward, for it will vindicate them over their oppressors. The Judgment is a completely separate event occurring much later, with several events taking place in between.

Paul's passages on the end times, as well as *Revelation*, suggest a combination of God's wrath and human persecution occurs. Then Christ returns to rule with those who were persecuted in His name (as well as any believers alive at that time). Then there's *another* round of God's wrath. Then everyone is resurrected. Then, and only then, does the grand Judgment occur.

Yet Another Problem for the Modern Gospel

The apostles of the 1st century thought Jesus was going to return very soon. Had they believed Christ's purpose was to deliver Christians from hell, it would mean they thought the vast majority of all people who ever lived had no hope, for they died before Jesus came. If this were true, there would have been exclamations of joy about how those of their era and locale were so fortunate as to have been in the right place at the right time.

If, conversely, those who came before Christ (that is, most people who had ever lived) did have some way to escape, there would be at least some indication of how faith in Christ was not required of *them*. The people who had access to Christ were the rare exception, not the other way around.

But we don't find anything like that at all, which makes perfect sense as the apostles were not building up grandiose theologies about how the Judgment worked, articulating rules God had to follow. Other than claiming that Jesus was the Judge and those who followed His commands would be rewarded, they had very little to say on the matter.

Key 4: Justification

I have purposely placed this section at the end because it is the most challenging. I promise not to tell anyone if you skip forward to chapter eleven and come back here later, though chapter eleven is no vat of tapioca pudding either!

Paul, like many modern pastors, often uses the term **justified**, particularly in stating we are **justified by faith**. What does he mean? This is another of those vague terms we use to make theology go down more smoothly. Some Bibles use the translation "declare righteous" instead, and the same word is translated **freed** in *Acts 13:39* and *Romans 6:7*.

The Greek term is **dikaioō**. Linguistically it should mean "to be made as one ought to be." The first part of the word means "to be as one ought." The -oō part normally means "to make." This is what the Holy Spirit does — it *makes us as we ought to be* by strengthening our spirit and informing our conscience to do the will of God. It's useful to point out here that the related word translated **righteous** does not have the nuance of *never-ever-having-sinned-ever-in-your-life* that it is often spun to mean.

The Greeks came to use the term secularly to mean "affirming someone," or "determining someone is acceptable." This is how Jesus uses it in *Matthew 12:36*, **For by your words you will be justified, and by your words you will be condemned.** When Paul says **. . . the doers of the law will be justified** in *Romans 2:13*, this is how he is using the term. James agrees in *James 2:21–25*.

The word also refers to a type of self-defense: "to show that one is as one ought to be." This is the sense of the term in *Luke 10:29*. N.T. Wright has suggested the term refers to demonstrating that one is in the covenant.

Evangelicals see justification as meaning "to declare righteous," but not in the sense that we actually are righteous. Justification, in their view, allows a type of "alien righteousness" where our sins are placed on Jesus, and we are considered righteous based not on our own actions but on Jesus'.

Why so Difficult?

It's useful to see why coming to an understanding of Paul's meaning is so difficult. One way to see the issue is by noting all the variables.

Initial, Ongoing, or Final?

Is Paul talking about something that occurs when we first believe, something that happens while we live in belief, or something that occurs at the Judgment?

Global or Individual?

Is Paul discussing the justification of individuals or groups? For example, he refers to scripture **foreseeing** the gospel that God would **justify the Gentiles** in *Galatians 3:8*, and the condemnation in *Romans 3:10–19* (which appears to be a parallel to *Galatians 3:22*) is an indictment of Israel as a nation. On the other hand, Paul is certainly concerned about the actions of individuals being compelled to follow the Mosaic law.

What Faith?

What faith is meant here? Is it our faith *in God*, as described in *Romans 4:24* (and, *very interestingly* referred to in *James 2:19*), our faith *in Christ* as described in *Galatians 2:16*, or does Paul refer to *Christ's faithfulness*? The Greek for "faith in Christ" is the same as the Greek for "faith of Christ," so several passages could be read in two different ways.

What Justification Might Mean

I'll be honest with you. I'm not certain what Paul means. It's hard to find a particular answer that makes sense when comparing scripture with scripture. In the end, we probably have to allow Paul to use the word more freely than we might deem responsible. After all, Paul was a proto-rabbinical 1st-century Jew writing to the masses. He uses the term **law** in at least five different ways within the book of Romans alone. It's quite possible that he reasons with individual believers about one type of justification using arguments that appeal to a different meaning when applied to the past. We must remember that Paul's *goal* takes priority over everything else. In his epistles, Paul's purpose lay in dealing with infighting within the church due to friction between Jews and Gentiles.

To be viable, it seems any theory on what Paul has in mind should make sense of three key things:

- His claim that justification is by faith
- His claim that justification is not by works of the Mosaic law
- His repeated use of *Genesis 15:6* as an example

One option that satisfies the above is the simplest one: Paul's point is that God determines our worth based on our faith. This is very different from our faith being used as a type of permission slip for God to transfer our sins to Jesus and Jesus' righteousness to us. Rather, the idea is that faith in God (rather than specific deeds) is the meter stick used to determine the merit of a person. This is what the Greek word meant in its common secular use.

While this simple idea has value, it is unlikely to make sense of all the ways Paul uses the term. I claim the linguistic definition of "to make as one ought to be" is an option worth considering. This is precisely what the Spirit does — it transforms us, turning spiritual death to spiritual life. Paul tips his hand in *Galatians 2:21* and *3:21* that he might mean this, speaking of how the law did not **give life**, and that righteousness could not come through the Law:

Galatians 3:2 **Did you receive the Spirit by doing the works of the Law or by believing what you heard?**

Galatians 3:16 **No one is justified by the works of the Law but by faith in Jesus Christ.**

This is a pretty powerful indication that justification is the work of the Spirit, which works to make us righteous (not merely "declares" us righteous).

This understanding of Justification satisfies the three bullet points I made above. The dependence on faith is obvious, for we receive the Spirit through faith. Furthermore, it was only through *Christ's faithfulness* that the Spirit could come. Paul's reference to **works of the Law** not achieving this refers on a small scale to circumcision's cutting the flesh without transforming the heart. It also makes sense on a large scale because God's sending the Spirit was not contingent on Israel keeping the Law (as Paul points out in *Galatians 3:17*) and the Law was unable to transform Israel into a righteous nation.

To see the relevance of the third bullet point (Paul's repeated use of *Genesis 15:6*), you have to wrap yourself in the cultural fabric of the 1st century, where stories had a more central position in society than they do today. Thus, Paul can refer to a single verse from Abram's story to bring the entire narrative to the mind of the reader. In this sense, the use of "justify" in the Abram example referred to God's calling Abram from idolatry in *Genesis 12:1*, hence bringing him to righteousness completely by grace. It is still *faith* that is causing the justification, for as *Hebrews 11:8* points out, **By faith Abraham obeyed when he was called to go out to a place he would later receive as an inheritance, and he went out without understanding where he was going.**

Speaking of grace, Paul says justification is by the **gift** (e.g., *Romans 3:24; 5:15–16;* and *6:23*). But what *gift* would Paul have in mind? To the apostles of the 1st century, **the gift** *was* the Spirit.[7] Seeing justification as transformation *by the gift* matches Paul's focus on freedom from slavery. The rest of *Romans 3–8* is about spiritual death and life; why shouldn't justification be as well?

Paul's gospel revolved about the destruction of the wall between Gentile and Jew. The Jewish Christians in *Acts 11:18* said **So then, God has granted the repentance that leads to life even to the Gentiles.** That is a statement about transformation! *Calling* someone to repentance *makes* them righteous; it does not *declare* them to be debt-free. To live in repentance, to turn from ungodliness and live a life faithful to God, is to live righteously (*Ezekiel 18:27*).

The Jews in *Acts 11:18* are responding to the outpouring of the Spirit (*10:45*), proof that the Gentiles are being shown "The Way," just as they have.[8] The Gentiles, kept out of God's special favor for millennia, are welcome in the new covenant. They are allowed **the life**, the **Promise**, the **gift** reserved for those children of Abraham God would call to righteousness (*Acts 2:39; 3:25–26*).

How does Paul refer to this *transformational* opening of **a door of faith for the Gentiles**, his gospel that the **Gentiles are fellow heirs, fellow members of the body, and fellow partakers of the promise in Christ Jesus**?[9] He says God is *justifying* them! Removing some rhetoric from *Galatians 3:7–14* we see this:

---

[7] *Acts 2:38; 8:30; 11:17; 10:45; Hebrews 6:4; 1st Timothy 4:14;* and *2nd Timothy 1:6*
[8] **The Way** was the name of the earliest Christians, see *Acts 9:2*
[9] *Acts 14:27* and *Ephesians 3:6*

> So then, understand that those who believe are the sons of
> Abraham. And the scripture, foreseeing that God would <u>justify</u>
> the Gentiles by faith, proclaimed the gospel to Abraham ahead
> of time. . . so then those who are by faith are blessed along with
> Abraham the believer.. . . Christ redeemed us from the curse of
> the law by becoming a curse for us in order that in Christ Jesus
> the blessing of Abraham would come to the Gentiles, so that
> <u>we could receive the promise of the Spirit by faith.</u>

I've compacted this passage to show what Paul sees as justification and the
purpose of Christ's death — that all who believe can receive the Spirit, which
God promised would come to all sons of Abraham. The parts I've removed contrast the physical descendants of Abraham, who relied on the Mosaic covenant
law to secure their identification with Abraham (and hence their share in the
blessing upon his progeny), with the spiritual descendants of Abraham who secure this blessing by having the same **faith** Abraham did.

What Justification is Not

Having proffered two possible definitions for justification, I'd like to demonstrate problems with the standard model. Evangelicals claim believers attain
an "alien righteousness" when God transfers their sins to Christ and transfers
Christ's merit to them. The context is that perfection is required (even if it is
contrived) to please God.

No Justification Through Works of the Law

The first problem with this idea, where we focus on God's appraisal rather
than our transformation, is that the Bible states quite clearly that people can be
righteous in God's sight by keeping whatever law they are given. Paul's own
student, Luke, claims that Elizabeth and Zechariah **were both righteous in the
sight of God, following all the commandments and ordinances of the Lord
blamelessly.** Paul describes himself as achieving the same type of righteousness
in *Philippians 3:6*. Paul never claims this righteousness does not exist, but
rather says it's a mere shadow of what he finds in Christ.

Before conversion, Paul was not concerned about his eternal security with
God. He had, after all, kept the law available to him at the time. Rather, he
yearned to be done with the anguish we see in *Romans 7:15–25*, and he found
that balm in Christ. We could learn a thing or two from Paul.

Similarly, as described in chapter five, the Old Testament is replete with
people who were righteous based on following the commands they were given,

without any mention of sacrifice. David's adultery and murder could not be covered with sacrifice, Noah lived before the sacrificial system was in place, and Rahab appears never to have converted to Judaism. The righteousness described over and over again in the Old Testament is not one accomplished by transfer of sin, which leads to the next problem.

No Transfer of Sin or Righteousness

Paul repeatedly refers to *Genesis 15:6* to illustrate that Abram was justified by faith and not works. But Paul's point is that Abram had not been circumcised or kept any other part of the Mosaic law, yet he was justified. The fundamental problem this passage poses for the modern definition of "justify" is that there is no transfer going on here. There's no transfer of sin discussed in the Genesis text, no transfer of sin discussed in Paul's description of the story in *Romans*, and no transfer mentioned in *Galatians*. Nor is the righteousness Abram is credited with transferred *from* anywhere. God seems perfectly content with judging Abram as righteous without having to withdraw that righteousness from somewhere else. It would be more reasonable to understand God *advancing* righteousness to Abram, who is *reckoned* a worthy investment. Faith here is like a credit rating describing whether someone will make good use of God's grace, likely to do God's work in the future (c.f. *Luke 14:28–34*).[10]

Not only is there no discussion of transfer in the original text or Paul's two commentaries on it, but there is obviously no place for sin to be transferred to. There is no sacrifice around to receive Abram's sin, and certainly no place to take righteousness from to deposit upon Abram. There is not even a mention of God forgiving Abram's past idolatry. **God is not considering Abram righteous by ignoring, forgiving, or removing his past sins — not in the Genesis story, not in Romans, not in Galatians.**

The Problem of Unjustification

There is one more problem with the understanding of justification found in many branches of conservative Christianity: the possibility of losing it.

Several times Paul shows concern for those who have *already* been justified. Examples include *1st Corinthians 15:2*; *2nd Corinthians 6:1*; *Galatians 4:11*; and in particular *Galatians 5:1–4*. Outside of Paul's writing, there are several more clear examples of concern for someone gaining freedom in Christ and then losing it, like *2nd Peter 2:20–21*.

---

[10]I'm not claiming this as a general rule, but it complements the analogy in *Romans 4:4–5*. In any event, that illustrative analogy should not dominate our understanding of the term.

Many Christians believe that Christ's blood wipes away all the sins they will ever have (past, present, future) when they come to belief (or, in the case of Calvinists, even before). It's hard to see how someone can lose the benefit of justification if that justification involves transferring all the sins they will ever do to Christ. Peter says someone who believes and then falls away is in a worse state than before they believed. That is hard to understand unless God somehow reneges on the transfer and puts the sins back on the ex-believer. Similarly, if grace is found in having sins removed freely, then how does one **fall from grace** as Paul claims in *Galatians 5:4*? If freedom occurs as part of a process where all sins are placed on Christ, then how can Paul speak of becoming **subject again to the yoke of slavery**? How is it possible to **destroy** a brother, as Paul describes in *Romans 14:15*, if all of his sins have already been removed? Note that this is a brother **for whom Christ died**. And why on earth is Paul worried about being **disqualified** in *1st Corinthians 9:27* if our forgiveness is assured once we believe?

These kinds of problems arise when we inflict Western philosophy on Jewish thought. We want to have Jesus as an antidote for individual believers' individual sins so that we can each have our individual immortality at the Judgment.

The discussions of Christ's blood in the Bible describe reconciliation and propitiation on a global scale, which makes perfect sense for Paul's gospel was largely one of the Gentiles being allowed into God's nation. Let's close this chapter by looking at such a passage.

A Key Passage

Romans 3:20–28 is crucial to evangelicals, having all the ingredients of the modern gospel. There is a talk of Jesus' blood, forgiveness, and a **free gift**; a word related to "atonement"[11]; and marginalization of the Law.

The first problem is that **the gift** (*Romans 3:24*) refers to the Holy Spirit, the agent of our justification. More issues present themselves when we look at the context. What is Paul's goal? What comes immediately before and after?

The lead-up to this passage focuses on Jews and Gentiles being equal before God. Paul explains that the Law did not show the Jews were more righteous but rather confirmed they had fallen short of their duty. But that's okay because God's plan (to make everyone as they should be through the free gift, the Holy Spirit) had nothing to do with the Law. God did not send the Spirit as a response to the Jews' keeping the Law. God sent the Spirit in spite of the sins the Jews

---

[11]Paul never uses the Greek word for "atonement," "expiation," or "propitiation" in any of his letters. A related word in *Romans 3:25* is the closest he ever comes.

had done (and the sins the Gentile nations did to them). God sent the Spirit as grace due to the **promise** made to Abraham, as described in *Galatians 3:18*.

This is why Paul specifies in *Romans 3:25* that God had passed over[12] the sins **previously committed**. These are the **violations committed under the first covenant** described in *Hebrews 9:15*. Even though the Jews and Gentiles had all screwed up, God sent Jesus anyway. God demonstrated righteousness (*Romans 3:21*) by keeping the Promise to Abraham. Thus, everyone (Jews under the Law and Gentiles not under the Law) has equal access to God through faith.

Look at another place in scripture where Paul refers to God's public demonstration of Christ crucified. Compare the verbiage of *Romans 3:25* with *Galatians 3:1*. Read *Galatians 2:11–3:22*, and compare it to the points Paul raises in the passage around *Romans 3:25*. Yet the discussion in Galatians is clearly about God accepting the Gentiles, who are given the Spirit when they believe, just as the Jews are.

---

[12]Indeed, Paul might be depicting Jesus as a Passover sacrifice. Jesus was crucified on the Passover. Paul oddly uses the Greek for "pass over" here. The word translated "propitiation" in this verse does not mean propitiation but refers to the places the blood of sacrificed animals were placed. It principally referred to the Mercy Seat in the original temple, but that object did not exist in Paul's day. It also refers to the lentils (*Amos 9:1*) on which the Passover blood was put or other places blood was placed (as in *Ezekiel 43:14,17,20* and *45:19*). In this sense, God was showing he had passed over the sins in the first covenant to free people spiritually, just as earlier the sins of Israel's idolatry were passed over to free the Israelites. I will show in chapter eleven why this notion of Jesus as Passover sacrifice for all creation makes a good deal of sense.

Summary and Final Notes

The message dominating almost all of Paul's work is the idea that Jew and Gentile are on equal footing with regard to being part of God's nation, the nation Jesus was returning soon to claim. The Mosaic law did not help the Jews receive the Spirit, and hence should not be forced upon Gentiles. Nor had the Mosaic law transformed Israel into a righteous nation, so why should any expect keeping the Law would help in the continuing transformation of those who follow Christ?

For Paul, salvation is all about transformation *from* the spiritual death in which creation languished before Christ *to* the life wrought through the Spirit. This salvation begins upon receipt of the Spirit, progresses as believers are transformed into Christ's likeness, and is complete upon receipt of the new body given at the resurrection.

Paul saw a believer's post-baptismal state as a marriage of a strengthened spirit and a fleshly body, a limited version of the salvation we will have later. Our transformation is a model of Christ's. He received the Spirit, so we shall as well. He rose again, and so shall we. He achieved a physical resurrection with a physical body, and so shall we.

Paul presents Christ as the true emperor, contrasting with the Roman world who taught that Caesar was the source of confidence. Not only should we follow Christ's commands, but we should also have confidence in Him, rather than putting our confidence elsewhere (such as in the temple, the Empire, or the Mosaic covenant).

Justify might be best defined as *to make righteous* in the sense of transforming or drawing someone to godliness. This occurred with Abram when God called him from idolatry. Christ's work justifies us in at least two ways. First, He works *genuine* righteousness through the general call to repentance His death brought. Second, transformation is one role of the Spirit He sent once God had given Him authority over creation. Justification is not the process by which God creates artificial righteousness by "removing sins from the book."

Paul and those to whom he wrote expected the second coming at any point, and so the word "saved" sometimes refers to deliverance from God's physical wrath upon the world. This occurs at a different time than the Judgment (and obviously only applies to those living in the end times, unlike the Judgment), so it should not be confused with it.

–XI–

ATONEMENT THROUGH MERIT

Evangelicals give the impression that the modern gospel is clearly stated in scripture and has been a staple of Christianity since its inception.

Nothing could be further from the truth.

We are told being a Christian means believing Jesus died for our sins so we could go to heaven. Were that the case, there were practically no Christians for the first several centuries of Christianity!

Both the *purpose* and the *content* of salvation taught in the early church differ in almost every way from what is taught today. That fact alone should give us pause since it not only indicates the apostles taught a gospel that does not match what we hear now, but obviously the modern message could not be *clearly* found in scripture if it lay undiscovered for 1000 years.

I have placed a short discussion of the early church's views on atonement in the appendix. I find this a particularly interesting topic as it grants us a window into how less indoctrinated minds conceived of the gospel. I recommend J.N.D. Kelly's *Early Christian Doctrines* to all who desire to take honest ownership of their beliefs. Here, I'll just note that even our current versions of the Nicene and Apostles' Creeds make no mention that our final destination is based on faith, nor do we find in them the emphasis on the Judgment found in today's church. Even hundreds of years after Christ, the idea that Christ's coming was about saving us from hell had not caught on.

One has to wonder why the Church ever came to consider Christ a sacrifice given to affect the final Judgment. Christ is the *mediator* of the new covenant. That is how the book of Hebrews repeatedly refers to Him (*7:22; 8:6; 9:15; 12:24*). He describes His own blood as the blood of the covenant in every description of the Final Supper found in the New Testament. (*Matthew 26:28; Mark 14:24; Luke 22:20;* and *1st Corinthians 11:25*). This covenant, described in *Jeremiah 31:31–34*, is a description of the new kingdom Christ is claiming today. The

Judgment has nothing to do with *mediation* between God and man because Jesus (not the Father) is quite clearly the Judge, not the defense attorney.

In this chapter, I try to give a more biblically motivated paradigm for Christ's work and atonement. While attempting to give a very general, biblically consistent picture, I also want to answer in some specificity the following questions:

- Why was a savior needed?
- How is Christ's work a sacrifice?
- How is Christ's work related to God's wrath?
- What roles do His earthly life, death, resurrection, and post-resurrection glory play in God's plan?
- How can we make sense of passages like John's calling Jesus the **propitiation for the whole world** and Paul's labeling Him the **savior for all men, especially those who believe**?

Jesus' Merit Before God

As I am trying to show that Christ's merit before God is the true lynchpin of atonement — and relevant in ways not commonly realized — it is useful to get a better understanding of that merit before moving forward to discuss details.

Jesus' Death as Proof of His Righteousness

Often, people see Christ's sinlessness as His chief merit — not too surprising given the picture of the Judgment often suggested, where only our sin really matters. Furthermore, this sinlessness is mostly seen as merely a qualification for His being a sufficient sacrifice, as though the whole point of His life up until Golgotha was to be a blemishless lamb.

I claim a more biblically acceptable view is to see Christ's death as the final display and test of Christ's righteousness, and the natural ending of a program of merit. It's useful to consider how Christ's death shows Christ's merit directly. I see four major parallel facets, each worthy of consideration: Obedience, Love, Perseverance, and Faith.

Obedience

The gospels give **The Law** a strange double-meaning. They present it:

1. as the collection of requirements for God's people
2. as a coded set of unrecognized prophecies Jesus fulfilled.

Christ's willingness to go to Jerusalem at the appointed time was but one of many done to fulfill **everything written about Me in the Law of Moses, and the Prophets, and the Psalms.**[1]

Nowhere are these two aspects so clearly interwoven as in *Matthew 5:18* where Jesus says **I tell you the truth, until heaven and earth pass away, not the smallest letter or stroke of a letter will pass from the law until everything takes place**, and then He launches into a discussion of "The Law" as a set of commandments. *Luke 16:16–17* is another interesting passage where Jesus claims **The Law and the Prophets** are no longer preached, but yet no part of the Law **can fail.** Christ's baptism by John in *Matthew 3:14–15* is another example. At first, John refuses to baptize Jesus. However, Jesus declares it is required **to fulfill all righteousness.**

There are several examples of Christ fulfilling various parts of scripture that have nothing to do with commands from God. John provides the final example of this in *John 19:28*, **After this Jesus, realizing that by this time everything was completed, said (in order to fulfill the scripture), "I am thirsty."** Those at the cross then hoisted up a sponge soaked with sour wine, fulfilling the 15th verse of *Psalm 22*, which Christ had already made reference to on the cross.

Love

While Christ's death was a command, it was also a choice. *John 10:15* clearly describes that Christ suffers for the sake of those who desire God. *John 15:13* echoes this sentiment, which Paul states explicitly in *Ephesians 5:2*. It is the same kind of love Moses shows repeatedly in protecting the wandering Israelites — a love similar to that portrayed in the parable of the fig tree (*Luke 13:6–9*).

There is nothing new to seeing Christ's work as a demonstration of love, but what is not considered strongly enough is that this love itself contributes to Jesus own righteousness. After all, Christ's loving work is so godly that it is the basis of a new command (*John 13:34*) while being the epitome of the second greatest commandment, given in *Matthew 22:39*. Indeed, a reading of the passage enveloping *John 10:17* suggests that God loves Christ *because of* His sacrificial love for us. It would not be too much of a reach to suggest this is one of the deepest points to the parable of the prodigal son. The elder son is shown to not be truly after his father's heart — if he were, he would have rejoiced with his dad. Jesus, the genuinely righteous son, rejoices at the welcoming back of the sinner, the son who had previously been dead to his father.

---

[1]*Luke 24:44*

Perseverance

Christ's willingness to suffer, even when He could call down angels to save Himself, is a separate contributor to Christ's merit. The value of suffering for God is referenced repeatedly in the gospels prior to Christ's death, and this pattern continues afterward. In many passages Christ's crucifixion is seen more as the death of the first Christian martyr rather than a separate, singular event.

For example, Jesus speaks of His coming death as **the cup** His Father has given Him at the Last Supper (*Matthew 20:22*), while praying in the Garden (*Matthew 26:39*), and while chastising Peter upon His arrest (*John 18:11*). What is often ignored when considering these verses is that Christ also says that the disciples will drink the same cup (*Matthew 20:23*). This makes perfect sense if we think of the cup as the sufferings in store for those who follow God, but it makes very little sense if we think of the cup as the wrath of God Jesus was to singularly endure in our place (as is commonly claimed).

Note that this idea of pre-determined persecution and suffering is common in the New Testament. I'm not suggesting anything that is not found in several other places. See *Mark 9:13; 10:30; John 21:19; Acts 5:41; 9:16;* and *21:11*.

Faith

Christ's death as a martyr is discussed significantly less than the first two, but the final facet receives even less attention. Christ's willingness to die not only says something about His *faithfulness* but also is a testament to the *contents* of His *faith*. Rather than merely showing a slavish willingness to do what God requires or live with the repercussions of His desire for God, Christ's surrender exposes how strongly He holds certain claims about God.

In particular, Jesus showed faith in God's righteousness, in the Almighty's resolve not to allow a righteous person to be put to shame. In accepting death, Christ was saying "It is God's judgment that matters, and God will judge Me as righteous." He was practicing what He preached in *Matthew 10:28*, **Do not be afraid of those who kill the body but cannot kill the soul. Instead, fear the one who is able to destroy both soul and body in hell.** The Greek term (***eulabeia***) in *Hebrews 5:7* describing Christ's prayers to God to save Him from death emphasizes this idea of choosing what is right due to fear of God.

Hence we read that Christ **entrusted Himself to the one who judges rightly** in *1st Peter 2:23*. He knew that God would not allow a sinless person to remain in the grave. In a broader sense, He was showing faith that God cared about righteousness and had the power to **reward those who seek Him**, as the writer of *Hebrews 11:6* claims is a key aspect of Christian faith.

Jesus' Death Related to His Life

Examining the four threads described above, we see that the merit in Christ's death is not genuinely disconnected from His righteousness portrayed in His life.

Obedience — Throughout Jesus' life He was obedient not only to God's general commands but also to the special plan set out for the Messiah.

Love — Jesus' love and compassion toward humanity is evident throughout the gospels.

Persecution — His final persecution was the product of years spent criticizing the Jewish leaders — criticism He knew would lead to His death, just as it had led to John's.

Faith — I discussed at length in chapter 7 that at the heart of Jesus' teachings is the type of faith shown in His willfully accepting death — faith that God has both the power and will to vindicate the righteous.

Two Key Blessings
What do Jesus and Darth Vader have in common?

Well, the short answer is "not much." But there is an eery similarity in how we form our perceptions of each.

If you are like most people born in the '60s or '70s, you saw the first three *Star Wars* movies (which are really the final three) early in life and then waited 10 to 20 years to see the rest. When you saw the original movies, you thought the story was about Luke Skywalker saving the universe from the evil Empire. However, when you watched the prequels later you realized that that is not what *Star Wars* is about at all. The six-movie saga is really a story of the rise, fall, and redemption of Anakin Skywalker, Luke's father.

Similarly, most Christians focus on Christ's work as it benefits them as individuals. We do not remember that Christianity is an outgrowth of a very community-based religion. We don't focus on our membership with God's people in a covenant relationship. We focus on forgiveness of sins because we place so much importance on the Judgment. We should stop seeing salvation as a saga built around our gain and instead see ourselves as part of a larger story whose plot revolves around the problems God has lamented since ancient times.

We should thank and praise God for all the goodness shown to us: providence, patience, mercy, and the opportunity to walk toward (and in) the Light. But any perspective that places our immortality as an end is thoroughly unacceptable. We should rather build our theory around God's Word. A plan is evident from Genesis to Revelation founded on the promise to Abraham:

1. Abraham's seed would inherit the Promised Land.

2. The world will be blessed through Abraham's seed.

The first of these promises originally referred to the land of Canaan, but later is seen as the entire world (*Romans 4:13*). The latter is described many times in the later prophets, where often **Israel** is seen as "the seed," but Paul claims the seed is Christ Himself in *Galatians 3:16*.

Rather than seeing Christ's death as paramount, a more biblical picture of His work and God's plan comes from studying how His suffering fits into the two promises above. It is better to see Christ's work as a whole, not only His death, as *sacrificial* than to see Him as a *sacrifice*, and there is very little to suggest or support that His death was a sacrifice *to God*.[2]

Moses and Christ

Jesus and others make clear how the Old Testament scriptures were a type of grand prophecy, a huge picture that both described the relationship between God and the Sons of Jacob and also, hidden within it, gave clues about the coming Christ so that the Jews of Jesus day could recognize Him. This is why Jesus is so exasperated in *Luke 24:25–27* that His own disciples had not figured out from the Jewish scriptures that the Christ had to die and rise again.

We can get a better feel for what these blessings mean by comparing Christ's work with Moses', who both liberated Abraham's descendants and, through that liberation, caused God's name to spread far beyond the sons of Jacob. *Exodus 9:16* presages this, and the theme is revisited in *Numbers 14:21–22*. A one-page summary comparing the two is on the next page.

---

[2]The only passage in the Bible where Jesus is referred to as a sacrifice *to God* is *Ephesians 5:2*, but the New Testament writers used this kind of language to refer to general good deeds or persecution. See *Romans 12:1*; *Hebrews 13:16*; and *1st Peter 2:5*. In particular, Paul uses similar terminology when referring to his own work for the sake of others in *Philippians 4:18*.

- Both fulfillments have two stages.
  - The Israelites wander in the desert for 40 years.
  - Christians languish in temptation-vulnerable flesh, waiting for the post-Judgment Kingdom. In particular, they wait for the **redemption of their bodies**. (*Romans 8:23*)
- Both Moses and Christ free people from slavery in the first stage.
  - The Israelites were physically forced into hard labor and spiritually had fallen into idolatry, worshiping the same gods the Egyptians did.
  - Christ frees people from the domination of sin.
- In both instances two confirmations are given to prove God has not forgotten the promise.
  - In the desert, the Israelites were given the manna as a sign and the Mosaic Covenant as a promise.
  - Christ's life, death, and resurrection is a sign, and the Spirit is the seal of Christ's covenant, a foretaste of the post-resurrection life.
- In both cases, the final blessing is seen as an **inheritance** given to Abraham's heirs according to the promise.
  - The Promised land is clearly an inheritance for the sons of Abraham. (*Exodus 15:17*; *Numbers 26:53–65*; and many more)
  - The coming kingdom is an inheritance for those who are sons of Abraham through faith. (*Acts 26:18*; *Romans 4:13–16*; and *Galatians 3–4*)
- In both instances the merit of the leaders safeguard the covenant community itself, but individuals can still be excluded for disobedience.
  - The exchange in *Exodus 32:7–35* regarding the golden calf and the aftermath of Israel's unfaithfulness on the edge of the promised land (*Numbers 14:10–38*) are two examples showing this combination
  - *Hebrews 7:22–25* describes Christ as the **surety of a better covenant** because He is continually able to make intercessions before God. However, this does not protect individual believers who do not do His will. (*Matthew 7:21*; *John 15:10*; *Acts 3:23*; *Galatians 5:21*; *1st Corinthians 6:9–10*; *Ephesians 5:5*; *Hebrews 4:11*; *5:9*; *Revelation 2:2–5*)

Seeing these parallels makes it easier to understand how the New Testament writers saw Christ's work. Moses led the Israelites out of slavery to found a Kingdom set apart for God. Christ is doing the same for Abraham's spiritual heirs, but the Promised Land is the kingdom Christ is coming back to claim. That kingdom has been promised to Christ as Abraham's seed,[3] and all of Christ's adopted brothers and sisters have a stake in it.[4] While the Israelites were in the desert, they were *heirs* but had not received their inheritance. In the same way, believers have not received the new, transformed, resurrected bodies attained when adoption as a fellow child of God is complete.[5]

Thus, we see that God's justice and wrath have no primary place in the description of salvation that is in Christ. Similarly, whatever importance Christ's death has in the gospel story, His exaltation and merit have far greater primacy.

Exaltation Based on Merit

Because we humans are largely interested in our own salvation, there is precious little discussion among Christians about why or how God exalted Christ after His work on earth was done. Some might be uncomfortable dwelling on the topic because it tends to brush up awkwardly against certain understandings of the Trinity. Others might not think there is anything interesting here because one could just as easily ask "Why *wouldn't* God exalt Christ?"

However, the reasons behind Christ's exaltation are intricately woven into our salvation, and something is lost by taking the simple perspective of "God exalted Christ because it was part of the Plan." For example, God could easily have equipped a random Israelite in Egypt with the power to work miracles and (with the aid of a few plagues) provoke Pharaoh to free the Sons of Jacob. But could such a leader have saved the Israelites time and time again when God was ready to wipe them out?

Similarly, God could have allowed Saul to remain king over Israel. Saul was not, in comparison with later kings, a particularly bad one. In fact, at the very end of his reign we see a very repentant, contrite ruler who still had faith in God.[6] But would Saul have pleased God so greatly that Judah would be shown mercy by God for centuries to come due to his memory?[7]

---

[3]*Galatians 3:16*
[4]*Romans 8:17* and *Galatians 4:5*
[5]*Luke 20:36* and *Romans 8:23*
[6]*1st Samuel 15:24–31*
[7]*2nd Chronicles 21:7; Isaiah 37:35;* and *Jeremiah 33:25–26*

Indeed, *1st Chronicles 14:2* has interesting wording: **David realized that the Lord had established him as king over Israel and that he had elevated his kingdom <u>for the sake of his people Israel</u>**. That sounds an awful lot like God blessing Israel through David's exaltation, just as the world is blessed through Christ.

Paul describes most clearly the reason for Christ's exaltation in *Philippians 2:8–9*, where the entire gamut of His obedience, from initial humbling all the way to His death, is credited. *Hebrews 12:2* refers to Christ enduring the cross **for the joy set before Him**. The same author also points out that it was because **of the suffering of death** He is now **crowned with glory and honor** in *Hebrews 2:9*. But *Hebrews 5:7* describes how ultimately God saved Him from death **because of His reverence.**

I claim that the various blessings we see as the fruit of atonement are actually the necessary consequences of Christ's exaltation. There are two principal ways in which such blessings can be a natural result of God blessing Christ:

- Certain things are *required* for Christ to be exalted, so God naturally brings them about as part of the exaltation process.
- Certain things are made *made possible because* of Christ's exaltation (or the merit that underlies it).

The works associated with atonement are some of the "Certain things" described above. We will go through three major examples, showing how each blessing is related to Jesus' work and God's exaltation of Christ.

Work 1: Repentance

Repentance is the most central and emphasized work of Christ. It was the core of both His and John the Baptist's message, and Christ cited it as His purpose in *Luke 5:32*. Describing Christ's fulfillment of the promise to Abraham, Peter says in *Acts 3:26*, **God raised up His servant and sent Him first to you, to bless you by turning each one of you from your iniquities.**

The question is, how does Christ do this? *John 3:20–21* gives an excellent picture:

> **For everyone who does evil deeds hates the light and does not come to the light, so that their deeds will not be exposed. But the one who practices the truth comes to the light, so that it may be plainly evident that his deeds have been done in God.**

Jesus is the light, and provides those who honestly desire to do God's work a sign to walk toward. Many Christians claim that none of us really want to do God's will, but John claims there are those who do desire this, and there are those who do not. Those who desire God will recognize Christ's words as the voice of God (*John 7:17*) and follow Jesus' commands. Those who do not desire God will not repent, **even if someone rises from the dead** (*Luke 16:30–31*).

Jesus does not provide mere guidance. His coming is also a wake-up call of sorts to those who desire God but have hitherto not known the Almighty. Christ's miraculous deeds and resurrection are a beacon to those looking for a guide and, at the same time, a resounding warning to everyone that there is no longer any excuse for ignorance. The time to repent is now. Paul says as much in *Acts 17:30–31*. Peter's message in *Acts 10:41–42* is similar.

Christ also brings about repentance by providing a perfect example for others to follow — teaching by example. This was particularly important for believers who would undergo persecution for their faith during the next several centuries. God's vindication of Christ after His execution strengthened the resolve of later martyrs. This is a separate way in which His life, death, and resurrection are important for atonement. Rather than seeing Christ's death as a completely fenced off act, the apostles appealed to others to follow in Christ's footsteps. Peter holds Christ up as an example in *1st Peter 2:21* and again in *3:17–18*. Paul does the same in *Romans 8:17* and *Ephesians 5:1–2*.

Christ's death as an example is shown in the gospels as well when Christ washes His disciples feet and then links this to His coming death,[8] and in John's version His example is the basis of a new command.[9]

Israel's history shows all the above was unlikely to be enough. God had sent prophets to Israel for centuries, but they had failed to call God's people to repentance. Elijah worked powerful miracles, raised the dead, and even was vindicated by God over death. Yet he and the other prophets were ignored by a nation who did not think righteousness was required. They had a relationship with God and believed they could safely ignore God's commands.

Jesus' ace-in-the-hole was the Spirit. The *power* of the Holy Spirit was routinely used to prove Jesus was Lord to unbelievers, while its *presence* was a continuing source of faith once someone believed.[10] We will be considering this blessing, the sending of the Spirit, separately.

---

[8]*Matthew 20:25–28; Mark 10:42–45;* and *John 13:15*
[9]*John 15:12–13*
[10]*John 15:26; Acts 3:6–16; 4:10; Romans 8:16; 1st John 3:24*

Work 2 – The Holy Spirit

The second major blessing of Christ's work is the availability of the Holy Spirit. From a metaphysical view, two things had to be done. The Spirit had to be sent *and* it had to be receivable.

Sending the Spirit

Christ said the Spirit could not be sent until after He had died.[11] The sending of the Spirit is seen as an answer to Jesus' prayer in *John 14:16*.

Why can Jesus cause this greatest of blessings by merely praying for it? John provides the answer to this as well in *John 16:15*, **Everything that the Father has is mine; that is why I said the Spirit will receive from me what is mine and will tell it to you.** The underlying idea is that God gave Jesus the Spirit, and so we can receive it by His **will** and in **in His name.**[12]

But the above should just make us ask, *Why has everything been given to Christ*, which brings us back to Christ's general exaltation due to His merit. Hence we see that the sending of the Spirit is a blessing based on Christ's merit rather than His death as a separate event. (Of course, as described already, Christ's willingness to die was a significant contributor to His merit.) Paul puts it nicely in *Romans 5:19*, Christ's **obedience** makes us righteous.

Receiving the Spirit

Receiving the Spirit is a separate issue altogether — one where Christ's sacrificial death rises to prominence. Our souls were not prepared to receive it.

As described by Jesus in all three synoptic gospels, **No one pours new wine into old wineskins; otherwise, the wine will burst the skins, and both the wine and the skins will be destroyed. Instead, new wine is poured into new wineskins.** He puts it differently in John, **I have many more things to say to you, but you cannot bear them now.**[13]

But why could his disciples not bear it then?

The short answer is given in *Hebrews 9–10*, but I think it is more interesting to see John's version. The third time Jesus says **where I am going you cannot follow** (*John 13:33*), it begins a discourse illuminating the purpose of His death.

After Judas leaves, Jesus speaks to His disciples. **Where I am going, you cannot come.** In *13:36* He adds **but you will follow later.**

---

[11]*John 16:7.* John affirms this in *John 7:39.*

[12]The clearest description of this is shown in *Acts 2:33*, but see *John 1:33; 5:21,26; 6:53; 14:26; 20:31; Galatians 4:6; Hebrews 9:15–17; 1st John 3:15;* and *5:11* for more.

[13]*Matthew 9:17; Mark 2:22; Luke 5:37–38;* and *John 16:12*

We get more information in *John 14:2–3*: **In My Father's house are many dwelling places...If I go and prepare a place for you, I will come again and take you to Myself, that where I am you may be, too.**

Many think Jesus refers to the second coming. But where *is* Jesus taking people? **I will...take you to Myself, that where I am, you may be, too.**

Huh?

The Greek behind this phrase is particularly interesting. The word for **take** here *already* means "to join with." In fact, the emphasis in that word is not the idea that you are *going* anywhere, but rather that you are *together.* It is an indication that someone is willing to be associated with another person. It is the term used when saying someone "takes" a wife. So, if the verb here *already* has the idea of association or joining, and then Jesus says He is taking them **to Myself**, we should understand that *Jesus is the destination.* As odd as it sounds, this is the same thing Jesus says in *John 12:32* when discussing His death: **And I, if I am lifted up from the Earth, will draw all men to Myself.**

You might be thinking, *Hey, shouldn't the Father's house be the destination? Isn't that where Jesus was going to prepare a place?*

For the Jews, the **House of God** could refer to two things. The primary meaning for **House of God** is the temple. There are about 100 instances of this usage in the Bible. The other possibility, which Peter, Paul, and the writer of Hebrews use, is to see **house** as referring to the members of a grand household. Just like House of Israel and House of Judah refer to all the people of those nations, the House of God would be believers in the new covenant — the new nation of God Christ rules. These meanings combine when we see the temple of the new covenant as being the body of believers.

Cleansing the Temple

Christ is the **cornerstone** of the new **House of God**, and believers are **living stones** being built upon Him. This temple had to be consecrated and purified, for sin pervaded creation, a preparation described in *John 14:2*. After this purification, the Spirit dwells within the temple, and hence within each believer.[14]

---

[14]The background for this summary: *Matthew 21:42; Mark 12:10; Luke 20:17; John 2:19–21* (Note all four of these come right after the cleansing of the temple and a discussion of the kingdom being taken away from the Jews and given to the Gentiles in the narrative, but the writers *chose* to place the story there: *Mark 11:27*, for example, shows these events did not happen immediately after one another, but all four writers chose to put these next to each other.) *Acts 4:10–12; Ephesians 2:20–21; 1st Peter 2:6–7; Hebrews 9:7–25; 13:11–20; 1st Corinthians 3:16–17;* and *6:19*

This might sound far-fetched, but look at the passage after *John 14:2*—Jesus refers time and time again to God dwelling inside believers. He first indicates that His own power comes because the Father is in Him (*14:10*); then He describes that believers will similarly do miraculous deeds (*14:12*), but this is only possible because Jesus is going to die. Why can they do these deeds? Because the Spirit will live inside them (*14:16*), and those who have the Spirit will know **I am in the Father and you are in Me, and I am in you.**

One disciple asks if only they will be given this revelation, and Jesus' answer (*14:23*) repeats the theme of God taking up **residence** in those who do God's will. This is what Jesus means when He says He will **come back to take you to Myself.** In *John 14:18–19* He speaks of returning **in a little while** and in a way invisible to the world — hardly a description of His Second Coming!

Leviticus' 16th chapter describes how and why the temple was consecrated. Israel's sin contaminated the temple. This was separate from the danger individual sinners faced. Once a year, the temple was washed of this contamination on the Day of Atonement. The high priest sprinkled the blood of a sacrificed bull or goat to cleanse the impurity caused by Israel's sin.

In the same way, Jesus' sacrifice purifies our souls [or **hearts** as described in *Acts 15:9* and *Hebrews 10:22*] from impurity so that the Spirit can reside there. The Day of Atonement sacrifice was to make the temple a fit house for God's Spirit, and Jesus' sacrifice did the same, but for a different temple.

So, the disciples **could not follow** Jesus yet because (as John comments in *John 7:39*) **the Spirit was not yet given because Jesus was not yet glorified.** But they could **follow later** because Jesus was going to come back and reside in them. The Pharisees could not follow because Jesus' word had no place in them (*John 8:37*). Contrast that with the disciples in *John 15:3*, who are clean already. Why are they clean already? **Because of the word I spoke.** The Word Christ spoke, which we noted in chapter 9 referred to commands from God, was essentially the initial requirements of the new covenant. The Pharisees rejected that covenant by rejecting Christ's commands. The disciples did not.

Cleansing the People

Christ's death cleansed the temple, but also cleansed the world so anyone (Jew or Gentile) could enter it.

Today we read in the Bible of being **cleansed** and tend to think of our sins being removed. But that's not what the term meant to the Jewish writers. Being clean was a requirement *to enter the temple.* This involved ritual cleansing to remove uncleanliness, which was not the same as sin. For example, a menstruating woman was unclean, as was anyone who touched a corpse. Cleanliness or uncleanliness did not have to do with punishment or sin, but rather dealt with separation. The unclean could not enter the temple (on pain of death).

Thus, being clean was the Jewish notion of *being holy*, which means "set apart." The temple and those who worshipped in it were to be set apart, divided from the rest of the world. We Christians have taken the term *holy* and transmogrified it to suit our needs. It isn't about sinlessness, but rather about consecration to the Lord.

And what does God say to Peter in *Acts 11:9* to signal that the Gentiles have been allowed into God's nation? **What God has made clean, you must not consider ritually unclean!** The New American Standard Bible quite accurately translates the **ritually unclean** term as **unholy**.

Thus, Christ's death cleansed the Gentiles to enter the temple of the new covenant, a living temple built with the souls of believers wherein the Spirit dwells. This makes baptism the perfect ritual for receiving the Spirit. The Jews had to undergo ritual cleansing to enter the temple of the old covenant, and we undergo ritual cleansing to enter the temple of the new. This is, of course, just another way of looking at how the forgiveness of sins described in the New Testament refers often to opening up of God's kingdom to all those who desire to serve the Almighty. We read **forgiveness of sins** and think the point is that the sins are going *unpunished*. While there is certainly an aspect of that in that the entire world was not destroyed due to the sins done in the centuries before Christ, it more commonly means that the stage is set for rapprochement. God had declared the sins of the past are no longer an obstacle to those who desire a relationship with the Almighty. That is, after all, what *Romans 3:25* says — God **proclaims** through Christ the **passing over of the sins previously committed**.

Indeed, it is possible to read *Romans 3:25* as making the same point as *Hebrews 10:19–20*, that Jesus' suffering allows us access to the most holy place in the temple of God. Indeed, this would be a rather shocking way of seeing what God has done through Christ. The Gentiles, who earlier could not even enter the main courts of the temple, are now allowed in the holiest of holies! (Some translations have the term **propitiation** in *Romans 3:25*, but that is not the word in the Greek. The Greek is the term used repeatedly in the Greek version of the Old Testament to refer to the Mercy Seat, which was in the holiest place of the temple, where earlier only the High Priest could go, as referenced in *Hebrews 9:7*.)

Work 3: Propitiation/Forgiveness of Sins

The final crucial work of Christ is the forgiveness of sins. It is important to realize that there are two kinds of forgiveness discussed. The forgiveness of sins *on an individual basis* is due to the repentance described as Christ's primary work (*Luke 24:47*). However, there is a larger-scale kind of forgiveness that has nothing to do with an individual's personal sins. It is this forgiveness that we will investigate since the above verse describes the basis for an individual's forgiveness. Repentance has always been a sufficient means for forgiveness: see *Jeremiah 36:3*; *Ezekiel 18:27*; *33:14–16*; *Mark 1:4*; and *Acts 3:19*.

Old Testament history is critical for understanding the purpose of this forgiveness. Israel (the northern tribes) had fallen into idolatry a thousand years ago. Having abandoned the Law, they intermingled with other peoples and lost their cultural identity. Judah (the southern tribes) maintained the covenant regulations, but their wickedness, in particular their mistreatment of the poor, kindled God's judgment nevertheless. In *Jeremiah 3:11*, God remarks **Faithless Israel has proved herself more righteous than treacherous Judah.**

God gave these nations over to the Gentiles as a form of chastisement. Those kingdoms then mistreated Israel and Judah, causing God's anger to flare up against them as well. Thus, there is wrath against all creation because both the Jews and Gentiles had sinned against God for several generations.

This sin acted as a barrier to peace with God. God would not take Judah back because Judah would not repent. God sent prophets, and they were ignored. Furthermore, centuries of Gentile oppression of Jews created hostility between the two, increasing the separation already present due to the Mosaic law.

So, we see the past sins are impediments to Christ's exaltation:

- Christ could not have a people until people repented.

- Christ was to rule over a united kingdom, just as David did. There could not be hostility between factions (Jew and Gentile) within.

- Wrath and destruction had been prophesied as fitting punishments on the earth for the generational, global sin of Jew and Gentile. Obviously, the destruction of creation works against Christ's interest as Lord over it.

The first of these has already been addressed in the repentance section. The second is found throughout the New Testament. Christ commands people to forgive others. Luke in particular attacks nationalism, highlighting Christ's teaching the Jews that they must accept all repenting people — even the Samaritans. Not only is forgiving others required, but Christ stresses in *Matthew 18:35* that our own eternal security depends on it. I've already spent considerable ink describing Paul's interest in peace. The early parts of Colossians and Ephesians describe how Christ reconciled all things, even angels, into a single kingdom.[15]

The final bullet is the subject of *1st John 2:2*, which calls Jesus a **propitiation for our sins, and not for ours only, but also for the whole world.** The question everyone cares about is *how* is Christ a propitiation? But perhaps the first thing we should discuss is *what does propitiation mean?*

The more conservative elements of the evangelical church talk a lot about propitiation. The idea is that it is not enough to merely deal with our *sin*. There is also a need to address *God's wrath* that exists in reaction to that sin. The cleansing and removal of sin is referred to as *expiation* and the addressing of God's wrath is referred to as *propitiation*.

Common Misunderstanding of Propitiation

There is no problem with understanding *propitiation* as the addressing of God's wrath. The problem is that those who do this tend to slip in *by sacrifice*, and it is assumed that Christ dealt with God's wrath by receiving it Himself or that His death was an appeasing sacrifice to God.

This claim, that *propitiation* is always through blood is propped up with *Leviticus 17:11*, which describes how God has **given it to you on the altar to make atonement for your lives.** This utilizes a basic principle that the blood of an animal is identified with its life.[16] What's so disconcerting about this leap of logic is that there are plenty of examples where propitiation occurs without blood. It is mind-boggling how often this verse is cited as proof that only blood can satisfy God in the face of so much scripture to the contrary.

In *Exodus 30:15*, propitiation is made through silver. In *Numbers 16:46*, God's wrath is averted by the burning of incense. Jewelry is used in *Numbers 31:50*. Grain is instituted as a means of propitiation for those who cannot afford to bring animals in *Leviticus 5:13*. And if one were to add on the examples where both animals and grain were required, dozens of examples could be given.

Furthermore, there is no need for any kind of gift to accomplish propitiation. *Exodus 32:30* shows Moses turning away God's wrath by simple intercession. *Numbers 8:21* describes Aaron as making atonement for the Levites without any sacrifice. Hezekiah's prayer in *2nd Chronicles 30:18* is another.

Note that *every* example I give above uses the same Hebrew word (**kaphar**) used in the blood sacrifices. This tight match prevails in the Greek version of the Old Testament written by Jewish scholars — the Greek word for propitiation in

---

[15]*Colossians 1:16–20; 2:13–17*; and *Ephesians 2:14*. It should be remembered that Paul has both the actual historic hostility and the division caused by the Mosaic Covenant in mind.

[16]*Hebrews 9:22* is also used to defend this view, but the context there is the consecration of the temple, which is the focus of most of *Hebrews 9–10*.

1st John 2:2 is the same word chosen for what Moses does for Israel with no sacrifice whatsoever. *Isaiah 27:9* describes how Israel will be pardoned purely by doing godly acts — the destruction of the altars to false gods.

Similar observations hold when we expand our study to include verses that do not use the exact Hebrew term for *propitiation*. *Genesis 20:17; Numbers 11:2; 14:19–20; 21:7; Deuteronomy 9:18–20; 2nd Samuel 24:25; 2nd Chronicles 12:5–12; 30:18;* and *Ezra 10:2–14* are a few examples where God's wrath due to sin has been averted due to righteous action or the intercession of a righteous person with no sacrifice whatsoever. As we will see in the next subsection, even the propitiation described in the context of rituals involving animal sacrifices appear to be based on intercession by the righteous priest.

Forgiveness by Intercession Even in the Temple Rituals

The heading above may sound strange. It is one thing to suggest, as I did in the last section, that forgiveness *requires* no sacrifice. Rather, the **prayer of a righteous man** is enough (*James 5:16*). It is quite another to claim the sacrifices themselves appear to have little to do with avoiding the punishment for sins.

I'm not saying the sacrifices had no atoning power. I would claim, however, that the *sacrifices* in the Levitical regulations addressed a different problem altogether — the *purification* and *cleansing* of the altar and temple. The sins of the Israelites defiled God's house, and the blood of the sin offerings were used to *purify* the temple. We will discuss this separately because it is inextricably linked to the sending of the Spirit, which is the third blessing.

I'm also not claiming that sin was being ignored. After all, in many regulations we read of someone who sins, brings the sacrifice, and then we are told **the priest makes atonement on his behalf, and it will be forgiven him.**[17] However, the sacrifice itself has little to do with this forgiveness. Note, some Bibles will try to make it appear that the **atonement** here is the actual ritual outlined, including the sacrifice. For example, their translation for a verse like *Leviticus 4:35* may read **In this way the priest will make atonement for him**. But, the Hebrew there is simply the word for **and: And the priest shall make atonement for him.** I'm grateful that the English Standard Version, one of the most conservative translations available, renders these verses accurately.

There are two standard views on how these sacrifices caused forgiveness. I want to describe each briefly and indicate some significant biblical problems. Then I'd like to show a third model where, even within the context of these sacrificial rituals, the forgiveness itself is due to the intercession by the priest.

---

[17] Many in *Leviticus 4–5*. Also see *Leviticus 6:2–7; 19:20–22;* and *Numbers 15:22–28*.

Standard Model 1: Appeasing God through Gifts

One model of propitiation is that someone "pays back" God or appeases God through the gifts brought to the temple.

Overall, this is not such an untenable view. The sacrifices were seen originally as a type of "food and drink" for God, and there are many discussions of a "soothing aroma." Furthermore, this model at least explains all the instances where someone could gain forgiveness without sacrificing a living creature (unlike Model 2, below). However, it does have some problems.

The main problem is that the guilt and sin offerings (the ones in *Leviticus 4–5* where rituals are prescribed for various sins) are not really gifts from the sinner to God. The *whole burnt offerings* were the ones dedicated to God. The sin and guilt offerings are eaten by the priests. Only a very small amount of them is burned up, and that is best seen as the *priests* giving God a portion of what has been given to them, as they did for *all* sacrifices. The Israelites are not allowed to eat the fat of any beast under any condition (*Leviticus 7:23–24*). Thus, the *sinner* is giving nothing to God at all! He is giving the animal to the priest, who gives a small part to God as a tithe. This is similar to the fraction of the grain offerings that are given to God (see *Leviticus 2:2; 5:12; 6:15;* and *24:7*)

You can check this by reading the regulations for the burnt offerings (*Leviticus 6:8–13*), the sin offerings (*Leviticus 6:24–30*), and the guilt offerings (*Leviticus 7:1–7*). If the sin and guilt offerings were supposed to be payments to God, the regulations ended up backwards.

Another problem with this model is that passages like *Leviticus 19:20–22* suggest the guilt offerings were actually the punishment itself. Rather than a bribe or payoff of God, the sacrifice is more like a fine designed to deter sin.

In addition to these, there are other points that this model has a hard time explaining. I will elaborate on these when discussing my model.

Standard Model 2: Vicarious Punishment

Conservative evangelicals stress this model. The idea is that the animal brought into the temple has the guilt/sin of the sinner placed upon it, and its death is God's wrath being executed. By this view, there is no forgiveness, really. Rather, someone else is getting the punishment. Strictly speaking, this is not even *propitiation*, which refers to wrath being cooled due to a change of disposition. Merriam-Webster's defines *propitiate* as "to gain or regain the favor or goodwill of." This was the meaning of the Greek word used in *1st John 2:2* as well. The Vicarious Punishment model does not provide actual propitiation. It simply claims the wrath was vented on someone else. Some claim the wrath had to be spent as a precondition to our regaining God's goodwill. As I described earlier, that is simply not the biblical picture of how God's favor works. When God relented of the wrath in store for Nineveh (*Jonah 3:10*), the Almighty didn't have to go blow up one of Jupiter's moons to exhaust the pent-up anger.

The above aside, there are all sorts of biblical problems with this view.

First, if the animal received the guilt/sin of the person, its very presence would defile the temple and the Altar.

Second, the treatment of the animal's remains shows the animal retains its purity throughout the ritual. Its meat is so holy that it actually sanctifies those who eat it (*Leviticus 6:29*). Furthermore, it must be eaten in a clean place. In those rare instances when the sacrifice could not be eaten, it had to be burned and its ashes disposed of in a clean place. This hardly sounds like the fate of a creature that has become forensically guilty before God!

Third, there is no indication whatsoever that the sins were laid on the animal. The exception to this, of course, was the scapegoat which was not sacrificed in the temple. Scripture makes clear the iniquity is put on the scapegoat (*Leviticus 16:21–22*), yet such verbiage is unseen anywhere else for the sacrifices killed in the temple. Instead, the Bible says that the priests, not the animal, bears the iniquity (*Leviticus 10:17*).

Fourth, if this was the way that guilt was defused, it would not explain how grain, silver, incense, etc. could procure propitiation.

Finally, this viewpoint suggests that death was the natural punishment for all sin, because in each case the sacrificed animal died. But that is not what the Bible says. There are instances, like intra-family sexual sins, where the punishment was less than death (but no sacrifice was allowed: *Leviticus 20:20*).

These middle-level sins cause a major problem with the Vicarious Punishment model, which claims the animal receives the punishment due for the offence. By that logic one must conclude that accidentally touching a dead animal (*Leviticus 5:2*) has the natural punishment of death while having sex with your uncle's wife is less offensive, having only the penalty of a closed womb.

If, instead, we see these sacrifices as penalties, the punishments match the crimes — giving up a sheep is less a punishment than being barren; touching a carcass is less an offense that having sex with your aunt. *Leviticus 20:20–22* specifies that having sex with a slave promised to another is not worthy of the same punishment as having sex with a free woman engaged to someone else.

But the idea that some sins have different natural penalties than others has no place in a framework where the sacrificed animal is seen as bearing the guilt and taking the punishment of the sinner. That framework requires all sins to have the same penalty, for the fate of the animal was always the same.

My Model: Priests Share Burden of Guilt — Propitiation by Intercession

I propose a model where the priests are representatives of Israel before God. When an individual sins, the priest shares in bearing that iniquity (*Leviticus 10:17*). This goes both ways, for the entire community bears the sin when the High Priest sins (*Leviticus 4:3*). This *sharing* in the lot is exactly what Moses was willing to do when he interceded for Israel in *Exodus 32:32*, **But now, if you would forgive their sin — but if not wipe me out from your book...**

Not only do the priests bear the iniquity, but they also lift up prayers (just as everywhere else we find wrath averted in the Bible) for pardon. The idea of the priests praying for people of the covenant is seen in *1st Samuel 12:23*; *Hebrews 7:25*; and *1st Timothy 2:5*. This last verse is likely a backhand to the Jewish cult. Paul is essentially saying "there are no longer an entire caste of mediators between God and humanity. There is only one." A particularly interesting example from the old testament where **prayer** is credited as the reason for deliverance *even in the midst of a sacrifice* is 2nd Samuel 24:25.

The sin and guilt offerings are then seen as given to the priests to help them fulfill their role. These sacrifices not only mean the priests have a supply of food (for they cannot be out doing other work if they are busy mediating for the people) but the sacrifices are so holy that they sanctify the priests who eat them, ritually addressing the iniquity they were continually bearing for the people.[18]

It was exactly this sanctification through *eating* the offerings (a privilege of the priests) that Samuel speaks of in *1st Samuel 3:14*. God *says* **I swore an oath to the house of Eli, "the sin of the house of Eli can never be forgiven by sacrifice or by grain offering.** But when one reads the rest of the story about this curse (*1st Samuel 2:27–36* and *1st Kings 2:27*) it becomes evident that what is meant is that Eli's descendants will be demoted from their priestly rank and privilege to eat the grain, sin, and guilt offerings that sanctified the eater. These sacrifices *only* priests could eat, as opposed to the peace, votive, etc. offerings that *did not* sanctify the eater, but that anyone in his household could eat.

It is particularly fitting that Eli's house be demoted and cursed so that they cannot eat of the grain or sin offerings anymore, for it was precisely because Eli's sons were being disrespectful in their eating of these sacrifices that the curse was laid in the first place. (*1st Samuel 2:15–17,29*)

---

[18]*6:18,27* shows the grain and sin offerings consecrate the priests who eat them. *Leviticus 7:7* suggests the guilt offering does the same.

Ritual Summary and Bigger Picture

Here is, then, how the sin offering "works" according to the observations of this section:

1. **The sinner brings the sacrifice to the temple.** This represents a confession of guilt (e.g. *Leviticus 5:5* — keep in mind that most of these offerings were for unintentional sins or sins done unwittingly.) It also represents a loss to the person, for he will receive nothing from the offering (the priests will end up being the one who eats his ram/goat/lamb/flour). This loss is a deterrent and memorial that sin is a serious issue with serious consequences. It is also an easement of sorts — the priests are bearing the guilt of the community, the guilt the sinner has contributed to. The priests are praying for the community. Thus his sacrifice both subsidizes their work and is meant to undo some of the damage, for the priests that eat of the sacrifice will be sanctified.

2. **The animal is killed and the blood is applied to the altar.** This cleanses the altar (and by extension the temple) from the taint of the sin. This makes the temple a more fit house for God's Spirit.

3. **A small amount of the animal is burned up (the fat, kidneys, etc.)** This is God's share of the animal the priest has received. The sinner has given the animal to the priests as a payment for bearing their sin. The blood and fat are God's portion. This goes back all the way to Abel (*Genesis 4:4*) and is a common facet to Jewish life. It was the breaking of this regulation that caused the curse on Eli (*1st Samuel 2:16* and later). Note that the original sinner is out of the picture. The fat is given to God because the priest gives some part of everything to God, regardless of what kind of sacrifice it is (c.f. *Leviticus 2:2; 5:12*; and *6:15*).

4. **The priest makes atonement for him, and he is forgiven.** The priest intercedes on his behalf, praying for the wrath to be turned away. Moses said **perhaps I can make atonement for your sin** in *Exodus 32:30* before going to pray for his people, when the Levitical accounts say **The priest will make atonement for him**, it refers to the same. Note that in the case where the High Priest himself sins, no such intercession is possible and there is no atonement. (Compare Leviticus 4:3-12 with the other 12 descriptions of offering in response to a particular sin.)

5. **The priests eat the sacrifice.** It is not only a form of sustenance, but an act of sanctification to absolve the sin whose guilt they bear.

Application to Eucharist

If the we see the sin offering in this way, the Eucharist gains a new meaning. In the old sacrifices the altar "drank the blood" of the sacrifice and the priests ate the flesh of the sacrifice. Each of these had a cleansing effect. The blood cleansed the temple from the taint of Israel's sin. The flesh sanctified the priests who were bearing that sin. In the new covenant, *we are the temple* and *we are the priests*, and the source of our sanctification is Christ.

In our covenant, sanctification refers to the work of the Holy Spirit inside us. John often uses the term **life** to refer to the Spirit. Hence (putting everything together) we arrive at *John 6:53*, **. . . unless you eat the flesh of the Son of Man and drink His blood, you have no life in yourselves.**

Summary of Forgiveness

This has been a long section. In summary, forgiveness of sins has always been available via the intercessions of righteous people, and that is how it is done with Christ, who **intercedes for us** now (*Romans 8:34* and *Hebrews 7:25*).

This forgiveness is not done with an eye toward the Final Judgment. There is little indication that forgiveness by the Father has any relevance at the Judgment, which makes sense as God has given all judgment over to the Son (*John 5:22*). In particular, the Bible clearly states this forgiveness does not automatically roll forward based only on faith. The writer, addressing those who have already been **made holy**, makes this abundantly clear in *Hebrews 10:26–31*. In *Revelation 2:3–5*, Christ directs John to write the church at Ephesus warning them of the consequences of their continued sins. This warning comes practically in the same stroke as a commendation for their steadfast faith in Him!

The purpose of the forgiveness is to allow for God's desired global, unified kingdom.[19] Christ has propitiated God's wrath against **the whole world** from destruction due to the **sins previously committed.**[20] In particular, the availability of this forgiveness on a global scale announced that the Gentiles, who were **without the Messiah, alienated from the citizenship of Israel, and strangers to the covenant of promise, having no hope and without God in the world**, were equally allowed to approach Christ.[21] The barriers of the past had been removed. It was now time for all people to repent for the forgiveness of their sins. That is the message given to the disciples to spread in *Luke 24:47*.

---

[19]*Colossians 1:20*
[20]*1st John 2:2* and *Romans 3:25*
[21]*Ephesians 2:12*

Summary and Final Notes

In Christ, God replays the Exodus story.

Before the Exodus, God shows power by the plagues visited on Egypt. In Jesus' time God shows power by the resurrection of Christ. In the Exodus story, after the Israelites wandered for 50 days, God inaugurates a covenant with them, gives them requirements, and directs them to build a tabernacle so the Almighty can dwell within their midst. In the apostles' time, *after the same 50 days,*[22] God gives the Holy Spirit, the sign of the new covenant, which itself instructs us in God's requirements. Jesus' blood acts to purify and strengthen our spirits so that the Holy Spirit can dwell in us, the temples of the new covenant, just as the Spirit dwelt in the tabernacle (the portable version of the temple) the Jews carried around in the desert.

Believers are wanderers in that desert, heirs to the kingdom that will come when Jesus returns. We have been freed from sin but have not attained our full inheritance — our transformed, resurrected bodies. For now we have "the Promise," which is the Holy Spirit — a down payment of sorts on our transformed bodies.

The life, death, and resurrection of Jesus, as well as the Spirit He sent, serve as a beacon for all those who earnestly desire God. Christ's commands allow anyone who desires God to do God's will. Those who have shown such an interest will claim their inheritance, unlike the generations of Israelites who failed to receive their inheritance due to disobedience (*Hebrews 4:11* and *Acts 3:23*)

Jesus' merit saved the world from destruction, and the same merit allows Him to pray as a High Priest for stumbling believers. His sacrificial death cleansed the temple of the new covenant and also cleansed the whole world so that any may enter that temple and receive this Holy Spirit, the seal of the new covenant.

The paradigm I suggest makes sense of passages that refer to the reconciling of **the whole world**, including **all things in earth and in heaven**. It also explains verses like *1st Timothy 4:10*[23] more adequately than the modern gospel.

Perhaps most satisfying — it finds critical meaning in all phases of Christ's story: His earthly ministry, His death, His resurrection, and His life after resurrection. This is a significant (and well known) deficiency with the version of salvation taught by most Christians. The "Jesus died so I could be forgiven" version of the gospel finds little import in anything other than Christ's death.

---

[22] Pentecost occurs on the exact day of the year as Moses' ascent of Mount Sinai.

[23] **...for He is the Savior of all men, especially those who believe**

Epilogue: What Now?

If you have diligently read this book and found yourself unimpacted, then I have failed. Even if you disagree with my paradigm, I would hope the wrestling you have done with scripture as you considered the arguments has, at the very least, left you a more mature Christian. To the extent that reading this has caused you to be more active and aware in your biblical study, the whole effort should be considered a success.

However, I assume most of those who have made it this far have found their viewpoints changed — if for no other reason than that we tend not to finish an entire book we don't find at least partially compelling, college texts excepted.

I fear that many readers will find themselves not only spiritually upended but feeling *uprooted* as well. If you are a member of a conservative church, and I have prevailed in swaying your beliefs, you likely feel conflicted about staying where you are. I have suffered this feeling, as have other readers with strong conservative backgrounds. You may find yourself in the unenviable condition of having upended your spiritual life, coming out of the chaos with a clearer understanding of the truth, and yet feel afraid to share with others this wonder. Conservative churches tend to restrict people from suggesting things outside orthodoxy. That's why we call them *conservative.*

Those who attend more liberal churches are likely in a more tolerable, but still frustrating, situation. You may not have had your views changed so much as crystallized by reading this book. For you, the gain may lie in seeing real, literal, biblical support for ideas that previously you had not seen defended biblically. You may want to share with others at your church but doubt the interest level your fellow parishioners have in finding support from a literal reading of the Bible. After all, I have in no way dealt with all the reservations most liberals have regarding the repercussions of a literal, serious take on the Bible. After years of downplaying a literal viewpoint, it might seem like a mere academic novelty that the Bible supports views liberal church bodies favor.

169

Nexus: www.John173.net

I have placed a nexus at www.John173.net to help connect people who generally agree with (or are intrigued by) the perspective I've fleshed out here. Hopefully, as time goes by, this will allow people to find others nearby for fellowship. I'm hoping a community of Christ-loving truth-seekers can share, discuss, and grow together there.

In the end, I am trying to expose the truth to as many people as possible, hoping to break the hegemony evangelicals have on a serious, reverent, literal reading of the Bible by showing their conclusions are centered on human psychology and philosophy rather than on God's Word and desires. If you believe that is a noble goal, I encourage and request that you support it in ways consistent with your own spiritual gifts and position within Christendom.

If you have an online presence or comment on others' webpages, you might consider linking to www.WhoReallyGoesToHell.com, where excerpts from this book reside. Even putting links on Myspace, Facebook, and Twitter can help. I also welcome you to join in the discussions and conversations at the blog www.authentic-christianity.net.

If you have an opportunity to suggest a topic for a small group, I encourage you to consider nominating this book for study. People are free to disagree with it, but I have to believe that the struggles that comes from considering these arguments are worthwhile and beneficial. Just breaking away from the 21st-century, Western mindset to consider how the Jews of Jesus' day would have taken His teachings and the written accounts and letters that much later became scripture opens you up to a whole new level of understanding.

If you are uncomfortable or unable to suggest this book to a small group, I encourage you to suggest it to others, Christian or non-Christian, who are open-minded and interested. If your pastor cares about truth and is humble, suggest the book to him or her. If your gifts and resources lie in other realms, I welcome you to prayerfully consider how they can be used to foster discussion and dialogue on what some would say is the most important doctrine of Christianity.

Related Topics

THE MODERN GOSPEL'S BIBLICAL PROBLEMS

The modern gospel states

- All people, having sinned, are unrighteous. Hence, due to God's perfect sense of justice, no one is naturally qualified for heaven.
- To address this, God sent Jesus as a sacrifice to grant forgiveness of sins to all believers. Alternatively, Jesus receives the sins and punishment of all believers, giving them a contrived perfection.
- Those who have faith in Christ, and only those who believe in Christ, can thus enter heaven as their sins have been addressed.
- God has no choice but to consign all others to hell for unforgiven sin.

Throughout this work, I have discussed several reasons why the above is biblically unacceptable. A summary of these is given below:

1. It presupposes the Judgment has the format of a court of law where only our offenses are relevant. Christ's teachings on the Judgment indicate godly deeds (which Jesus and others say can be done even by those who have no knowledge of Christ) are as relevant as our failings.

2. The Bible depicts many people, including those who never knew of Jesus, as righteous. The idea that a single sin makes someone unrighteous in God's eyes is thoroughly destroyed by any reasonable reading of scripture.

3. The modern gospel claims faith in Christ is the only means by which sins can be forgiven, but scripture gives at least six different routes to forgiveness, most available to non-believers.

4. It fails to make any sense of why the original apostles only spread the gospel of Christ to other Jews during the decade after Christ's death. These men were full of the Holy Spirit and had been given a complete teaching of God's work through Jesus [*Luke 24:27*]. To suggest they believed Christ's purpose was to save believers from hell would indicate they wanted all non-Jews to be consigned to eternal torment.

173

5. It assumes God holds all people to the same standard of conduct, a claim without biblical support. Dozens of passages demonstrate otherwise.

6. It fails to show the relevance of Christ's life and resurrection in God's salvific plan. If we are saved through Christ's sacrifice, then the resurrection itself is rather unneeded. Yet the early apostles and church fathers based their theories of salvation squarely upon the resurrection rather than the sacrificial aspect of Christ's death. Jesus is never referred to as a sacrifice or propitiation anywhere in all the evangelism captured in Acts (the most comprehensive repository of the apostles' actual teachings to unbelievers), and very rarely is He so described elsewhere.

7. It declares Jesus' sacrifice grants forgiveness of all sins to believers when the Bible specifically says otherwise.

8. It is not consistent with the context and purpose of the Messiah as found in the later prophets.

9. Jesus' own disciples did not know of His coming death and resurrection even though He attempted to tell them privately about it. Thus, it is impossible for the modern gospel to have had any real place in the general message Jesus and His apostles proclaimed to the crowds during Christ's earthly ministry.

10. Jesus, Paul, and many others indicate that believers and unbelievers are *both* in danger of hell due to their sins.

11. The modern gospel cannot explain how Enoch and Elijah were allowed to ascend to God's presence before Christ's sacrifice. Suggesting God forgave people before Jesus by looking forward to Christ's sacrifice would render nonsensical much of the Old Testament.

12. It is impossible to read Matthew, Mark, or Luke in isolation and come away with any semblance of the modern gospel. Thus, we must reject the modern gospel or else claim these writers cruelly and willfully misled their readers, for they could not assume their audience had access to any other specific commentary on Christ's purpose.

13. It violates Jesus' own teachings regarding how those who came before Him are judged. In particular it fails to explain how those who never knew of a coming Christ (much less that Jesus was He) could possibly be saved from hell.

14. It claims forgiveness of sins is the prevailing aspect of the Judgment while the vast majority of Judgment portrayals in the Bible make no mention of forgiveness at all.

15. It does not explain how the *entire creation*, including animals and God's angels, were reconciled to God through Christ's blood, for we do not generally believe either of these kinds of creatures guilty of sin.

16. Jesus was sent to mediate the new covenant, so it is unnatural to suggest His sacrifice was aimed at the Judgment (which transcends covenant, for all are judged).

17. The Bible proclaims the **entire world** and **all people** have been saved through Christ. If salvation is derived from forgiveness of individuals' sins, such would imply that all have been forgiven of their sins, not just those who believe in Christ.

18. All the original apostles, and all Jewish Christians of the first century, continued to obey the cultural Jewish laws. The modern gospel has trouble explaining why Peter, nine years after Christ's death, still believed he could not enter a Gentile's house. It also leaves one bewildered as to why Paul was just as ardent about keeping the Mosaic laws after his conversion as before.

19. It does not respect the Jewish understanding of salvation, a rather serious issue given that all the books of the New Testament were written by Jews, the original Christian church was almost entirely Jewish, and the gospels relate Jesus' interactions with Jews.

WHAT JESUS DIDN'T PREACH

It often comes as a shock to Christians to hear what *wasn't* part of Jesus' message during His ministry on earth. By *message* I mean *what He and His disciples preached to the Jewish crowds before His death.* (Jesus sends out His disciples to preach the gospel in *Matthew 10:5ff*; *Mark 6:7*; and *Luke 9:1*.)

In particular:

- His message did not include *anything* about His death or resurrection, and it certainly didn't indicate anything about His being a sacrifice.
- Until the very end of His ministry, His message did not even include anything about His being the Messiah.

I realize the above may look idiotic. A few points to consider:

- We must separate what He taught His disciples from what He preached to the crowds.
- We must recall that His message to the crowds who came to hear Him was of a different nature than His answers to Pharisees who questioned Him.
- We must understand that the gospel writers chose items from Jesus' ministry that got across points they wanted their readers to know. Much of this happened at the very end of His ministry and is not representative of what He taught during the years He preached throughout the land earlier.
- We must separate what Jesus says from commentary by the gospel writer (like *John 3:13–21*).
- We must realize that we see (after the fact) hints Jesus gave which even His disciples did not understand at the time.

The above points should help clear up the confusion you are bound to have as I show that it simply cannot be the case that Jesus preached the modern gospel to the crowds He encountered for a day or two each while traveling throughout the holy land.

Of course, *after* His death, Jesus' apostles did preach these truths. I'm certainly not claiming that Jesus is not the Christ or that He didn't rise from the dead. I'm merely pointing out that He did not preach these things before dying, and hence nothing like the modern gospel could have been in His general message. This is extremely important to keep in mind while interpreting His teachings found in the gospel accounts.

For example, as you read through Jesus' descriptions of the Judgment highlighted in the first two chapters, it is useful to know there was no implicit understanding of Jesus dying for people's sins or saving those who "believed in Him." When the gospel writers speak of people **believing** in Jesus, it does not mean what that phrase conjures up for most people today. His disciples **believed** in Him and knew nothing of His death and resurrection. Even in John, the gospel most likely to be used to support the modern gospel, it often just meant to believe Jesus was sent from God.[1]

What Did Jesus Preach about His Death?

While Jesus certainly dropped hints about His coming death, it wasn't part of His and His disciples' message since not even His disciples understood that He was going to die and rise again. Furthermore, it was not until the last nine months or so that He even **began** telling *them* about it. (I'll explain the importance of the **began** part later.)

This all becomes easier to understand if we look through the eyes of the Jews of Jesus' day. Some, but not all, believed there would be a resurrection, but it would be far, far in the future and it would happen for everyone at once. The idea that the Messiah would die and rise again *before everyone else* was completely unknown. While it was encoded in the prophets, no one got it.

No one.

That's why the disciples were totally disheartened (*Luke 24:20*) when Jesus died, because they thought that was the end. **But we had hoped that He was the one who was going to redeem Israel.** (Note the verb is in the imperfect tense in the Greek as well. "Were hoping" or "used to hope" would be, strictly speaking, more accurate translations. In any event, the point is that they no longer were hopeful.) *John 20:9* also explicitly indicates the disciples did not know He was going to rise from the dead.

It's understandable that the disciples had not figured any of this out due to their understanding of what the Messiah would do. Today we demonize the

---

[1] E.g., *John 6:42; 8:42–43; 9:33; 11:42; 16:30;* and *17:21*

Pharisees as rejecting Jesus "because they wanted a political leader." That can hardly be the reason they rejected Jesus, for it was the same expectation His own disciples had! They assumed, like anyone else, that He was going to eventually be king over Israel. Just as David had lived in hiding as the rightful king of Israel until Saul's reign ended, they assumed Jesus would eventually be exalted. The idea that He would die made no sense to them. This is why there is the curious conversation in *Mark 9:9–13*. The disciples wonder what **rising from the dead meant** because it *couldn't possibly mean Jesus was going to die.*

They wondered what figurative meaning it had. The prophets occasionally used the idea of resurrection metaphorically, and Jesus was known to speak in parables, so it is not surprising that they heard Christ describe His future suffering and assumed it referred to something else. The crowd in *John 12:34* shows a similar understanding that the Christ would not die.

In *Matthew 16:21*; *Mark 8:31*; and *Luke 9:22* Jesus **began** to tell the disciples of the things that would happen to Him. Matthew and Mark explicitly use that phrase — **began to tell**. It might look like Luke indicates otherwise, but then in *Luke 9:45* Jesus is telling them about His imminent betrayal and they don't understand. *Mark 9:9–13* would also look odd if we thought Jesus had told them everything earlier. I believe Peter's confession marks the time Jesus started warning His disciples a little at a time of what would happen.

Peter gets upset in *Matthew 16:21–22* that any dishonor at all would be shown to Christ, the rightful King of Israel. The idea that Peter was upset about Jesus undergoing suffering makes far more sense than suggesting Peter was upset that Christ would die and rise again as Lord. Every other piece of scripture indicates the apostles were oblivious until after His resurrection, and the notion that any of this discussion was taught to the public makes no sense given that Jesus did not even want them telling others He was the Christ.

Later when He tells them clearly (*Matthew 17:23*; *Luke 18:32–33*; *Mark 9:31–33*; *John 13:33*; and *16:16–18*), they still don't get it. In *Matthew 17:23* we read the disciples were **deeply grieved**, which suggests their understanding was obviously misconceived. The other passages clearly say they did not know what He meant.

Since Jesus didn't even hint of any of these things to His disciples until nine months before His death, and they never figured it out anyway, it certainly could not be considered part of His general message. He sent out His disciples to preach in all the villages *before* He began to speak on this topic at all.

The above information might make *Matthew 20:28* confusing. In that verse Jesus says ...**just as the Son of Man did not come to be served but to serve, and to give His life as a ransom for many**.

There are four important points to be made about this snippet:

- This pronouncement comes right before Jesus' death and is not representative of His teachings during His earlier ministry. Further, it was evidently not vital enough for Luke to include it in his narrative.

- He is speaking only to the disciples, and even they did not understand. *Luke 24:21–27* shows no one had an inkling of His coming death. *John 20:9* confirms this.

- Many early church fathers saw Christ as a ransom paid to *Satan*. It would take the church about 1000 years to fully reject this, so we cannot with any intellectual integrity claim Jesus is clearly describing Himself as an atoning sacrifice to God. We read that into the text based on what we have been told, but early church fathers did not see it that way.

- *Hebrews 9:15* and *Romans 3:25* show this ransom was for sins committed under the first covenant by humanity at large. (Israel sinned directly against God by failing to keep the Law given to them, the Gentiles sinned against God by oppressing God's people.)

Did Jesus Preach He is the Christ?

Jesus did tell the (Samaritan) woman at the well that He was the Christ in *John 4:26*. Otherwise we see instance after instance where He tries to keep that information under wraps. He silences demons to stop them from proclaiming this (*Luke 4:41*), and every description of Peter's confession shows Christ earnestly commanding them not to tell anyone (*Matthew 16:20*; *Mark 8:30*; and *Luke 9:21*). This all happened *after* the disciples were sent out to preach around Judea.

People later start to think that perhaps He is the Christ, but not because He is saying so. When Peter declares it, the reason is due to divine revelation (*Matthew 16:17*), and the disciples don't indicate the crowds had drawn that conclusion from all the teachings and healing they had seen up to that point (*Matthew 16:13–15*).

This last verse is revealing in another way. Jesus was calling Himself the **Son of Man**, but that was not understood as a title for the Christ. *Matthew 16:13–14* and *John 12:34* both show this. Thus, Jesus' long dialogue with the Pharisees in *John 10* cannot be considered declaring Himself as the Christ. It isn't until seven months before His death that people start thinking He might be the Christ or someone as powerful.[2]

Other than during the trial before the Sanhedrin, the only time Jesus directly indicated He was the Christ to a Jewish crowd was out of exasperation with the Pharisees four months before His death (*John 10:36*), after they had misconstrued His claim in *John 10:30*. In all other instances, He gave indirect answers. And the fact that He had to be asked about it indicates that it was not the focus of His teachings. After all, if Jesus' message had anything to do with His being the Christ, the Pharisees would not have been so frustrated in *John 10:24*. Note His answer **I told you and you do not believe. The deeds I do in my Father's name testify about me**. This is one example of many where Jesus does not make a claim but wants people to decide one way or the other about Him based on the commands He gave (*John 7:17*) and His works (*Luke 7:22*), but primarily on the former (*John 10:38*).

We read His words and see things that look like direct claims to Messiah that were not. For example, we take His use of the title **Son of Man** as a claim to Messiah, but the Jews did not understand it that way. Similarly, He says the scriptures speak of Him in *John 5:39–*. We take that as an indication that He is the Christ, but the scriptures also speak of Elijah (the one who comes before Christ). Indeed, it appears that most people thought that Jesus was Elijah.[3]

This observation also proves Jesus' general message could not have been that He was the Messiah. Had He been telling people He was the Christ, people would not have declared He was **the prophet** (*John 6:14* and *7:40*) instead or believed He might be Elijah.[4] Once we accept that Jesus was not telling people He was the Christ, it becomes much easier to understand why people thought He might be Elijah. Elijah has to come first, and John the Baptist told people (*John 1:21*) he was not Elijah. Jesus was doing the things great prophets, like Elijah, had done in the past: give God's Word and perform powerful miracles. Since Jesus wasn't claiming to be the Christ, Elijah had to come first, and Jesus was doing the things a great prophet like Elijah did, it's no wonder the Jews thought Jesus was Elijah. The apostles illustrated these claims by their confusion right after Jesus confirms Peter's confession. The disciples wonder (*Matthew 17:10*) how it is possible that Jesus can really be the Christ when **the scribes say that Elijah must come first.**

---

[2]*John 7:26–52* occurred around the Feast of Tabernacles (*John 7:2*) the August before Christ's death.

[3]*Matthew 16:14*; *Mark 6:15*; and *Luke 9:8*

[4]Note the Jews evidently saw **the prophet** as someone different from both the Christ and Elijah — *John 1:20–21* and *7:40–42*. In any event, it would be impossible for people to think He were Elijah if He were claiming to be the Christ.

Final Reminder

I'm certainly not suggesting Jesus was not the Christ or that Jesus did not rise from the dead. My point is that nothing like the modern gospel was preached to the crowds Jesus ministered to, and we absolutely must keep this in mind when interpreting His teachings during that time.

Furthermore, since Jesus *did* have a gospel message, but that message did not include anything we normally associate with the gospel, we should be very curious what that message was and why it could be called **the gospel**. This information is critical if we are to really understand Christ's purpose and the reason for His death.

COMPARISON OF BIBLICAL AND CONSERVATIVE EVANGELICAL CHRISTIANITY

Biblical	Conservative Evangelical
God judges people relative to • how they judge others (*Luke 6:37*; *James 2:13*; *Matthew 7:2*; and *John 9:41*) • their own enlightenment (*Matthew 23:29–33*; *John 15:22–24*; *Isaiah 65:12*; *Jeremiah 36:31*; *1st Samuel 3:13*; *James 3:1*; and the entire book of Zephaniah) • their conscience (*Genesis 20:5–6*; *Romans 1:18–19*; *1st Corinthians 8:10*; and *James 4:17*) • comparison with other humans (*Matthew 11:21–24*; *23:29–33*; and *Luke 11:31–32*)	God judges people against a perfect standard no mortal can satisfy.
The central truth is Jesus as King sent to turn God's people back to God as proved by His prophesied crucifixion and resurrection. This is shown by too many verses to cite, but it is showcased where we expect to see the gospel portrayed most clearly: the conclusion of each gospel as well as the entirety of Acts. Particular verses include *Matthew 28:18*; *Mark 16:6*; *Luke 24:25–27*; *45–48*; *John 20:29–30*; *21:12–14*; *Acts 2:14–41*; *3:12–26*; *4:8–12*; *5:30–32*; *10:34–43*; *13:16–41*; *17:2–4*; *18:31*; *22:1–21*; and *26:1–29*	The central truth is that God is unable to forgive sin without sacrifice, so God sacrificed Jesus to Godself as a way to get around this limit on God's ability.

Biblical	Conservative Evangelical
Christ's purpose is to call people out of spiritual bondage to serve God faithfully. This is the conclusion of Peter's pentecostal sermon: *Acts 3:26*, but is also found throughout the Bible (e.g., *Romans 6:4–6; Titus 2:14; Hebrews 9:14; 1st Peter 2:24; 1st John 3:4–5*). Jesus characterized this as His purpose during His earthly ministry as well (*Luke 5:32; 13:6–9; John 8:34–36*). Indeed, that was bulk of both Jesus' and John the Baptists' gospel — *Repent! for the time of the new covenant was at hand.* Throughout the prophets we see repentance as the crucial requirement for forgiveness that allowed a return to healthy covenant relationship with God. This exhortation to do God's will was exactly what Jesus and John preached before their deaths (*Matthew 3:2; 4:17; 5:19-20; 7:21; Mark 1:4; 15; 6:12; Luke 3:3; 6:46-49*), what Jesus told His disciples to preach afterward (*Luke 24:47*), and what the apostles themselves did preach (*Acts 3:19–20,26; 5:31; 11:18; 13:24*)	Christ's principal purpose was to save us from Hell.
Jesus is seen as protecting believers from the physical wrath God had prophesied upon the earth.	Jesus is seen as saving believers from His own righteous Judgment after the grand resurrection, which Revelation depicts as occurring only after God has poured physical, global wrath on the earth (twice), 1000 years after Christ's return.
Jesus' blood mediates the New Covenant prophesied in *Jeremiah 34:31–34* by sending the Holy Spirit to those who have received forgiveness through repentance and obey His commandments (*Luke 10:45; John 7:39; 16:7; Acts 2:38; 5:32; 8:30; 11:17-18; 15:9; 26:20;* and *Hebrews 6:4*)	The "New Covenant" is not clearly defined.

Biblical	Conservative Evangelical
Christ's blood allows Gentiles to enjoy the gift of the Holy Spirit through faith (*Galatians 3:14*), removing the wall of partition and hostility between Jews and Gentiles (*Ephesians 2:14*) so that the ordinances of the Mosaic law no longer deterred people from being in God's Kingdom (*Colossians 2:14*). While this blood allows those who convert to receive the Holy Spirit after receiving forgiveness for earlier sins through repentance, it does not work as a blanket atonement for ongoing sins of believers. Neither Christ's sacrifice nor those in the Old Testament worked forgiveness for intentional sins (*Numbers 15:30*; *John 5:29*; *Hebrews 10:26*; *1st Corinthians 6:9–10*; *2nd Corinthians 5:10*; *Colossians 3:24–25*; *Ephesians 5:4–5*; *Revelation 21:8*) Most of these were written to people who were already believers. Paul's own concern for his future in *1st Corinthians 9:24–27* and *Acts 24:15–16* should be a warning to any believer.	Jesus blood is seen as plenary payment of debt each individual owes toward God due to sins committed. Since the smallest debt toward God would leave one subject to wrath, and there is no way for anyone to atone for the smallest amount of wrong, a single unforgiven sin leaves one consigned to Hell.
There are many ways for someone to receive forgiveness: • Forgiving others (*Matthew 6:14*) • Repentance (*2nd Chronicles 7:14*; *Jeremiah 36:3*; *Ezekiel 18:27*; *33:14–16*; *Luke 3:3*; and many other verses already cited) • Church intervention (*John 20:23*) • Prayers of the righteous (*1st John 5:16*, and many, many times in the Old Testament) • Confession of sins (*1st John 1:9*) Note that many of these are available to people who have no understanding or knowledge of the gospel. Stephen prayed for the forgiveness of those who were stoning him. It is hard to understand why confession, having others pray for you, etc. are given as routes to forgiveness if those sins are assumed to already be forgiven through faith in Christ. (*James 5:14–16*)	The only way to have sins forgiven is through faith in Christ.
People can be pleasing to God through faith in God without any knowledge of the gospel of Christ. (Rahab [*James 2:25–26*], the denizens of Nineveh [*Jonah 3:9–10*], Cornelius before Peter arrived [*Acts 10:4*])	Only those with faith in Christ (not mere faith in God) can please God.

Biblical	Conservative Evangelical
Judgment is seen as an evaluation of disposition with the totality of one's actions, words, and thoughts considered. Believers are not dealt with any differently than non-believers. (*Matthew 7:21; 12:36–37; 13:49-50; 25:31-46; Luke 6:46; John 5:29; Acts 24:15–16; Romans 2:15–16; 1st Corinthians 9:24–27; 2nd Corinthians 5:10; Colossians 3:25; Hebrews 10:29; 2nd Peter 1:17;* and *Revelation 20:13*)	Judgment is seen as a trial where the principal question is whether someone is guilty of even one (unforgiven) sin. Believers are dealt with entirely differently than non-believers.
Jesus fulfills the promise made to Abraham and the covenant made to David. Gentiles are able to take part because through grace they become sons of Abraham. (*Isaiah 37:35; Jeremiah 23:5; 30:9; 33:15-21; Ezekiel 34:2324; 37:24-25; Hosea 3:5; Amos 9:11; Matthew 1:1; 9:27; 12:23; 15:22; 20:30; 21:9; Mark 10:47–48; 11:10; Luke 1:27,32,69–76; 3:8; 13:16; 18:38-39; 19:9; 24:49; John 7:42; Acts 2:33–39; 3:25; 7:17; 13:23–2424; 26:7; Romans 1:3; 4:16; 9:7; Galatians 3:7–8; 14:29; 2nd Timothy 2:8; Hebrews 2:16; Revelation 5:5;* and *22:16*)	Jesus fulfills the curse in *Genesis 3:15* that explains why snakes have no legs. No gospel writer found this verse (or the fall in general) worth mentioning even once, nor does it show up in the evangelism shown in Acts, even when apostles brought the gospel to non-Jews. The single semi-reference in the New Testament (*Romans 16:20*) in set in the future, and it is **God** doing the crushing.
The fall of Adam is seen as the cause of spiritual death, human weakness to selfishness (*Romans 5:14; 6:6;* and *7:15-25*) See *Romans 5:12* and *7:10* where Paul uses **death** in this way. It is not true that **all** died (physically) after Adam (Enoch[*Genesis 5:24*] and Elijah[*2nd Kings 2:11–12*] being examples of people who did not), and of course Paul had not **died** prior to writing the book of Romans but says that he **died** when the commandment came, for only through the commandment did temptation, and human domination by it, begin (*Romans 7:7–11*).	The fall of Adam is seen as the condemning the entire human race to eternal punishment.

Early Christian Atonement

Evangelicals try to put their theory in early Christian mouths, suggesting *Penal Substitution*[5] was taught in some form very early on. It wasn't.

Steve Jeffery, Micahel Ovey, and Andrew Sach spend 20 pages in *Pierced for Our Transgressions* quoting 13 of the most influential Christian leaders prior to Calvin. They claim these passages show overwhelming support for this theory throughout church history, but the quotes actually reflect the opposite.

No account before the late 4th century shows God *transferring* sin or its guilt to Christ. The early fathers saw Christ as *sharing* in our sin so we could *share* in His glorification, or else they got hung up on ideas where God paid Satan a "ransom" for humanity (an idea that lived in minor form into the 11th century!)

Even after the idea of transferral of sins gained some prominence (often in the same theories that gave Satan some role in salvation), it was not until the 16th century (!) that any writing is produced where it is *eternal damnation* that is being mitigated.

This should not be too surprising — recall how apostles focused on the *resurrection* not the Judgment.

The earliest theories of *atonement* describing God's work in Christ had nothing to do with legal figures or payment of debts. Early Christian thinkers claimed Jesus had taken humanity (as a whole) into His being. Therefore, since Christ beat death by His resurrection, humanity (united with Him by His incarnation) can now accomplish the same. Furthermore, since He rose again in power with a physical body, we can hope for the same.

There were different ideas about how exactly this defeat happened. But in general the early church thought the question was *How did Jesus thwart Satan or Death?* not *How did Jesus protect us from God's eternal wrath?* They were

---

[5]Penal Substitution is the term for the type of atonement most commonly taught by Evangelical churches. Christ's goodness is transferred to us. Our sins are transferred to Christ, and God punishes Christ for those sins at the cross. The "price" having been paid, and God's anger assuaged, there is therefore no condemnation for those in Christ.

trying to get around the universal principle that *All who sin must die.* This principle had to be reversed, somehow, for Christ to cheat Death and raise us.

For example, Athanasius[6] believed it was possible to lead a sinless life. He believed Jeremiah and John the Baptist were examples of people who had. They still died since they inherited humanity's physical frailty; Adam's sin had caused humanity to lose the "divine image" which staved off decay.

Athanasius wrote that if it were merely our transgression against God that had to be dealt with, then simple repentance would be enough. Christ's sacrifice was needed to undo the corruption that Adam's deed had invoked into the human race. This general interest in the *effect,* but not the *guilt,* of original sin was quite prominent throughout the first 300 years of the church.

Athanasius also wrote, "He was made man that we might be made gods." Gregory of Nazianzus, the only major figure in the first millennium to attack wholeheartedly the "Jesus as ransom to Satan" idea, wrote, "That which was not assumed (by Christ) is not healed; but that which is united to God is saved."

Athanasius makes clear that the church taught this lifting up and deification to be effectual to all the world, not just believers: "For the presence of the Saviour in the flesh was the price of death and the saving of the whole creation."

There are several reasons it is hard for anything the early writers wrote to support the dogma of evangelicals:

- The focus was on the resurrection, not the Judgment.
- The church was primarily concerned with the principle articulated by Paul in *Romans 6:23* that **the wages of sin is death**. This means that Christ *shared* (with us) rather than *took* (from us) the penalty for sins. We do, after all, still die.
- Since Christ shared in our death to defeat death, it's hard to see how His work had anything to do with the Judgment because He did *not* suffer what we would otherwise suffer (i.e., hellfire according to current Christians).

---

[6]Athanasius was the most important Christian Father from 254 until 396. Origen, the premiere theologian prior to him, believed God paid Christ as a ransom to Satan, which is certainly not doing any favors to Evangelicals.

Scripture Index

Genesis
3:14–16	32
3:22	67
4:4	165
5:24	16
6:8	32
6:9	69
6:11–14	80
7:1	69
12:1	139
15:2	121
15:6	69, 71, 138, 139, 141
18:24–32	73
20:5–6	70
20:17	73, 161
26:4–5	69
26:24	53
31:34	80
49:10	121

Exodus
9:16	150
15:1–19	29
15:17	151
16:3	29
16:31–35	115
30:15	160
32:7–35	151
32:9–14	73
32:30	160, 165
32:31–32	116
32:32	164

Leviticus
2:2	162, 165
4:3	164
4:35	161
5:2	163
5:5	165
5:12	162, 165
5:13	160
6:2–7	161
6:8–13	162
6:15	162, 165
6:18	164
6:24–30	162

6:27	164
6:29	163
7:1–7	162
7:7	164
7:23–24	162
10:17	163, 164
16:21–22	163
17:11	160
18:5	102
19:18	9, 113
19:20–22	161, 162
20:20	74, 163
20:20–22	163
22:9	74
24:7	162

Numbers
8:21	160
11:2	161
12:1–3	29
14:10–38	151
14:19–20	73, 161
14:20	72
14:21–22	150
15:22–28	161
15:27–31	42
16:46	160
16:46–47	73
18:22	74
18:32	74
21:5–9	116
21:7	161
25:13	53
26:53–65	151
27:3	74
31:50	160

Deuteronomy
6:5	9
8:3	115
9:18–20	161
15:7	113
24:20	113

Joshua
2:1–3	31
2:1–4	16

2:11	32

Judges
1:7	74

1st Samuel
2:15–17	164
2:16	165
2:27–36	164
2:29	164
3:13	70
3:14	164
12:23	164
24:21	53
28:3–15	120

2nd Samuel
12:13	74
15:24–31	152
22:20–27	69
24:25	161, 164

1st Kings
2:27	164
8:47	73
9:4	68
15:3	69
15:14	69

2nd Kings
2:11	16
5:18–19	73
5:27	53
8:19	73
9:26	74

1st Chronicles
14:2	153

2nd Chronicles
7:14	72
12:5–12	161
21:7	68, 152
30:18	160, 161
30:18–20	72, 73
32:25–26	73

13:15	154	**Acts**		11:17–18	112

LaVergne, TN USA
11 December 2009
166734LV00002B/2/P